Battleships

Battleships

igloo

igloo

First published in 2010
by Igloo Books Ltd
Cottage Farm
Sywell
NN6 0BJ

www.igloo-books.com

The measurements used are approximate.

10 9 8 7 6 5 4 3 2 1
ISBN 978-0-85734-421-2

Author: Leo Marriott

Printed and manufactured in China

Contents

USS Tennessee *at speed with her powerful battery of 14-inch guns trained to starboard encapsulates the power of the battleship.*

INTRODUCTION

Introduction

Below: *Between the two world wars the battlecruiser HMS* Hood *was the pride of the Royal Navy.*

What is a battleship? There is a tendency today for some not versed in the intricacies of naval terminology to apply the term *battleship* to any warship, but this is analogous to calling any airplane a jumbo or any car a Ford Mustang. A simple description would be to say that battleships are (or were) the most heavily armed and armored warships of their time, and in general could only be defeated by another battleship. Other warships, such as cruisers, destroyers, sloops and patrol vessels, were basically subsidiary to the battleship, and a nation's maritime strength and status was measured by the number and characteristics of the battleships that made up its fleet.

The evolution of the ironclad battleship began in the mid-19th century, when Britain was the world's foremost naval power by a considerable margin, a position it held until the end of the First World War in 1918. Thereafter, this supremacy was gradually eroded, more by political decisions and financial constraint rather than any military force, and by the end of the Second World War in 1945 it had ceded maritime supremacy to the United States. In many ways, this change was also reflected in the status of the battleship which, having reigned supreme as the arbiter of sea power until 1914, began to find itself increasingly vulnerable to new technologies in the form of aircraft and submarines. However, it was a slow process, and between the wars battleships were still regarded as the necessary backbone of any fleet. Considerable effort was put into improving their effectiveness.

Even when the Second World War broke out in 1939 most naval observers still regarded the battleship as all-powerful, and it was only a far-sighted few who saw that the future lay over or under the sea. Events were to show that such visions were correct, and the decline of the battleship was particularly hastened by the events at Pearl Harbor in December 1941. A surprise attack by Japanese carrier-based aircraft effectively eliminated the US Navy's fleet in the Pacific. This event not only confirmed that battleships were vulnerable to strong air attack but also meant that the US Navy had no option but to respond in kind. They based their attempts to halt and eventually defeat the Japanese forces on fleets and task forces built around the new capital ship – the aircraft carrier. From that time on battleships played an important but subsidiary role in this new type of naval warfare, although there were still a few classic battleship engagements to be played out.

When the war ended in August 1945, the battleship was effectively consigned to history. Although individual ships remained in service, either for reasons of national prestige or for limited military roles, the likelihood of a classic naval battle between opposing surface fleets had virtually disappeared. Even the post-war rise of Soviet sea power in the Cold War era did not alter this situation. (Nevertheless, today it is the Russian fleet that maintains vestiges of the battleship tradition with a class of modern missile-armed battlecruisers, which are as large and impressive looking as their historic predecessors.)

This book will trace the fascinating story of the battleship, commencing in Victorian times when, the whole nature of the fighting warship was being transformed. Changes included the introduction of steam propulsion to replace sail, iron and steel hulls to replace the old 'wooden walls,' and the introduction of new powerful breech-loading guns firing explosive shells to replace muzzle-loading cannons that lobbed solid shot. Any one of these factors required thought, skill and imagination by admirals, sailors and naval architects in order to apply the new technology in

Below: *The ill-fated HMS* Captain *completed in 1870 was a fully rigged turret ship designed by Cowper Coles.*

Battleships

Launched in 1871, HMS Devastation *was the first major warship to dispense with any form of sail and set the pattern for future battleship development.*

the most effective manner. The fact that the changes all occurred within a few decades led to an amazing variety of ships, each having a proponent claiming it to be representative of the future. In practice there were more failures than successes, many ships being thoroughly impractical and some even downright dangerous. A classic example of the latter was the turret ship HMS *Captain*, which sank in 1870 during a fierce gale, taking 473 sailors down with her.

However, by the 1880s some of the more outlandish ideas had been discarded, and the modern battleship began to emerge in recognizable form. The story really started with HMS *Devastation* which was commissioned in 1873. This was the first major seagoing warship to dispense entirely with any pretence of relying on sail, even as an auxiliary form of propulsion, and was armed with four heavy muzzle-loading guns in two revolving turrets. From this grew the early ironclad battleships, which typically displaced around 10,000 tons, armed with four large breech-loading guns and capable of 15 knots on coal-burning reciprocating steam machinery. Such ships were built in substantial numbers by Britain and, to a lesser extent, by other nations with the industrial capacity and expertize to build such complex vessels. Effectively this meant France, Germany, Russia, Italy, Austria and the United States – more or less in order of relative fleet strengths. At that time, the US Navy was a relatively minor player on the world stage.

By the start of the 20th century, the battleship had grown to around 15,000 tons. Although the main armament still comprised four large caliber guns, typically 12-inch caliber mounted in twin armored turrets, a substantial battery of smaller calibers, such as 9.2-inch or 7.5-inch guns, were also carried with the fastest ships still capable of 18 knots. In Europe, the situation was dominated by an aggressive arms race as Germany attempted to assert itself by building a large seagoing fleet capable of challenging the Royal Navy. By 1905, Germany had laid down or completed no less than 24 battleships in little more than 15 years. Although this was an impressive achievement, the Royal Navy still retained a comfortable margin of superiority with almost twice as many battleships. At this time the French navy was in decline, building few battleships and concentrating on powerful cruisers, which were judged to be better suited to maintaining the security of France's far-flung colonial possessions.

In the Far East, Russia had felt threatened by the rise of Japan as a modern maritime power and dispatched a fleet to sail around the world from the Baltic to secure its Yellow Sea base at Port Arthur (now Lüshunko, China) after a Japanese surprise attack had all but eliminated the Russian Asiatic Fleet. Led by Admiral Rozhestvensky, the Russian ships were intercepted in the Tsushima Straits by a modern and well-organized Japanese force under the command of Admiral Togo in the 15,2000-ton battleship *Mikasa*. The outcome was a crushing victory for the Japanese fleet with all the Russian ships being sunk or captured. This victory established Japan as the major maritime power in the Pacific.

Above: *HMS* Dreadnought *revolutionized naval warfare when she was launched in 1906.*

Below: *Older battleships such as the USS* Maine *(BB10) completed in 1902 were rendered obsolete by the arrival of* Dreadnought*.*

However, the naval world was about to experience a revolution that which would completely transform the nature of warfare and start an arms race that would factor in the outbreak of war in 1914. In October 1904, Admiral Sir John Fisher became First Sea Lord, the professional head of the Royal Navy. He had already been responsible for numerous reforms within the navy but was now in a position to push forward his ideas for the battleship of the future. Heavily influenced by the events at Tsushima, but also by the nature of new Japanese and American ships being laid down, he was the driving force behind the construction of a revolutionary new battleship – HMS *Dreadnought*. Speed was of the essence, and the keel was laid down on October 2, 1905, the hull was launched on February 10, 1906, and the ship was commissioned on New Year's Day, 1907. This was an incredible achievement by any standard, given the size and complexity of the new ship, which at 18,100 tons was larger than any of her predecessors. However, it was not just size that made the difference. Apart from a few light guns, her sole armament comprised no less than ten 12 inch guns in five armored turrets organized in action by a central firing control system. Despite her great size, she was capable of 21 knots, power being provided by the newly developed steam turbines, the first application of this type of propulsion to a large warship.

The effect of HMS *Dreadnought* was dramatic. Overnight every other battleship was rendered obsolete as a Dreadnought-class ship could maneuver at will into a favorable tactical position due to its speed advantage before opening heavy fire at long range. So marked was that superiority that the term *battleship* dropped out of use for a decade or more as capital ships were divided into *dreadnoughts* and *pre-dreadnoughts*. As far as the Royal Navy was concerned, the construction of HMS *Dreadnought* was a calculated gamble. Overnight, Britain's overwhelming superiority in pre-dreadnought battleships became irrelevant as other navies could now start to build up new fleets composed of dreadnoughts. Inevitably, Germany took up the challenge but given its flying start, the Royal Navy was able to keep comfortably ahead so that by the time the First World War broke out it had no less than 20 in commission and another 12 under construction. The German figures were 15 and six respectively.

When Admiral Fisher initiated the design of HMS *Dreadnought*, he also encouraged a further new class of warship, the fast battlecruiser. Like the new battleship, these carried a standard armament of 12-inch guns (eight in four turrets) and were driven by steam turbines. However, they were not intended to form part of the line-of-battle but instead would act as scouts to the main battle fleet and also be capable

The German High Seas Fleet at sea led by the pre-dreadnought SMS Preussen.

of independent deployment to catch and defeat enemy cruisers operating in a raiding role. The first three battlecruisers were commissioned in 1908, and their high speed (25 knots, rising to 27 knots in later classes) and dashing lines caught the public imagination. However, the speed was achieved by a reduction in armor protection which reduced weight and made space available for the installation of more powerful engines. The balance between hitting power, mobility and protection is a complex equation, which has existed throughout military and naval history, and the battlecruiser represented an imaginative solution for a particular set of tasks. Experience was to show that it was not necessarily a good one.

When war broke out in 1914, the Royal Navy was already mobilized and sailed immediately to its war stations. Things started badly with the loss of three armored cruisers to U-boat attack in the English Channel. (U-boat is short for *Unterseeboot*, the German for submarine.) This immediately demonstrated the threat to capital ships posed by the relatively new underwater weapon and, until countermeasures and tactics could be developed, the threat considerably inhibited operations by the battle fleet. Even worse was the total defeat of a Royal Navy cruiser squadron off the coast of Chile by the German Asiatic Fleet under Admiral von Spee. To avenge this, Admiral Fisher acted quickly and dispatched two battlecruisers to the South Atlantic where they met up with Von Spee off the Falkland Islands – and completely annihilated his force.

However, the focus of the naval war remained in the North Sea, where the British public confidently awaited a major naval engagement that would result in a Trafalgar-style total victory over the German High Seas Fleet. Despite a number of minor actions with variable outcomes, it was not until May 1916 that the British Grand Fleet under Admiral Jellicoe met with the German ships under Admiral Scheer at the Battle of Jutland. The result, fought in the late afternoon and gathering dusk, remains the largest battleship engagement ever fought, but the outcome was inconclusive. From the British point of view at least, it could only be regarded as a draw. Indeed, the Royal Navy had suffered grievously, losing no less than three of the new battlecruisers, while in terms of capital

ships the Germans lost a battlecruiser and a pre-dreadnought battleship. Nevertheless, as a result of their experience at Jutland, the High Seas Fleet did not seriously challenge the Royal Navy again, and the whole fleet sailed to surrender and internment in November 1918. Subsequently, the entire German fleet was scuttled while impounded as Scapa Flow in Orkney by its crews in June 1919.

Despite the experience at Jutland, the Royal Navy persisted with the construction of new battlecruisers, and HMS *Hood* was completed in 1920. With a displacement of 41,000 tons, she was the largest

warship in the world during the period between the wars. Despite the Armistice, plans still existed for large battlecruisers displacing 48,000 tons armed with 16-inch guns, and these were to be followed by even larger battleships armed with 18-inch guns. The driving policy behind these plans was to maintain a margin of superiority over Japan and the United States, both now emerging as major maritime powers.

It was not until the start of the 20th century that the US Navy made serious efforts to build up a strong blue-water force, and it was not involved in hostilities in the First World War until 1917 at which point a squadron was dispatched to serve with the British Grand Fleet based at Scapa Flow. By 1919, the United States had a declared policy of parity with the Royal Navy and was laying down 40,000-ton battleships armed with 16-inch guns as well as large battlecruisers.

HMS Hood *at Scapa Flow in 1940, framed by the 15-inch guns of a Queen Elizabeth-class battleship.*

HMS Nelson *was one of two battleships armed with 16-inch guns that Britain was permitted to build under the terms of the 1921 Washington Treaty.*

With Japan building similar ships, another major naval arms race was getting underway, and there seemed no limit to the size and cost of battleships. Whether the nations concerned could afford such massive vessels was open to question, and it was therefore not surprising that an agreement was reached at the Washington Naval Conference of 1921 (initiated by the United States) to limit the abilities of battleships and the size of the world's naval fleets.

It was agreed that, with a few specific exceptions, all battleship construction would cease and no more would be started for at least ten years (this period was later extended). In addition, the displacement of any new battleship would not exceed 35,000 tons and the largest permitted gun caliber would be 16 inches. Finally, a wholesale program of scrapping older ships was put in place so that an approximate parity of strength existed between the US and British navies, and Japan was restricted to a total capital-ship tonnage equal to three-fifths of that of the two major powers, while France and Italy were forced to accept a figure approximating to one third.

As a result of these decisions, the US Navy completed three Maryland-class battleships, Japan completed two Mutsu-class ships and Britain was permitted to lay down and build two Nelson-class ones. All of these were armed with 16-inch guns, but in accordance with the provisions of the Washington Treaty and the 1930 London Treaty, no further battleships were laid down by USA and Britain for nearly a decade. One side effect of the Washington Treaty that had a major impact on the subsequent development of the battleship was that several surplus hulls which would otherwise have been broken up were permitted to be retained and converted into aircraft carriers.

The first event to lead to resumption of battleship construction was the appearance of the German *Panzerschiffe* (armored ship) *Deutschland* launched in 1931. Under the terms of the 1919 Versailles Treaty, Germany was permitted to replace some of the old pre-dreadnoughts it had retained after the First World War. These were limited to 10,000 tons and 11-inch guns, and the Allies assumed a like-for-like replacement that would offer no threat to their larger navies. However, by adopting diesel propulsion, the German ships were fast (26 knots) and had a long range. A relatively heavy armament of six 11-inch guns in two triple turrets made these so-called 'pocket battleships' ideal for commerce raiding on the high seas. On paper they could easily defeat any cruiser sent against them and could outrun virtually any better-armed capital ship. Alarmed by this threat, the French navy laid down two 26,000-ton battlecruisers armed with 13.5-inch guns in 1934, but these were matched by the Italian Littorio-class battleship armed with 15-inch guns laid down the same year. France followed up with the Richelieu-class battleships of 1935, also armed with 15-inch guns. Having initiated these escalations, Germany continued by laying down two battlecruiser (the *Scharnhorst* and *Gneisenau*) between 1934 and 1935 and two battleships (the *Bismarck* and *Tirpitz*) in 1936.

Abiding by treaty limitations, Britain and the United States did not start building new battleships until 1937 when the first of five King George V-class battleships for the Royal Navy were laid down. However, these were only armed with 14-inch guns, which British politicians vainly hoped would be accepted by other competing nations. The two US battleships (*North Carolina* and *Washington*) retained the 16-inch gun as did all subsequent US battleships, of which a further eight were completed during the Second World War. Japan had publicly renounced treaty limitations in 1937, and unknown to the Allies was proceeding with the building of three massive 64,000-ton battleships armed with 18-inch guns. In the event only two (the *Yamato* and *Musashi*) were completed as designed, the third being completed as an aircraft carrier.

All of the battleships and battlecruisers laid down from 1934 onwards had one thing in common – they were much faster than their First World War predecessors and were variously capable of between 28 and 33 knots. This effectively made the conventional idea of a lightly armored battlecruiser unnecessary although the German Scharnhorst and US Alaska classes (laid down 1941) put a different slant on the equation, mounting only 11-inch or 12-inch guns in fast yet well-protected hulls.

Below: *The USS* Washington *(BB56) was one of two US battleships ordered in 1937. She was completed in 1941.*

Battleships

Despite hardly ever putting to sea, the German battleship Tirpitz *was a major threat to the Arctic convoys to Russia until she was finally destroyed in late 1944.*

When war broke out in 1939 very few of the new ships were ready and many early actions involved battleships and battlecruisers from the First World War, although a lot of these had been extensively rebuilt and modernized in the 1930s. The great battle fleets of the earlier war no longer existed and such battleship actions as were fought involved much smaller numbers of warships. The nearest approaches to a fleet action occurred in the Mediterranean where on at least two occasions (Calabria in 1940 and Matapan in 1941) substantial British and Italian forces came into contact. Also in July, 1940, a British force including two battleships and the battlecruiser HMS *Hood* bombarded the French fleet at Oran in order to prevent their ships falling into German hands.

Major events demonstrating the potential power of battleships included the dramatic chase to catch and sink the *Bismarck* after she had sunk HMS *Hood*. Her sister ship *Tirpitz* did not even have to leave harbor to cause the destruction of convoy PQ17 off Norway. The British Admiralty ordered the convoy to scatter due to the perceived threat posed by the German ship. Alone and undefended, the convoy's merchant vessels were steadily picked off by German attacks.

HMS Repulse *was one of two British ships sunk off Malaya by Japanese aircraft in December 1941 – an incident that finally ended the battleships predominant position in the war at sea.*

A dramatic shot taken from the cruiser Prinz Eugen *showing the German battleship* Bismarck *firing at HMS* Hood.

Despite these surface actions, it was quickly apparent that the days of the battleship were numbered and it was aircraft which held the balance of power at sea. The Royal Navy had demonstrated the potential of air power by disabling the Italian Fleet at Taranto in November 1940 using almost obsolete Swordfish biplanes. The Japanese were quick to note this success and repeated the operation on a grander scale at Pearl Harbor in December 1941, sinking or disabling seven US battleships. Even more serious for the battleship was the sinking of British ships HMS *Prince of Wales* and HMS *Repulse* off Malaysia on December 10, 1941. These ships were free to maneuver in open waters, had the latest anti-aircraft armaments and were escorted by four destroyers. Advocates of the battleship had maintained that in these circumstances, a battleship was quite capable of defending itself. The success of the Japanese air-borne attack put paid to that idea for ever.

For the rest of the war, battleships were mostly used to support major operations such as assault landings (e.g. Sicily, Italy, Iwo Jima) where the firepower of their big guns was a tremendous asset to the invading troops, or acting as anti aircraft escorts to the fast carrier forces. There were brief moments of glory such as the sinking of the *Scharnhorst* by HMS *Duke of York* (December 1943) and the night action of the Pearl Harbor survivors during the Battle of Leyte when they were involved in the sinking of the Japanese battleship *Yamashiro*. Later in the same campaign the monster battleship *Musashi* was sunk by air attack from US Navy carrier-based aircraft and her sister, *Yamato*, was also lost to air attack in April 1945.

When the war ended in 1945, none of the Axis battleships remained in commission, all having been either sunk, scuttled, disabled or interned. Many that did survive were expended in the US atomic bomb tests in 1946. On the Allied side some battleships were kept in commission for a while, either as training ships or for reasons of national prestige, and at various times there were plans to convert them to carry guided missiles but in general they had all been laid up and scrapped by around 1960. A major exception was the US Navy's Iowa-class battleships which saw a brief resurgence in the Korean War and again in the Vietnam conflict. Amazingly they saw further service in the 1980s when they were adapted to carry cruise missiles. Some even took part in the first Gulf War in 1991 although that proved to be their swan song. Today, the only surviving examples from the era of great battleships are museum pieces.

But that is not quite the end of the story. The Russian navy created a modern iteration of the battlecruiser concept in the 1980s and at least one of these ships remains in service today. The serried ranks of great guns were replaced by modern missile silos and launchers but the sight of a 30,000-ton warship cutting through the seas at 30 knots still recalls the long gone days when the battleship and battlecruiser ruled the world's oceans.

Below: *HMS* Duke of York, *the ship that sank the German battlecruiser* Scharnhorst.

Introduction

April 16, 2010 the end of an era: USS Wisconsin*, the US Navy's last battleship, is handed over to the city of Norfolk, Virginia, for safekeeping as a memorial and museum ship.*

THE PRE-DREADNOUGHT ERA

The might and power of HMS Devastation *is conveyed by this oil painting.*

The Pre-Dreadnought Era

Above: *The Battle of Trafalgar.*

In October 1805, Admiral Lord Nelson led the Royal Navy to an historic victory over the combined French and Spanish fleets off Cape Trafalgar, Spain. Although not quite the last major battle fought by sailing ships of the line (that distinction goes to the Battle of Navarino in 1828), it represented the culmination of three centuries of naval warfare in which the nature of the ships and their weapons had not changed to any significant extent. Nelson's genius lay in the way he inspired his men, organized his fleet and applied bold new tactics to achieve victory. Nevertheless, the fighting at Trafalgar inevitably reduced to individual ships fighting at very close quarters – Nelson himself was fatally wounded by a musket ball fired from only a matter of feet away. The outcome of such encounters was substantially dependent on the speed with which the crews could serve their muzzle-loaded cannons.

Almost exactly one hundred years later, on May 27, 1905, a battle of almost equal significance was fought on the other side of the world where a Japanese fleet led by Admiral Togo intercepted a Russian fleet that had steamed half way round the world from the Baltic port of Kronstadt. The Russian intention was to relieve the Russian-held Port Arthur in Manchuria, then under siege by Japanese forces. This action was to be fought by heavily armored ironclad steamships armed with powerful breech-loading guns capable of accurate fire over thousands of meters. The contrast between the two battles could hardly be greater.

The hundred years that separated these two actions had seen a total transformation in the nature of fighting ships, and their weapons and equipment. This in turn had resulted in entirely new tactics and methods of command in order to utilize the opportunities offered by the new technologies. In particular the period saw the advent and evolution of the ironclad, steam-powered battleship, ultimately leading to the great armored vessels of the 20th century that were to play such an important role in two major world conflicts.

In the early decades following Trafalgar, the pace of change was slow, if not non-existent. As the world's most powerful maritime force, the Royal Navy was reluctant to deviate from tried and tested principles. Although the introduction of diagonal framing allowed wooden hulls of greater length to be built, the sailing warship was otherwise little altered. But already factors were at work that would force change and the introduction of steam propulsion was one. A steam ship could maneuver freely, disregarding the wind, and this obviously conferred tactical advantages. However, it required adequate supplies of coal, which necessitated the establishment of a worldwide network of coaling stations. Early steam vessels were propelled by side paddles that were vulnerable in action and took up space where guns had previously been mounted. It was not until the superiority of the screw

Above: *At the Battle of Tsushima the Japanese navy inflicted a humiliating defeat on the Russian fleet and the outcome had a major influence on warship design*

Below: *The French* Gloire *was the first major seagoing armoured ship, although it was based on a wooden hull.*

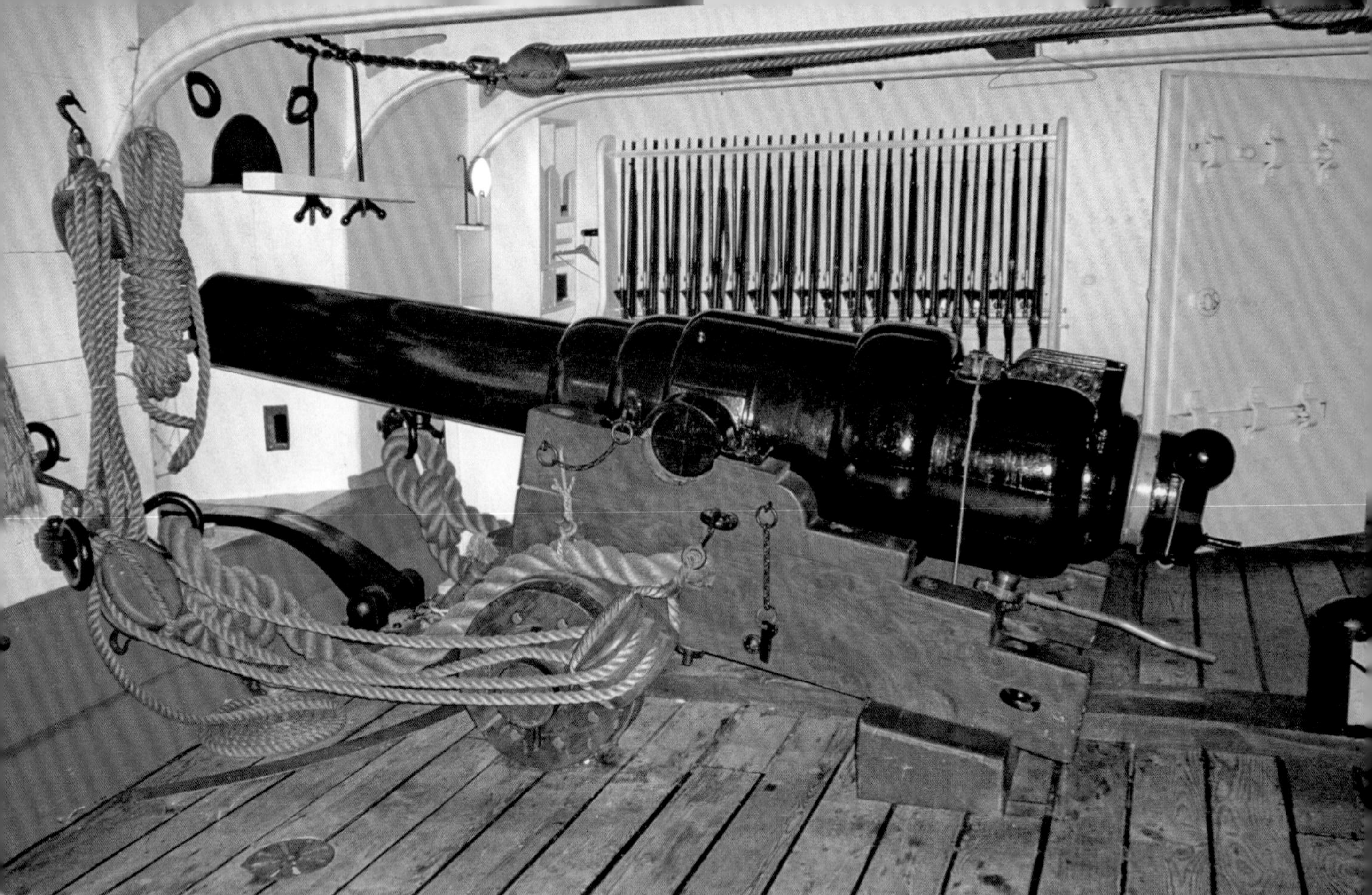

Above: *One of the 70-pounder breech-loading guns carried by HMS* Warrior. *These were not successful, and the navy reverted to smooth-bore muzzle loaders for another two decades.*

propeller was demonstrated in the 1840s that navies began to seriously adopt steam propulsion, although full sail rigging was still carried. The last fully rigged sailing ship of the line was launched as late as 1848 (HMS *Aboukir*, a 90-gun two-decker) although by then similar ships were already being converted to steam propulsion while still on the building stocks.

The new steam frigates still retained the traditional broadsides of muzzle-loading cannon, but the nature of naval guns was about to change dramatically as shell-firing guns with barrels rifled for greater accuracy began to enter service. Actions in the Crimea War had shown how effective these could be, particularly against wooden-hulled ships, and some form of armored defense was obviously required. As was often the case in this period, it was France who initiated new ideas, but with its superior industrial resources of the time, Britain was then able to match or even better the concept. In 1858, the French navy laid down *La Gloire* and three sister ships. These were armored steam frigates with a speed of 13 knots and carried a total of 52 guns, a mix of muzzle-loading cannon and breech-loading rifled shell-firing guns. Although claimed to be the first major armored warships, they were actually wooden-hulled ships with a 11.5-cm (4.5-inch) thick wrought iron armored belt around the ship, covering the hull sides above and below the waterline. The British response was immediate, laying down the armored ships HMS *Warrior* and HMS *Black Prince* in 1859. Constructed entirely of iron, they displaced 9,210 tons and had an overall length of 127 meters (419 feet), making them almost twice the size of *La Gloire*. The main armament of HMS *Warrior* comprised twenty-six 68-pounder muzzle loaders (ML) and four 70-pounders and ten 110-pounder breech-loading guns arranged in traditional broadside manner protected by the armored belt. Although the Royal Navy had introduced large caliber breech-loading guns at this stage, they were not a success, and the service subsequently reverted to muzzle loaders of increasing size an weight for another two decades.

The traditional broadside disposition of the guns was retained in several ships built after *Warrior*, and contemporary French ships were similar. However,

Above: *The CSS* Virginia, *a floating gun battery converted in 1863 from the captured Federal steam frigate,* Merrimack.

Below: *The turret of a Federal Navy monitor. Although it shows impact damage from roundshot, the armor has not been penetrated.*

across the Atlantic a fierce action was fought in 1863 during the American Civil War, which was to have a profound effect on warship development. Confederate forces had captured the screw frigate *Merrimack* when they occupied the Federal Navy Yard at Norfolk, Virginia. Numerically inferior, the Confederate Navy decided to convert her into an impregnable armored floating gun battery. The hull was cut down to the waterline so that an armored citadel could be built over it. This consisted of stout sections of pine and oak tapering inwards at 45 degrees, the whole covered with 5-cm (2-inch) thick iron plates. The

gun battery, firing through ports cut in the armor, was made up of four 7-inch rifled ML and six 9-inch smooth bore guns. On March 8, 1863, the *Merrimack* (now renamed *Virginia*) set out from Norfolk to attack blockading wooden Federal warships in the Hampton Roads. She played havoc. The shots from the Federal ships were easily deflected by the sloping armor, and the two of them were destroyed. By sheer co-incidence, the Federal forces had been working on a revolutionary warship design by Swedish engineer John Ericsson. Based on a wooden hull, the USS *Monitor* had an armored deck and overhanging armored sides but its most significant feature was that its armament of only two 11-inch Dahlgren smooth-bore muzzle loaders was contained within an armored revolving turret. On the morning of May 8, the two ironclads met and thundered away at each other for almost four hours. At best, the result was a draw with neither able to inflict significant damage on the other, which at least demonstrated the benefits conferred by the armor plating. The event is significant as the first engagement between two ironclad armored ships.

Despite this dramatic contemporary sketch, the engagement between the Monitor *and the* Merrimack *was inconclusive as neither could penetrate the other's armor.*
Inset. *Plan of the* Monitor *showing the raft-like hull and internal arrangement of the rotating turret.*

Fig. 2.
A
B
B
C
D
Fig 1
A
B
C
K
Fig.3.
A
K
G
PLANS OF THE MONITOR.

Above: *HMS* Monarch, *a fully rigged turret ship designed by Reed was completed in 1869.*

Detail below: *A close up view of one of the turrets aboard HMS* Captain.

Although the guns in the *Monitor* had a very slow rate of fire – it took around seven minutes to ready the guns between shots – the fact that a ship armed with only two guns had stood up to one armed with ten guns was a clear demonstration of the advantages to be conferred by the use of revolving turrets. In fact, such an arrangement already had its advocates in Europe, notably the Royal Navy's Captain Cowper Coles, who had already patented the idea as early as 1859. In theory, the great advantage of a ship armed with turrets was that it only required half the number of guns carried by the equivalent broadside ship as its guns could be pointed in both directions. In practice, there were numerous difficulties, one of which was the effect of the heavy armored turrets on the stability of the ship. In addition, at that time ships were still fully rigged and the various masts and shrouds obstructed the gun's field of fire. Nevertheless, Coles succeeded in building a small ship, HMS *Prince Albert*, to prove the concept in 1862. In 1866, the 8,300-ton HMS *Monarch* was laid down. Armed with four 12-inch rifled muzzle-loaded guns (MLRs) in two turrets amidships, *Monarch* was the first such ship intended for deployment as part of the seagoing battle fleet and carried a full three-masted sailing rig. Designed by Sir Edward Reed, the chief naval constructor, she did not meet with Coles' approval, having a high freeboard, which in his opinion made her a larger target, and having fore and aft fire obstructed by the forecastle and supports for the flying deck superstructure. Consequently, he persuaded the Admiralty to build a further turret ship, HMS *Captain*, to his own complete design. The result was another steam-powered three-masted ship but with the turrets mounted much lower down. Despite doubts about her stability, she was commissioned in January 1870. In September that year, she encountered a strong, but not unusual, gale off Finisterre, Spain.

Above: *The changing face of naval warfare in Victorian times is clearly illustrated this view of HMS* Devastation, *completed in 1873, passing HMS* Victory *in Portsmouth Harbour.*

Suddenly, even as the crew were reducing sail, she rolled over and sank taking all but 18 men with her, including the captain and Cowper Coles himself.

Despite this grievous loss of life, the turret was still seen as the way forward, and Reed solved the problem of stability under sail in a simple and revolutionary way – he discarded all the sails and associated masts and rigging. The result was HMS *Devastation*, the first major warship to rely entirely on steam power and effectively the first recognizable modern battleship. *Devastation* displaced 9,330 tons on a length of 87 meters (285 feet) and a beam (maximum width) of 18 meters (58 feet), the hull protected by 30 cm (12 inches) of wrought iron backed by 45 cm (18 inches) of teak. The freeboard was only 135 cm (4 foot 6 inches) so the main deck was constantly awash when the ship was under way, but a 2-meter (7-foot) armored breastwork occupied the middle two-thirds of the ship and at either end were turret rings with revolving mountings each carrying a pair of 12-inch MLRs contained in an armored gun house. Between the turrets was a superstructure carrying a flying deck through which the two funnels were led and in which the single pole mainmast was stepped. Despite the low freeboard, the ship was intended for ocean-going duties, and her bunkerage of up to 1,800 tons of coal gave a respectable range of action.

As well her heavy guns, *Devastation* was also fitted with a bow ram – a piece of equipment that was *de rigeur* for ironclad warships of the day. There were few naval actions involving the early ironclads and those which did occur were eagerly analyzed to study the effectiveness of new weapons or new construction. On July 20, 1866, an Austro-Hungarian fleet under Rear-Admiral Teggethoff clashed with a superior Italian force under Admiral Count Persano off the island of Lissa in the Adriatic. The Italian fleet included large ironclads, both armed with numerous

Above: *The Italian flagship* Re d'Italia *was sunk by ramming at the Battle of Lissa (1866), an event that was to have a major influence on warship design.*

Armstrong rifled guns firing shells weighing between 45 and 135 kg (100 and 300 pounds), as well as five well-armed ironclad frigates. There was also a rather odd 4,000-ton vessel known as a turret ram that was fitted with a 79-meter (26-foot) sharpened iron prow as well as carrying two 300-pounder Armstrong guns. Teggethoff's ships were a much more varied group consisting of two armored frigates including the flagship *Ferdinand Max*, four smaller ironclads and a number of other vessels including a steam-driven wooden ship-of-the-line.

When the fleets met, their initial sailing formations quickly disintegrated and a close-range mêlée resulted. In the course of this, the *Ferdinand Max* rammed and sank the Italian flagship *Re d'Italia* but despite the great quantities of ammunition expended by both sides, the only other ship sunk was a small Italian gunboat when a fire started by a shell-hit caused the magazine to ignite. The apparent lesson of this engagement was that shells were generally unable to penetrate armor, and the only effective way to sink an enemy was to ram him. Consequently, for at least the following two decades, every major warship was fitted with a ram, and although no other ships were sunk in this way during a battle, there were several accidental losses. HMS *Vanguard* was rammed in a fog by HMS *Northumberland* in 1872, and an infamous incident in 1892 when the battleship *Camperdown* rammed and sank the Mediterranean fleet flagship HMS *Victoria* in broad daylight. The latter was caused by a badly thought out fleet maneuver ordered by the Commander-in-Chief, Admiral Sir George Tyron.

The Battle of Lissa also had another effect on warship design. Teggethoff had led his fleet against the Italian line in an arrowhead formation, and this was seen as a factor in his success. As a consequence great emphasis was placed on ships being able to deploy the maximum possible firepower directly ahead. This was obviously not possible with the traditional broadside battery of the early ironclads and even a ship with fore and aft turrets could only fire forward with half of its armament. Consequently, some rather curious ships were built in an effort to concentrate fire ahead. With the *Admiral Duperre*, launched in 1877, the French navy came up with one solution that was subsequently incorporated in several of their subsequent ironclads.

France introduced the concept of an armored barbette to protect the guns in the Admiral Duperre *launched in 1879.*

Displacing almost 10,500 tons, the ship was characterized by the significant tumblehome of the hull sides – in other words they were angled steeply inwards – and this allowed structures to be built up on either beam clear of the superstructure to act as gun mountings. In fact, these structures, and the similar ones protecting other guns mounted on the centerline fore and aft, were another French innovation known as a barbette. They were heavily armored breastworks behind which the guns could be loaded and trained, and were a popular alternative to the more complex and heavier armored turret. The *Admiral Duperre* carried four 340-mm (13.5-inch) guns in single mountings, one on either beam, and one fore and aft. In this configuration, three of the guns could fire directly ahead or directly astern.

In the meantime, the Royal Navy had built several central battery ships in which the main armament was carried in an armored citadel amidships, with the decks above main deck level recessed fore and aft of the citadel to allow some guns to fire directly ahead or astern. The first of these was the 9,490-ton HMS *Alexandra* launched in 1873 and armed with two 11-inch MLR, ten 10-inch MLR and six 13-hundredweight breach loaders. (At that period it was quite common to designate guns in terms of their weight rather than caliber). However, the introduction of barbettes and turrets required a different arrangement, and it was Italy that came up with the idea of mounting the guns on either beam in echelons amidships. With

Below: *HMS* Alexandra *was one of several central battery ships with the guns protected by an armored citadel built for the Royal Navy before turrets were widely adopted.*

Armed with massive 16-inch guns, the Dandalo **(above)** *and her sister ship* Duillio **(below)** *were potentially the most powerful battleships in the world when laid down in 1873.*

Above: *The* Lepanto *was laid down in 1876 but was obsolete by the time she was completed 11 years later. Large and fast, her hull was unprotected, and only the central redoubt was armored.*

recessed superstructure fore and aft, both turrets could train directly ahead or astern and, because of the staggered echelon arrangement, both could also train simultaneously on either beam. The Italian chief naval constructor, Benedetto Brin was responsible for the design of the *Dandalo* and *Duillio* which, when laid down in 1873, were potentially the most powerful warships in the world. The main armament of these 11,138-ton ironclads was four massive Armstrong 100-ton, 450-mm (17.7-inch) ML guns mounted in two large armored turrets amidships, the forward one slightly offset to starboard and the aft offset to port. This allowed the outside gun of each turret to fire directly ahead although in practice the blast damage to the superstructure proved unacceptable. These two ships were followed by the *Lepanto* and *Italia* laid down in 1876, which were even larger (14,000-tons) but carried four slightly smaller guns in twin barbettes enclosed in a central armored redoubt.

Britain's response to these monsters was HMS *Inflexible*, designed by Nathaniel Barnaby very much along the lines of the Italian ships. Like them, the main armament of four 16-inch ML guns was carried in two armored turrets echeloned port and starboard amidships. The loading and firing of these great guns was a complex and time-consuming business even though the turrets and loading mechanisms were hydraulically powered. After firing, the turret was trained, and the guns depressed to line up with upwardly angled loading tubes protected by an armored wall. Once lined up, the turret was locked and hydraulic rams forced sponges up the barrels that were also washed out with water sprays. The sponges were withdrawn, and the bagged cartridges placed by hand onto the loading trays, followed by the shells that were on trolleys manhandled into position in line with the loading tubes. The whole combination was then pushed up the loading tube and into the gun barrel by hydraulic rams. Once these were withdrawn, the turret was unlocked and could be trained onto the target. A firing tube was inserted into the vent, and this could be ignited remotely by an electric spark or manually by a percussion mechanism. Fire control was still rudimentary with individual gun layers sighting

Above: *HMS* Inflexible *was built in reply to the Italian Duillio class and was also armed with 16-inch guns in offset turrets.*

through an armored hood atop the turret, although it was envisaged that any engagements would occur at ranges of 900 meters (1,000 yards) or less. A well-trained crew could fire off one round per gun every two minutes but this was in ideal conditions and anything up to five minutes was not uncommon.

Apart from carrying very heavy guns, *Inflexible* also boasted the thickest armor ever carried by any warship. The amidships waterline belt and the armored citadel on which the turrets were mounted were protected by no less than 60 cm (24 inches) of compound armor interleaved with 43 cm (17 inches) of teak backing. This was thought to be proof against any existing weapon that could conceivably be fired against it. In later ships improved steels and different methods of protection meant that this figure was never exceeded. *Inflexible* was also built with a brig sailing rig, but this was never seriously intended as a prime method of propulsion. It was there as much as anything to cater for the Victorian Royal Navy's fetish for sail drill as means of training seamen.

The concepts embodied in the *Inflexible* were embodied in two smaller 8,500-ton ships (*Ajax* and *Agamemnon*) laid down in 1876 and having the distinction of being the last British battleships to be armed with muzzle-loading guns, in this case four 12.5-inch. They were followed by two more (*Colossus* and *Edinburgh*), which at 9,150-tons were slightly larger and were the first to be armed with the new breed of Armstrong breech-loading 12-inch guns.

Despite problems with earlier breech-loading guns, such weapons had become necessary due to improvements in explosives. The introduction of slow-burning gunpowder, which released its energy over a period of time as the shell progressed through the barrel, resulted in higher muzzle velocities and longer ranges. In order to take full advantage of this process, longer barrels were required which, together with the rifling that imparted a stabilizing spin to the shell, much increased accuracy. Ramming tight-fitting shells against the rifling up a long barrel was becoming mechanically very difficult, and the obvious solution was breech loading. Once again, it was French invention that held the key to a simple method of sealing the closed breech. Early breech loaders had used a screw plug to seal the open breech but this was difficult to operate, requiring several complete turns to achieve a firm seal. In the French interrupted screw principle, matching segments were cut out of the male and female screw threads so that the plug could be inserted right up against the breech and sealed by a turn of around 30 degrees. This allowed a much quicker loading rates and was initially applied to smaller-caliber weapons, where shells and cartridges could be loaded by hand. Such weapons were officially designated Quick-Firing (QF). With larger weapons, such as a battleship's 12-inch guns, mechanical loading was still required, but even so the rates of firing increased dramatically.

The development of QF guns occurred at an opportune moment as the great ironclads and battleships were beginning to face a new threat in the 1870s. This was the locomotive torpedo that had to be successfully developed in Italy by the Englishman Robert Whitehead. It was well understood that one of the best ways of sinking an enemy warship was to place an explosive charge on the hull under the waterline. Although various methods had been tried it was Whitehead's development of a self-propelled underwater weapon that could be accurately aimed at a target that made it a practical proposition. Although such devices had been tried before, his breakthrough was the invention of a device to ensure that the torpedo ran on a steady course and, more importantly, at a constant depth. Early examples only carried a small charge over a distance of a few hundred yards at 6 knots, but once the basic principles were understood, development proceeded rapidly although in the 1870s maximum range was only around 900 meters (1,000 yards).

Above: *The French invention of the interrupted screw provided a simple and effective method of sealing a gun breech, leading to the introduction of Quick-Firing (QF) guns.*

The French navy in particular saw the torpedo as a valuable weapon, and a school of naval officers

HMS Colossus *had the distinction of being the first British battleship with breech-loading guns as the main armament, and also the first to have compound armor.*

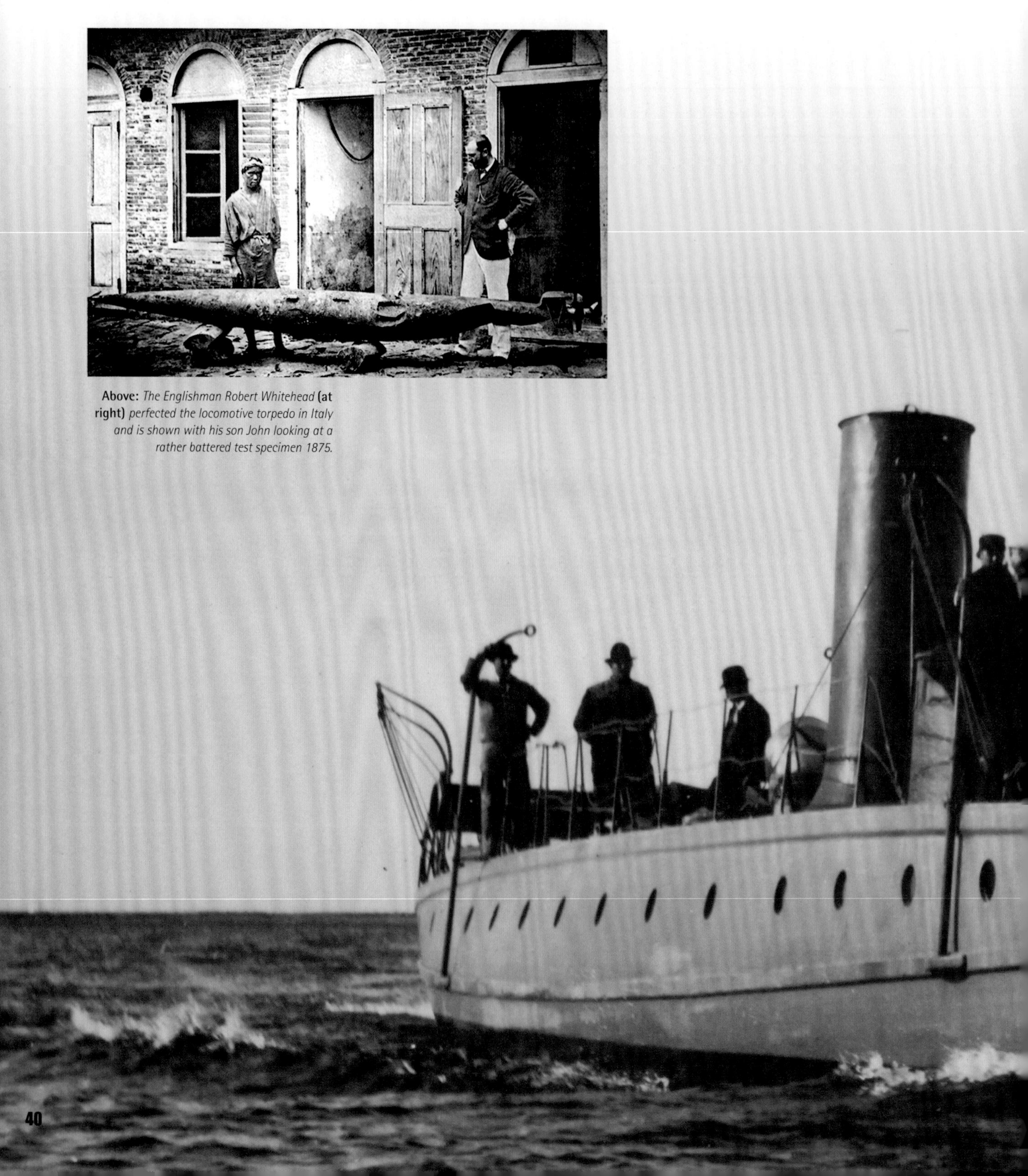

Above: *The Englishman Robert Whitehead* **(at right)** *perfected the locomotive torpedo in Italy and is shown with his son John looking at a rather battered test specimen 1875.*

advocated a great fleet of fast and small torpedo-armed craft that would out-maneuver the lumbering battleships, easily evade their ponderous heavy gunfire and deliver crippling attacks at short range. Such was the attraction of the policy that France actually stopped building first-class battleships for a while in the 1880s, and the existence of such a threat led the Royal Navy to consider countermeasures. Most of these related to defending battleships in anchorages. These were fitted with anti torpedo nets, searchlights, and fast-firing Gatling guns or Nordenfelts. (A rather similar situation exists today where warships are forced to take precautions against terrorist attacks by suicide motor boats, and the answer is much the same – detection systems and fast-firing automatic response). Initially, there was concern over protecting the battle

THE GATLING GUN AS USED IN THE BRITISH NAVY.

Above: *The threat of attack by torpedo boats led to battleships being fitted with rapid-firing Gatling guns and Nordenfelt machine guns to protect themselves while at anchor.*

The USS Stiletto, *shown at the moment of firing a torpedo, was typical of the early small torpedo boats. Despite their small size, they had the potential to damage much larger ships.*

Above: *This view of HMS* Collingwood *(launched in 1882) clearly shows how the 12-inch guns were mounted in open barbettes.*

fleet at sea but exercises showed that torpedo boats would find it difficult to get close enough to deliver their attacks, especially as battleships began to be armed with the new quick-firing guns as a deterrent. Also the Royal Navy decided to fight like with like and introduced larger and faster craft known as torpedo-boat destroyers, whose express purpose was to sink the enemy craft and deliver their own attacks.

By the start of the 1880s, the experience with the various ironclads already in commission or building led towards a more standardized design that could be built as a class and operate as a homogenous battle fleet. Nicholas Barnaby produced HMS *Collingwood*, laid down in 1880, the design being based on HMS *Dreadnought* completed in 1879. *Dreadnought* in turn was basically an enlarged version of the twin-turret HMS *Devastation*. The even larger *Collingwood* was armed with four 12-inch BL guns in twin barbette mountings symmetrically placed fore and aft and a secondary armament of six 6-inch QF guns was distributed on either beam in the superstructure between the barbettes. Although useful in fighting off attacking torpedo boats, these guns were mainly intended to be directed at the unarmored sections of an enemy ironclad. Compared to earlier ships, Barnaby's design abandoned any pretence of retaining a sailing rig and stepped only a single mainmast, for signaling and lookout purposes, behind the twin funnels. HMS *Collingwood* presented a pleasing profile and set the pattern for future battleship construction for the next 20 years. She was followed by four slightly larger 10,600-ton ships to the same overall design, which were known as the Admiral class, and shipped heavier 13.5-inch guns. A fifth ship of this class, HMS *Benbow*, carried two single 16.25-inch BL guns, one in each barbette. However, the next two ships (*Victoria* and *Sans Pareil*) were also armed with two of the 100-ton 16.25-inch guns, but in this case they were contained in an armored revolving turret. The weight of this meant that only one could be carried and this was fitted forward, with the superstructure occupying the after section of the ship. There was little advantage in this arrangement, and the huge guns took more than five minutes to load and fire. As already noted,

Above: *Despite mounting huge 16.25-inch guns, HMS* Victoria *was a retrograde step. She was lost in a tragic collision in 1893.*

Victoria was to be lost in a tragic accident after only three years in active service.

Apart from the Victoria class, British battleship construction now began to proceed along more orthodox lines, and successive classes of battleship were built in significant numbers. Indeed it was around about this time, towards the end of the 1880s that the term *battleship* came into common use. Previously the generic term *ironclad* was more commonly applied to the variety of armored ships produced over the two preceding decades. Britain's new chief naval constructor, William White, sought to improve on Barnaby's Admiral class and produced the highly successful and much admired Royal Sovereign class of which the lead ship was laid down in 1889 with another seven following over the next two years. Compared to the Admiral class displacement rose to 14,150 tons, and the most noticeable difference was the addition of an extra deck for the whole length of the hull. This substantially increased freeboard making these ships much more seaworthy and raised the four 13.5-inch guns in twin barbette mountings to 7 meters (23 feet) above the waterline, where they could be fought in virtually any weather. Secondary armament was doubled to twelve 6-inch QF and numerous light 6-pounders and 3-pounders were carried in the upper superstructure, and there were also seven fixed 18-inch torpedo tubes. (Most battleships of the time carried a torpedo armament.) A foremast and mainmast were stepped and the twin funnels were unusually set side by side abaft (behind) the bridge.

One of the Royal Sovereigns, HMS *Hood*, was completed to modified design in which the main armament was carried in two armored turrets instead of the open barbettes. However, the weight of these meant that the additional deck was discarded so that the gun mountings were lower down. This negated the advantages enjoyed by the other ships, and the idea was not repeated in this form. When, in 1894, the British government approved a massive naval expansion program it included no less than seven new battleships of the Majestic class, whose design was a natural progression of the Royal Sovereigns. The basic outline remained the same, but the 13.5-inch guns were replaced by a new type of 12-inch gun, which although of smaller caliber, offered a similar performance and greater accuracy due a longer 35-caliber barrel and being designed to use the new cordite propellant. In addition, they were protected by an armored gun house that rotated with the guns and overhung the barbette. This arrangement was lighter than former turrets, which had contained all the loading mechanism and eventually became the norm. Although the Majestics were only slightly heavier than their predecessors, they were much better armored due to the use of Harvey-steel plate, which was twice

Below: *The Royal Sovereign class designed by Sir William White set the standard for battleship design during the last decade of the 19th century.*

as effective as wrought iron. Consequently weight saved on the main belt and barbette armor could be utilized for increased protection of the superstructure and other areas.

The next British battleships were the Canopus class of six ships laid down in 1897 and 1898. These were basically repeat Majestics with improved machinery so that they could make 18.75 knots as against 17 knots. The new installation resulted in the twin funnels being on the fore and aft axis of the ship instead of side by side. The Canopus class was followed by another eight ships of the Formidable class, built in three sub-groups with minor differences and laid down between 1898 and 1901. Although retaining the same basic outline, displacement had risen to 15,000 tons due to increased protection, and the main armament 12-inch guns were of an improved 40-caliber type with a maximum range of 15,000 meters (16,500 yards). Next came another six ships of the Duncan class, all laid down in 1899 and completed 1903–4, which repeated the successful formula except that protection was slightly reduced to save weight, and the horse power of the reciprocating steam machinery rose to 18,000 shaft horsepower (shp), resulting in a speed of 19 knots.

Above: *HMS* Majestic, *name ship of a class of nine battleships.*

William White's final group of battleships were a further iteration of the Majestics, the eight King

HMS Hood's *guns were mounted in heavy armored turrets, the weight of which necessitated a reduction of freeboard.*

Left: *HMS* Canopus *was launched in 1897 and completed in 1899.*

Edward VII class laid down between 1901 and 1903. While retaining the basic characteristics, a significant change was made to the secondary armament, which comprised four 9.2-inch guns sited in single armored casemates at each corner of the central superstructure, as well as the usual battery of 6-inch QF guns, now reduced to ten.

A less obvious but very important change was that central fire control positions were now carried aloft on the masts, replacing the traditional method of guns being aimed individually on the mountings. This was a recognition of the increasing ranges at which any engagement was likely to be fought.

The 9.2-inch gun also featured in the two Lord Nelson-class ships laid down in 1904 and designed by the new chief constructor, Sir Philip Watts. While following the basic form of his predecessor's ships,

Right: *The King Edward VII class introduced the 9.2-inch gun as secondary armament.*

The eight Duncan class laid down in 1898 and '99 repeated the Majestic formula but were slightly faster.

he eliminated the 6-inch QF guns and upgraded the secondary armament to a battery of ten 9.2-inch guns carried in fully enclosed turrets, one twin mounting at each corner of the superstructure and one single mount on either beam. Vibrations at the fire control positions on the pole masts of the King Edward VII class led Watts to incorporate stiffer tripod masts.

Including the two Lord Nelsons, the Royal Navy had laid down no less than 39 battleships based on the original Majestic between 1895 and 1904, to which could be added the earlier Royal Soveriegns and two Swiftsure class originally laid down for Chile in 1902, but purchased by Britain in 1903. This was a great fleet by any standards, and with each ship costing an average of around £1 million in contemporary values, a substantial financial investment. Fortunately with her extensive empire, and a worldwide trade network

Above: *The* Lord Nelson *and her sister ship* Agamemnon *represented the ultimate British pre-dreadnought battleships.*

Below: *HMS* Swiftsure *was one of two battleships designed for the Chilean navy by Sir William White and purchased by the Royal Navy in 1903.*

dependent on an enormous merchant fleet, the United Kingdom could afford to spend this sort of money, and the political situation of the time made it absolutely necessary that she so do.

Until the end of the 19th century, France was still seen as Britain's most likely potential enemy. This view came partly from the historical perspective but also because of French colonial ambitions. In addition, France began to edge increasingly closer to an alliance with imperial Russia who, under Tsars Alexander III and Nicholas II, was also intent on becoming a significant naval power. Bases were established in the Black Sea following the Russo-Turkish war of 1877 and also at Port Arthur in the Far East. At one point the Russian navy even had a small base on the French Mediterranean coast. It was this sort of alliance that led Britain to declare a two-power standard whereby the strength of the Royal Navy should be sufficient to successfully engage any two other naval powers. However, the threat from the Franco-Russian alliance gradually receded in the face of a far more potent threat from a newer potential enemy – Germany. The new German nation had already flexed its muscles in the Franco-Prussian War of 1870–1. Although its Prussian-led army was victorious, its small navy had been completely blockaded into ineffectiveness by the much more powerful French fleet. Even so, it was not until the accession of Kaiser Wilhelm II in 1888 that Germany had a leader with the vision to make the country a maritime power. And when he appointed Admiral Tirpitz as his minster of marine in 1897, things really got moving.

Although various coast defense ships and armored barbette vessels had been built in small numbers, it was not until the four Brandenburg-class battleships were laid down in 1890 that the Imperial German Navy began to build ships up to the standard of contemporary European navies. On a displacement of 10,000 tons the Brandenburgs were 115-meters (380-feet) long and smaller and slower than the British Majestic class. The main armament comprised six 280mm (11-inch) guns in three twin armored turrets, one each fore and aft, and the third amidships between the funnels and the mainmast where its arcs of fire were restricted. While the main guns had a

Above: *Admiral Alfred von Tirpitz was the architect of German naval expansion at the end of the 19th century*

barrel length of 40 calibers, the midship guns were reduced to 35 calibers due to the restricted training space. A secondary armament of six 105-mm (4.1-inch) and eight 88-mm (3.5-inch) guns was carried as well as six fixed torpedo tubes.

In many ways, the next group of five ships comprising the Kaiser Friedrich III class (1895–8) were a retrograde step. Although slightly larger and heavier, the main armament comprised only four 240-mm (9.4-inch) guns in twin turrets fore and aft, backed up by no less than eighteen 150-mm (5.9-inch) guns of which six were in single turrets at upper deck level, and the rest in single casemate mountings at main and upper deck levels. Bearing in mind that the 9.2-inch gun was adopted as the secondary armament in

Above: Kurfürst Friedrich Wilhelm, *a Brandenburg-class battleship launched in 1890.*

British battleships, the German vessels were distinctly under-armed for a battleship. Indeed, the Royal Navy might have classified them as armored cruisers except for the fact that their speed of 17.5 knots was well below that of any self-respecting cruiser. The following Mecklenburg class of another five ships (1898–1900) were little better and apart from a redistribution of the secondary armament and more powerful machinery that boosted speed to 18 knots were more or less repeats of the earlier ships.

It was not until the Braunschweig class was laid down in 1901–2 that the main armament reverted to the 11-inch gun and secondary armament was reduced to fourteen 150-mm (5.9-inch) guns although twelve 88-mm (3.5-inch) were also carried. These ships could be distinguished from their predecessors by having three funnels instead of two, and this feature was repeated in the five Deutschland class that followed in 1903–4. By this time, displacement had risen to 13,190-tons due to better armor protection, and length was 127 meters (419 feet) – figures very similar to the contemporary British Duncan class. The German 11-inch gun in these ships fired a 240-kg (528-lb) shell over a range of 19,100 meters (20,700 yards), which compared with an 455-kg (850-lb) shell over a similar distance the best British 12-inch gun. Thus by 1905 the German navy possessed 23 modern battleships either in commission or under construction – barely half that of the Royal Navy and distinctly inferior on a case-by-case comparison of individual ships.

As Germany began to flex its maritime muscles, a similar pattern of events was beginning to unfold across the Atlantic. Despite being involved in the first ironclad naval battle during the American Civil War, the Federal Navy had made little progress since then and indeed, many of its finest ships had been laid up and allowed to rot. By 1881, the US Navy was in a parlous state, being composed almost entirely of wooden vessels, most of which were in need of repair. Even so, it was not until 1889 that the first attempt to build a major warship to international standards was attempted. The battleship USS *Texas* was completed in 1895. On a displacement of only 6,300 tons, she was armed with two single 12-inch guns mounted in turrets amidships and six 6-inch QF guns, two in single turrets fore and aft at upper deck level, and the remainder in

Braunschweig *was one of a class of five battleships launched between 1902 and 1904 that could be distinguished by their three tall funnels.*

Right: *The Kaiser Friedrich III-class battleships were lightly armed with 9.4-inch guns.*

single casemate mounts at main deck level. The main belt carried 30-cm (12-inch) compound armor, which was also extended to the central redoubt and the main armament turrets. Of similar size and layout was the USS *Maine*, which was also completed in 1895, but the main armament comprised four 10-inch guns in two twin turrets, backed up by six 6-inch guns.

The first US battleships to bear full comparison with their European contemporaries were the three Indiana-class ships laid down in 1891 and similar to the British Royal Sovereigns in outline. However, in accordance with US Navy policy at the time, they were much more heavily armed with four 13-inch, eight 8-inch and four 6-inch guns, all in twin turrets except for the 6-inch guns that were in single casemate mountings on either beam. The armor belt was varied between 45 cm (18 inches) and 36 cm (15 inches), and on a displacement of 10,300 tons the ships made only 16 knots.

The heavy weight of the turrets reduced the freeboard and these were very wet ships, unable to operate the main armament in a seaway. This was

Above: *The USS* Texas *was the first American ironclad battleship that attempted to match the standards of European navies.*

addressed in the subsequent USS *Iowa* (laid down 1893), which had a lighter main armament of four 12-inch guns and less armor protection so that freeboard increased to a reasonable level. The next pair of ships, USS *Kearsage* and *Kentucky*, featured a distinctly unusual arrangement of the main and secondary armament, which comprised four 13-inch guns in two twin turrets, each of which carried a twin 8-inch mounting on its roof, the combination rotating as one unit. In addition, a broadside battery of fourteen 5-inch guns was carried at upper deck level. Although this arrangement was adopted to save weight, it was dangerous from a tactical point of view. A single shot could disable the whole combination, quite apart from the fact that unprotected ammunition hoists between the two turrets and the magazines below were a hazard.

It was not until the Alabama class (laid down in 1896–7) that US battleship design began to approach Royal Navy standards, and these ships bore comparison with the Majestic class in most respects except speed, which remained at 16 knots, as with all the earlier ships. However, the main armament of four 13-inch guns in twin turrets fore and aft fired an 499 kg (1100-lb) shell as against the 385 kg (850-lb) shell of the British 12-inch gun. These were followed by the similarly armed *Maine* class in which more powerful machine increased speed to 18 knots and resulted in three very tall funnels replacing the previous two in the Alabamas. Consequently, these ships had an appearance not unlike some of the contemporary German battleships.

Despite the drawbacks of the combined 12-inch and 8-inch turrets introduced in the USS *Kearsage*, this arrangement was repeated in a class of five battleships laid down in 1902. The Virginia class also represented a step up in size with a length of 134 meters (441 feet) and a displacement of almost 15,000 tons, while the twin screw 19,000 ihp machinery gave a speed of 19 knots – very fast for a battleship of that period. Apart from the combined mountings fore and aft, a further

The USS Maine*, launched in 1901, was named for its predecessor that was destroyed by an explosion in Havana harbor. The early U.S. submarine passing in front of the ship hints at the underwater threat to the dominance of the battleship.*

four 8-inch guns were mounted on a pair of twin turrets, one on either beam, and twelve 6-inch guns were carried in casemate mountings on the broadside. The basic design was repeated with six Connecticut-class ships (1903–5) except that the combined mountings were finally discarded, and the secondary armament of eight 8-inch guns was carried in four twin turrets placed at the corners of the central superstructure. Displacement rose to 16,000 tons but less powerful machinery meant that speed was reduced to 18 knots.

The increasing size of these battleships caused concern, and in an effort to reverse the trend, two Mississippi-class ships were laid down in 1904. The hull length was reduced to 116 meters (382 feet), less

USS North Dakota *at the same Naval Review, only a year after being completed.*

Left: *USS* Mississippi *at a Naval Review in 1911. She and her sister ship* Idaho *were sold to Greece in 1914.*

powerful machinery requiring only two funnels was installed, and although the main and secondary armament remained the same, displacement was reduced to 13,000 tons. However, speed fell to only 17 knots, which made it difficult for these ships to combine tactically with their sisters, and the experiment was not repeated. Indeed, as will be seen, the next generation of battleships were to start a trend to much larger and more heavily armed vessels.

Thus by 1905, the US Navy had in service or under construction some 31 relatively modern battleships. This lifted the service from being only the world's 12th-ranking navy in 1883, behind countries such as Spain, Chile and China, to the second most powerful in 1905, although still a long way behind the Royal Navy. The reasons for this massive expansion were complex, but one factor was the publication by the American naval historian Captain Alfred Mahan of his acclaimed book *The Influence of Seapower on History.* Here, for the first time was a reasoned analysis of why Britain was such a successful trading nation and how this was inextricably linked with the strength of her navy. The ideas expressed in this publication added strength to the ideas of some American politicians and naval officers, who realized that the United States could no longer rely on the vast stretches of

the Pacific and the Atlantic to deter the expansion of other nationalist forces. In particular, the continued presence of powerful Spanish warships in the Caribbean and in the Pacific was seen as a threat and an affront to US security.

Matters came to a head with a rebellion of the inhabitants of Cuba against their Spanish masters. US Navy ships were dispatched in a neutral capacity to assist American citizens caught up in the fighting. On February 15, 1898, the battleship USS *Maine* was anchored off Havana when she was destroyed by a massive internal explosion. Although later investigations pointed to an accidental ignition of coal gas, at the time a sabotage theory was rampant and this was enough to cause the United States to declare war on Spain. In the Pacific, a squadron of US Navy cruisers and gunboats destroyed a force of Spanish ships at anchor in Manila Bay in the Philippines, while in the Atlantic efforts were made to locate and intercept a force of Spanish cruisers dispatched to assist the Cuban garrison. However, the Spanish ships under Admiral Cervera reached Cuba without being brought to battle and were secured in Santiago Harbor on May 19, 1899, where a US blockading force was quickly established. After several weeks under siege, Cervera decided to make a run for it and sailed with his four cruisers. Ranged against him was a considerable force which included the battleships *Iowa*, *Oregon*, *Texas* and *New York*. Initially the US ships were caught by surprise and a confused mêlée resulted, but the battle then developed into a chase before all of the Spanish ships were sunk or run aground and destroyed. Analysis of the action showed that most of the damage had been caused by the fast-firing 8-inch and 6-inch guns of the battleships secondary armaments and only two hits from the larger 12-inch guns appear to have been recorded.

It was not only Spain that had caused concern to the United States. Across the Pacific Ocean, Japan was rapidly emerging as a major maritime force and pursued expansionist policies in China. From being an almost medieval backwater until around 1860, Japan was rapidly turning itself into a modern state with increasing industrial capacity. However, at the start of the 20th century, its efficient and well-trained navy was mostly equipped with ships built in Europe. It had already shown its prowess in the Battle of the Yalu River on September 17, 1894, when a Japanese force intercepted Chinese warships covering troop transports. The Chinese fleet included two German-built 7,200-ton battleships each armed with four 12-inch guns carried in two barbette mountings set in echelon in the style of HMS *Inflexible*. There were two smaller barbette ships and six small cruisers but all of the ships were slow, their crews badly trained and there was a lack of modern quick-firing medium-caliber guns. This contrasted with the Japanese cruiser force, which was well handled and operated with the ruthless efficiency that was to characterize Japan's naval actions. The faster cruisers literally ran rings around the ponderous Chinese vessels, of which five were sunk and both of the battleships badly damaged, although one of them managed a hit on the Japanese cruiser *Matsushima* with a 12-inch shell, forcing it to pull out of the battle. The action was broken off as darkness fell and was a notable Japanese victory.

One of the side-effects of the Sino-Japanese war and the subsequent peace negotiations in which European parties were involved, was that Russia gained the strategically important harbor at Port Arthur – now the port of Lüshunko – on the Yellow Sea. This was connected to an extension of the Trans-Siberian railroad, enabling troop reinforcements to be rapidly

The wreck of the Spanish armored cruiser Viscaya *after the Battle of Santiago.*

dispatched. A Russian Asiatic Fleet was established, which included no less than six battleships. An inconclusive fleet action was fought in February 1904, when the Russian fleet consisting of six battleships and three cruisers came out and was met by the Japanese with four battleships and four armored cruisers. A long-range gunnery battle followed in which the Russians appeared to be getting the best of the action. Then a lucky hit from a 12-inch shell hit the armored conning tower of the Russian 13,000-ton French-built flagship *Tsarevitch*, killing Admiral Vitgeft and causing the ship to veer out of control. The Russian line dissolved in confusion, and their ships headed back to Port Arthur where they were subsequently destroyed by land-based artillery.

The Japanese navy drew some valuable lessons from this engagement, particularly the need to practice and refine accurate long-range gunnery. That they were successful in this was to be clearly illustrated in the Battle of Tsushima, which was to provide a dramatic climax to the era of the ironclad. To defend interests in the Far East, a Russian fleet under Admiral Rojestvensky was dispatched from Europe. When the opposing forces met approaching the Straits of Tsushima on May 27, 1905, the Russian admiral appeared to lead a numerically superior force with a substantial advantage in firepower. In practice, all was not well. His main strength was concentrated in four large battleships and four older battleships. Although his fleet numbered more than 30 vessels, many of these were obsolete, and some of the support ships could only manage 10 knots, which reduced the speed of the whole fleet.

For Japan, Admiral Togo's fleet was smaller, the main force being four battleships and eight armored cruisers, but his ships were faster, and the crews well drilled. Interestingly virtually all of his battleships were British-built including his 15,200-ton flagship *Mikasa*. Initially, he maneuvered his ships into line ahead running parallel to the Russian fleet. At this point his superior speed enabled him to pull ahead and then steam across the bows of the advancing enemy line, achieving the classic maneuver of crossing the enemy's 'T' so that his ships could concentrate their fire onto

the leading ships. The Russian flagship *Suvoroff* was soon hit and pulled out of line, and other ships began to take heavy fire. Within a few hours, the Japanese had secured a major victory, sinking or capturing every one of the Russian fleet. It was perhaps no coincidence that the Japanese Admiral Togo was a professed admirer of Admiral Nelson and his methods, even to the extent of flying a dramatic moral-boosting flag signal as his ships went into action.

Today, his flagship *Mikasa* is still preserved as a museum and memorial at Yokosuka in Japan, the only surviving battleship of this era anywhere in the world and one with a battle-proven history.

The Mikasa*, a British-built battleship that was Admiral Togo's flagship at the Battle of Tsushima in 1905.*

The French-built Russian pre-dreadnought Tserarevich *completed in 1903 illustrates the pronounced tumblehome, which was characteristic of French battleships of the period. This ship was damaged in the Battle of the Yellow Sea in 1904.*

The Loss of the HMS Victoria

Above: *HMS* Camperdown, *flagship of Rear-Admiral Markham.*

In 1893, HMS *Victoria* was the flagship of the Royal Navy's prestigious Mediterranean Fleet when she was lost as the result of a collision with her sister ship HMS *Camperdown*. The event became perhaps the most infamous in Royal Navy history, and was the naval incident satirized in the 1949 British film *Kind Hearts and Coronets.*

The sinking occurred on June 22, 1893, at around 3 p.m., during exercises off the coast of Syria in full view of an onshore audience. The fleet of 11 pre-dreadnoughts was preparing to come to anchor under the command of 61-year-old Vice-Admiral Sir George Tryon, aboard the *Victoria*. Tryon was regarded as a highly competent officer with original ideas but was also an iron disciplinarian possessed of a strong and overbearing personality. He liked to develop initiative among his commanders by confronting them with testing situations at short notice. These characteristics made him a difficult man to serve under.

Tryon had decided on a flamboyant maneuver to bring the fleet to anchor. Starting off cruising in two columns of six and five ships, the lead ships of each column would reverse course by turning inwards towards each other, the rest doing the same in

Above: *Vice-Admiral Sir George Tyron RN.*

succession as they reached the position of turn of the lead ships. The columns would then proceed a short distance in the new direction before anchoring. The turning diameter of the ships meant that the columns would have to start a minimum of eight cables (1,450 meters; 1,600 yards) apart to avoid the ships meeting in the middle.

Below: *HMS* Victoria *showing the massive single 16.25-inch gun turret.*

Tryon's original idea was to start the turn with the columns six cables apart. He accepted a correction that eight cables was required, but inexplicably went back to ordering the six cable distance soon after, despite queries from his staff. Tryon led the starboard column of six ships, while the port column of five ships was led by his deputy, Rear-Admiral Albert Hastings Markham, in *Camperdown*.

The two signals hoisted ordering the turn were: 'Second Division alter course in succession 16 points to starboard preserving the order of the fleet' and 'First Division alter course in succession 16 points to port preserving the order of the fleet.' Seeing the hoists, Markham openly declared the maneuver impossible, and delayed raising the necessary flags to acknowledge. But before Markham could query the order, Tryon semaphored 'What are you waiting for?' This rebuke stung Markham into acknowledging, and both columns began their turns. Markham rationalized that Tryon intended to turn outside him, as this would mean that Tryon would remain in the starboard column once course had been reversed, thus preserving the order of the fleet. Nevertheless, Markham took the precaution of having his men sent to collision stations.

As the ships headed towards each other at about 9 knots, various officers on both vessels were waiting for some last-minute change of order from Tryon that would resolve the situation. Tryon himself was apparently watching the turns of the ships behind him, until he was asked by the captain of the *Victoria* for permission to go full astern with the port engine to tighten the turn. Tryon then saw that the *Victoria* and *Camperdown* were less than 460 meters (500 yards) apart. He gave permission, but it was too late. Markham ordered his engines full astern at around the same time.

Camperdown struck the *Victoria* on her starboard bow at an angle of about 80 degrees, and as the ships continued to swing a hole of 9 square meters (100 square feet) was torn in the flagships' hull. *Camperdown*, in common with most contemporary battleships, was fitted with a ram at the bow designed to strike below the waterline. Ramming remained a standard tactic at this time, as gunnery engagements between ironclads were still potentially inconclusive.

With engines reversed, the ram was quickly withdrawn, which only served to allow more water into the *Victoria*. Tryon had ordered all watertight doors closed a minute before the collision, but it was too late. In the hot weather all possible doors, hatches and vents had been left open. Within ten minutes the low forward deck was awash, with the gun turret forming an island, water pouring into the turret ports, and the stern of the ship rising from the water. Thirteen minutes after the collision, the *Victoria* rolled to starboard and sank quickly, bow first. Most of the crew got into the water, but many were then killed by the suction of the descending ship and the still rapidly turning propellers. Although 357 crew were rescued, another 358 perished, including Tryon who stayed on the bridge in the traditional manner. *Camperdown* had also taken on hundreds of tons of water but stayed afloat. The two ships following the leading vessels only narrowly avoided collisions themselves.

Two issues had to be resolved in the subsequent investigation: Why had *Victoria* gone down so quickly, and who was to blame? Design features of the *Victoria*, such as the arrangement of watertight bulkheads and doors, and the massive main turret mounted on the

The last moments of HMS Victoria *dramatically caught on camera.*

low foredeck, had created instability. Another point was that *Victoria's* side armor did not extend to the bow area, where *Camperdown's* ram struck. However, it was concluded that had the watertight doors been secured prior to the collision, the ship would not sunk.

As to blame, there was little doubt of Tryon's culpability. He was heard by more than one officer to say, 'It was all my fault!' immediately after the collision. However, the reasons for his behavior remain unclear. Tryon had issued a similar turn order to two columns too close together during the 1890 Home Fleet maneuvers. On that occasion, the order was declined by the other column leader. If the 1893 order was not a mistake, perhaps he intended Markham to turn outside him (the opposite of what Markham believed), or perhaps Tryon was testing Markham to see what he would do. If the orders *were* a mistake, it has been suggested Tryon confused radius of turn with diameter, or had in mind the shorter distance required for the more common 90-degree turn. There have also been suggestions that Tryon was physically or mentally ill at the time. Markham received some blame for blindly obeying dangerous orders, and his reputation and operational career were blighted, although he eventually received promotion to admiral.

As a postscript, the wreck of the *Victoria* was relocated in 2004, stuck vertically in the mud of the seabed with her stern pointing to the surface, the combined weight of the flooded forward compartments and the massive guns taking her straight to the bottom bow first.

Victorian Naval Constructors

Above: *HMS* Sultan, *a fully rigged central battery ship of the type initially preferred by Reed over the turret ship.*

From Tudor times, the design of sailing warships had rested with master shipwrights at the yards that built the ships, but by the end of the 17th century the post of Surveyor of the Navy had been created. Under his direction, each class of warship was laid down according to certain specifications. In the 18th century, the French were quick to apply scientific principles to warship design and produced ships with superior sailing qualities to their Royal Navy contemporaries, but it was not until 1811 that the Admiralty first established a school of naval architecture at Portsmouth. One of its graduates was Isaac Watts who later, as Surveyor and Chief Constructor of the Navy, was responsible for the design of HMS *Warrior*, Britain's first ironclad battleship launched in 1860.

Watts was succeeded as chief constructor by Edward Reed in 1863, a post he held for seven years during which some of the most dramatic developments in warship design and construction occurred. Born in 1830, Reed began his career as a shipwright apprentice at Sheerness dockyard in Kent, but in 1849 won a place at the School of Mathematics and Naval Construction at Portsmouth. Graduating in 1852, he returned to Sheerness where the only employment available was as a supernumerary draughtsman. Frustrated at the lack of career opportunities, he resigned and worked as a technical journalist, editing the influential *Mechanic's Magazine*. In 1860, Reed became secretary to the newly formed Institute of Naval Architects. At the same time he offered the

Above: *Sir Edward James Reed KCB, FRS, Chief Constructor of the Royal Navy from 1863–70.*

Above: *HMS* Neptune *was a fully rigged turret ship originally designed by Reed for the Brazilian navy but was purchased by the Royal Navy while still being built in 1878.*

Admiralty Board designs for various armored ships that eventually resulted in a contract to design HMS *Bellerophon*, a 7,500-ton central-battery armored ship launched in 1865. Reed's work in this field led to his appointment as chief constructor in 1863 at the age of 33, even before *Bellerophon* was laid down.

Although Reed favored the central-battery ship, he was responsible for the design of HMS *Monarch*. This was the Royal Navy's first major seagoing armored ship fitted with revolving turrets – although a full sailing rig was also carried. Subsequently, Reed refined his ideas for a turret-armed ship and produced HMS *Devastation*, which was laid down in 1869 and completed four years later. Here, Reed did away with any form of sail rig and mounted the twin 12-inch muzzle-loading rifled (MLR) guns within

Below: *HMS* Neptune *right elevation and deck plan (with masts truncated).*

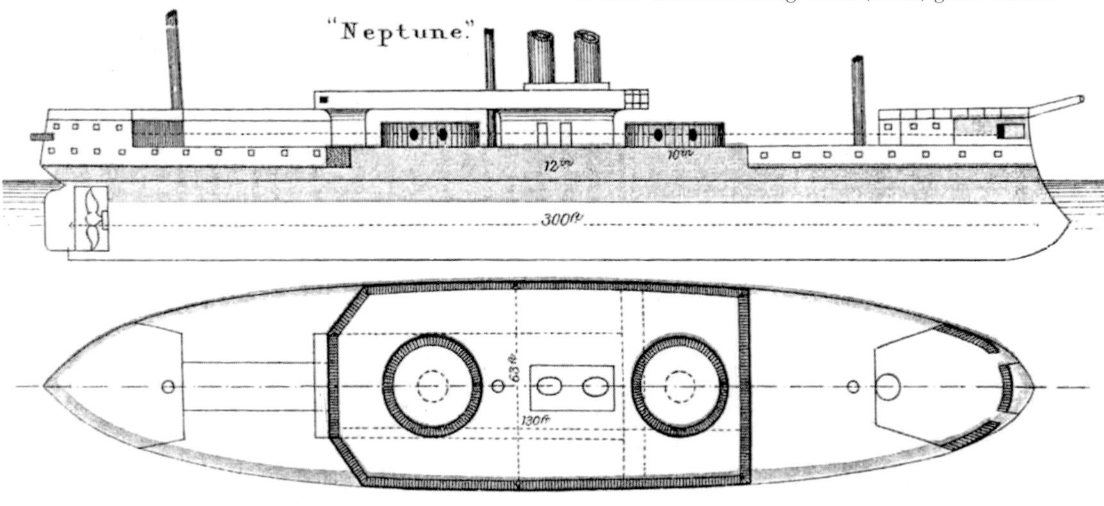

Above: *HMS* Warrior *the first iron-hulled, armor-plated warship.*

a raised breastwork that gave added protection as well as keeping them clear of heavy seas. In this ship Reed began a line of development that resulted in

Below: *Sir Nathaniel Barnaby KCB, Chief Constructor of the Royal Navy from 1872–85.*

the evolution of the battleship up to the end of the Second World War.

By the time *Devastation* was completed, Reed had resigned as chief constructor in protest at the Admiralty's actions in allowing Captain Cowper Coles to design and build a sail-rigged steam-powered turret ship, HMS *Captain*, without any reference to Reed's department. His action was shown to be fully justified when the *Captain* foundered in a gale in September 1870 with the loss of all hands – including Coles. Reed continued to design warships for other navies, and in 1874 became a Member of Parliament, where he had a successful political career before dying of a stroke in November 1906.

Reed's successor in 1870 was actually his brother-in-law, Nathaniel Barnaby, who had also started his career in Sheerness dockyard and trained at the same school of naval architecture. Barnaby then went to Woolwich dockyard as a draughtsman before joining the Department of Naval Construction in 1854, subsequently assisting with the design of HMS *Warrior*.

After acting as Reed's assistant, he was eventually appointed chief constructor in 1870, although the title was changed to Director of Naval Construction (DNC) in 1875. During his period of office, Barnaby had to grapple with the increasing size and power of naval guns, and the resulting requirement to increase armor protection of his ships. Inevitably, this gave rise to a significant increase in the size of the armored ships, and his first major project was HMS *Dreadnought*, a successor to Reed's *Devastation*, displacing 10,800 tons. Next he designed HMS *Inflexible*, which was armed with the largest muzzle-loading guns ever mounted in a British warship, 81-ton, 16-inch-caliber monsters in two twin turrets amidships. Eventually, Barnaby returned to a more conventional layout, and in HMS *Collingwood* (1879) he set the standard for British battleships for the next 25 years. Armed with 12-inch guns, their low freeboard and breastwork superstructure made them wet ships on the open seas.

A desire to mount heavier weapons resulted in one of the Collingwood class being modified to carry two single 110-ton 16.25-inch guns, while two Victoria class armored rams carried the two guns in a twin barbette mounting. The rate of fire of these large guns made the tactical employment of these ships a dubious prospect, and Barnaby's last designs were based on the Collingwood class except that the main armament comprised 13.5-inch guns and displacement rose to over 12,500 tons. By 1885, Barnaby was suffering from health problems caused by the strain of his work, and he resigned although he continued to take a professional interest in naval developments until his death in 1915, aged 86.

The new DNC was William White, the last of the constructors of the Victorian navy, who remained in his post until 1901 and whose early career was similar to his predecessor's. Born in 1845, he served as an apprentice at Devonport dockyard and attended the new School of Naval Architecture at South Kensington, London, in 1864, the year of its opening. White then worked as a draughtsman before moving on to work with Sir Edward Reed and later with Nathaniel Barnaby. During this time, he worked on *Dreadnought* and *Inflexible*, and undertook a commission to design a cruiser for the Argentinian navy. He also wrote a book, *The Manual of Naval Architecture*, which became a standard reference source and was translated into many languages.

White's most famous creations were the Royal Sovereign-class battleships, the first of which was laid down in 1889. These improved on the Collingwood class by lengthening the hull and adding a deck to increase freeboard, with a consequent dramatic improvement in sea-keeping qualities. The design was repeated, with improvements to armor protection, in the Majestic class, which also had an armored gunhouse protecting the barbette-mounted 12-inch guns, an arrangement repeated in all subsequent battleships. White also designed the Canopus, Formidable, Duncan and King Edward VII classes of battleship, and in all was responsible for the staggering total of 47 battleships, 26 armored cruisers, 102 protected cruisers and 75 other warships. Following his retirement in 1901, White assisted with the design of the Cunard liner RMS *Mauritania*, and held the presidency of several engineering institutions before his death in 1913.

The constructors and naval architects of the Victorian period were outstanding engineers who embraced new technologies. They were the front runners in the arms race to ensure that Britain's maritime supremacy remained unchallenged at the dawn of the 20th century.

Below: *Sir William Henry White, Director of Naval Construction 1885–1901.*

DREADNOUGHT

HMS Dreadnought *– the start of a new era for battleships.*

Dreadnought

On February 10, 1906, King George VII traveled to Portsmouth Dockyard to launch the latest battleship for the Royal Navy. As part of Britain's ongoing program of building up her naval strength, the launch of yet another battleship was not such an unusual occurrence – but this one was different. As the King spoke the traditional words, 'I name this ship *Dreadnought*, may God bless all who sail in her,' and smashed the bottle of Australian wine over bows, he might as well have fired a starting pistol for one of the greatest arms races of all time. (In fact, the bottle required a second attempt to make it smash.)

HMS *Dreadnought* represented a break from the steady evolution of the battleship that had taken place until that time. At the direction of the brilliant and imaginative Admiral Sir John Fisher, the naval staff and ship constructors had come up with a design that outclassed all existing battleships and made them obsolete at a stroke. The ship had been laid down in great secrecy only a few months earlier on October 2, 1905, and with many important components previously ordered and manufactured, the construction of the hull proceeded apace to make her ready for launching just over four months later – a tremendous achievement under any circumstances. Once launched, the hull was towed into dry dock for fitting out with machinery and her full armament of heavy guns. There was no let up in the pace of working and by the beginning of September, HMS *Dreadnought* was commissioned into the Royal Navy, ready to commence trials. Total construction time was only 12 months (two months less than planned) and set a record for battleship construction that has never been surpassed since.

There was good reason for this haste. Even as the ship was being built and details of its features became known, it was recognized by other navies that their own battleships were suddenly outclassed and, if they wanted to remain as a front rank naval power, they would have to start constructing dreadnoughts of their own. By developing the dreadnought, Britain was also putting its own maritime strength at risk. Any potential enemy armed with dreadnoughts would be a threat to the Royal Navy's own battle fleet built at

Below: *Completed in only twelve months, HMS* Dreadnought *outclassed every battleship afloat when she commissioned at the end of 1906.*

The brilliant Admiral Sir John Fisher was the driving force behind the concept of HMS Dreadnought.

Above: *Battleships such as the French* Justice*, completed in 1908 and armed with a mix of 12-inch and 7.6-inch guns were rendered obsolete by the faster and more heavily armed* Dreadnought.

great expense over the previous two decades. The only course open was to build dreadnoughts at a greater rate than anyone else and ensure that supremacy was immediately regained and maintained.

So what made HMS *Dreadnought* such a revolutionary weapon and how had she come into existence? As already mentioned, the driving force behind her creation was Sir John Fisher who rose to the post of First Sea Lord, the professional head of the Royal Navy, in October 1904. Before that, he had held several important posts including command of the Mediterranean Fleet, regarded by all as the most prestigious seagoing appointment in the navy. The post offered every opportunity to try new ideas and encourage and develop younger officers into his forward way of thinking. In 1902 he was appointed Second Sea Lord, responsible for manning and training issues throughout the Royal Navy. Here he made his mark with several major reforms in the selection and training of officers, making promotion on merit much more the norm, re-organizing and improving conditions for both officers and men, and placing considerable emphasis on the importance of gunnery training.

Fisher was always receptive to new ideas and was quick to take advantage of new weapons and systems as they became available, although his apparent lack of regard for tradition inevitable made enemies in some quarters. Nevertheless, while in the Mediterranean his ideas concerning a new capital ship began to crystallize, and he was able to take them further when acting as Commander-in-Chief (C-in-C) Portsmouth in 1903 in conjunction with the dockyard's naval constructors. At that point he envisaged a ship, which he named HMS *Untakeable*, armed with eight heavy caliber guns, at least six of which would be capable of firing on either broadside. High speed in excess of current battleships was essential so that she could choose her own tactical position and also successfully engage enemy cruisers. No secondary armament was required as she could fight battles at long ranges of her own choosing, and the heaviest practical armor would be carried. The hull would have high freeboard for good seaworthiness and to enable the guns to be fought in all but the worst weather conditions. Rigid tripod masts would carry the latest fire control systems and all other command functions would be enclosed in an armored conning tower below the bridge.

In 1904, Fisher formed a Committee on Designs to look into the project in more detail, and a series of important decisions stemmed from this. Fisher himself initially proposed an armament of 10-inch guns on the basis that they had a higher rate of fire but soon came round to the idea of the 12-inch guns firing a heavier projectile. He was adamant that the ship should be capable of heavy fire directly forward so the final configuration was ten 12-inch guns in five twin turrets – one on the centerline on the forecastle and two on the centerline aft – while the other two were winged out on either beam between the funnels. In this way a broadside of eight guns could be fired, and six could fire directly ahead or astern. This single-caliber main armament was one of the features that distinguished *Dreadnought* from her predecessors, and it conferred significant advantages in controlling long-range gunfire. With the guns under a central control firing salvoes or broadsides, the shells would all land together making it relatively easy to spot and make adjustments, something that was not easy when guns of different calibers were engaging at the same time.

In order to achieve the required speed (at least 21 knots to give a 3-knot advantage over most contemporary battleships) a bold decision was made to install the newly developed steam turbines. These had been successfully tested in the destroyers *Cobra* and *Viper* of 1899 and fitted in the cruiser *Amethyst* in 1904. The great success of these installations gave the design committee the confidence to specify them for their new battleship.

In designing HMS *Dreadnought*, the committee gave due consideration to intelligence gathered from the results of the few engagements in which pre-dreadnought battleships had been involved – notably the recently fought Battle of Tsushima in the Far East. This appeared to confirm the correctness of

Above: *In* Dreadnought *the elegantly simple steam turbine replaced complex reciprocating machinery such as this installation destined for the cruiser HMS* Andromeda.

the emphasis on long-range gunnery and the tactical advantage accruing from higher speeds. Consideration was also given to the effects of battle damage, and as a result *Dreadnought* was designed so that her transverse bulkheads were watertight right up to main deck level. There was no provision for watertight doors to allow for access through the bulkheads so, in order to move fore and aft at the lower levels of the ship, it was necessary to climb up to main deck level and then descend again into the relevant section. Although this was inconvenient, it removed any likelihood of the watertight integrity of the ship being compromised by a watertight door being left open – a significant factor in the loss of the battleship *Victoria* after she was rammed by the *Camperdown* (*see page 62*). The completed *Dreadnought* displaced 17,900 tons of which no less than 5,000 tons was devoted to armor protection including an 28-cm (11-inch) belt of armor and similar thickness of protection for the turrets, barbettes and conning tower.

While Fisher and the Royal Navy are rightly credited with the breakthrough in naval construction that HMS *Dreadnought* represented, there were others thinking along the same lines hence the haste with which the ship was built. In 1903, the influential reference book *Jane's Fighting Ships* had published an article by the Italian naval architect Vittorio Cuniberti in which he set out ideas for 'an ideal battleship for Britain's Royal Navy.' This proposed a 17,000-ton ship armed with twelve 12-inch guns and capable of 24 knots – not so different from Fisher's own ideas. Meanwhile, in North America the US Navy had been authorized as early as March 1905, even before *Dreadnought* was laid down, to construct two new battleships of the *South Carolina* class. In fact, they were not laid down until the end of 1906, but they subscribed to the big-gun school with an armament of eight 12-inch guns arranged in four twin turrets, two forward and two aft. For the first time, these were placed in super-firing positions. In other words, within each pair the inner turret was mounted on a higher barbette so that it could fire over the top of the one in front. This arrangement allowed the turrets to be grouped more closely together so that less armor was require to protect the turret trunkings and magazines. A light secondary armament of 3-inch guns was carried but the outdated reciprocating engine was retained, which only allowed a speed of 18 knots.

Fisher's fertile mind was not only concerned with battleships. The Royal Navy already possessed several armored cruisers that displaced around 14,000 tons, the same as many battleships. These were armed with 9.2-inch guns and could make around 23 knots. They were intended for the traditional trade-protection role, intercepting and sinking enemy commerce-raiders, but were also expected to work with the battle fleet by scouting ahead and acting in a support role when battle was joined. Fisher decided to improve this type of vessel by equipping them with the same 12-inch

The American South Carolina class (commissioned 1910) introduced the concept of super-firing turrets.

guns as the battleships so that they would be more useful as an adjunct to the fleet and also raising speed to 25 knots so as to be able to catch any existing cruiser, as well as having a useful excess margin over dreadnought-type battleships. In order to achieve such speeds, installed horsepower rose to 41,000 shaft horsepower (shp) compared to only 23,000 shp in *Dreadnought*, and the hull was lengthened to 173 meters (567 feet) overall. To save weight the main armament was reduced to eight 12-inch guns in four turrets, one each fore and aft and two *en echelon* amidships, allowing six guns to fire in any direction including directly ahead and astern and eight guns could be brought to bear on a restricted broadside arc. As these ships were not intended to form part of the line of battle, and to save weight, armor was reduced to a 15-cm (6-inch) main belt and 18-cm (7-inch) plates for turret fronts and barbettes. Despite this, the ships were still very large and imposing, and the term *battlecruiser* was coined to describe them. In the public mind, and to many politicians and even admirals, they were capital ships and were an important component when comparing strengths with other navies.

As a deliberate decision, no battlecruisers or further dreadnoughts were laid down until HMS *Dreadnought* had completed her initial trials. Given the novel nature of the new ship this was a sensible approach but she soon showed her worth, and the steam turbines in particular were a great success. Consequently no less than three battlecruisers (*Invincible, Inflexible* and *Indomitable*) were laid down in early 1906 while the first of three dreadnought battleships, HMS *Bellerophon*, was also laid down in December 1906 and the others in the following January and February. These were of similar dimensions to *Dreadnought*, although displacement

Above: The *Bellerophon class could be distinguished by having tripod fore masts and mainmasts to support the fire control platforms.*

Below: *The St. Vincent class repeated the Dreadnought formula but were armed with a new longer ranged 12-inch, 50-caliber gun.*

rose to 18,600 tons, and the layout of the main armament was the same. However, the close-range anti-torpedo boat armament was strengthened to sixteen 4-inch QF guns in place of the 12-pounders carried in *Dreadnought*. An obvious external difference was the repositioning of the tripod foremast forward of the fore funnel, where it was not affected by the smoke fumes (as experienced aboard *Dreadnought*), and a second mast was added ahead of the second funnel.

The pace of construction continued with three more dreadnoughts of the St. Vincent class laid down 1907–8. Externally these differed little from the Bellerophons, but a significant change was the fitting of a new 12-inch, 50-caliber gun in place of the older 45-caliber weapons. These boosted a maximum range from 17,000 meters (18,600 yards) to almost 91,200 meters (21,000 yards), a substantial improvement although each mounting was heavier and displacement

rose to 19,250 tons. A slightly longer hull and increased power maintained speed at 21 knots.

Up to this point, the case for continued battleship construction had full political support, but with six dreadnoughts and three battlecruisers on plan, the Liberal government of the time decided there were other priorities and consequently only one battleship and one battlecruiser were authorized in 1908. The battleship was HMS *Neptune*, and her keel was laid in January 1909. The arrangement of the wing turrets in the earlier dreadnoughts had drawn criticism as not all guns could fire on the broadside. Neptune's design was therefore altered with the wing turrets amidships staggered in echelon fore and aft of the second funnel

Above: *HMS* Indefatigable, *the first of a new class of battlecruisers, was also armed with the new 12-inch, 50-caliber gun.*

Left: *Germany's answer to the* Dreadnought *was the Nassau class but these were armed with 11-inch guns and could only make 19 knots using reciprocating machinery.*

so that both could train on either beam, echoing the arrangement in the battlecruisers. In order to give these guns enough space to train, the fourth (X) turret was raised to fire over the after (Y) turret so that they could be moved closer together. A flying deck over the midship turrets connected the fore and aft superstructures so that the appearance of this ship was substantially altered although the hull, machinery and scale of armor was largely unaltered.

The 1908 battlecruiser was HMS *Indefatigable,* which was similar to the earlier ships except that she also carried the new 12-inch, 50-caliber guns and her hull was lengthened slightly to give improved arcs of fire to the midship turrets. The port-side wing turret was moved forward and could train through an arc of around 30 degrees to starboard in the gap between the fore funnel and the repositioned second funnel, which now stood clear of the main superstructure. Similarly, the starboard wing turret could train on the port broadside between the second and third funnel, which was now at the forward end of the superstructure.

In any potential war, Britain could count on the manpower provided by the nations of her large empire. Discussion were held with various governments, and this resulted in the Commonwealth Defence Program under which, among other provisions, Australia and New Zealand agreed to each pay for the construction of a Indefatigable-class battlecruiser. These two ships were laid down at Scottish shipyards in June 1910 and were named after their respective donor countries. HMAS *Australia* was commissioned into the Australian navy in June 1913, which accepted responsibility for running costs and retained command of the ship, although she would be put at the disposal of the Royal Navy if the need arose. On the other hand, New Zealand was too small a country to afford such an expense, and its ship was donated to the Royal Navy on completion in November 1911.

It was hoped that the slowdown in the building program would be noted by other nations, which might then be persuaded to cut back their own construction. This was particularly directed at Germany, who initially had appeared slow to react to the advent of the dreadnoughts. The four pre-dreadnought *Deutschland* class had been laid down in 1904–5 and all had entered service by 1908, but two more years were to elapse before any new dreadnoughts were laid down. The German Navy under Admiral Tirpitz had not been surprised by the appearance of HMS *Dreadnought*, but they realized that their own ships would have to be larger and more powerful to match the British ships. This posed a severe problem as the main German navy base at Kiel in the Baltic was separated from Wilhelmshaven on the North Sea coast by the Jutland peninsula, and the two were linked through Schleswig Holstein by the Kiel Canal. While this could accommodate ships up to the size of the pre-dreadnoughts, larger ships could not use it unless it was dredged and widened, and new lock gates fitted. This was a major engineering task and naturally took time.

Eventually four Nassau-class dreadnoughts were laid down by Germany in 1907, although in many respects they were still inferior to the British ships. Displacing 18,850 tons, they were armed with twelve 280-mm (11-inch) guns in six twin turrets, one fore and aft, and two on each beam. This was not a particularly practical layout as despite the number of guns only eight could be trained on either broadside. Also, a considerable secondary battery was shipped consisting of twelve 150-mm (5.9-inch) and sixteen 88-mm (3.5-inch) guns, which rather went against the big-gun concept demonstrated by *Dreadnought*. An even greater drawback was that they were still powered by reciprocating machinery capable of a speed of just 19.5 knots. On the plus side they were well armored and particular attention had been paid to underwater protection, which included steel bulkheads behind the lateral coal bunkers and watertight cofferdams that would absorb the initial damage. This attention to underwater protection was a significant feature of all the German dreadnoughts and was to prove its worth in the heat of battle.

Having started construction of dreadnoughts, the German navy then began laying down new ships at an increasing rate. The four ships of the Helgoland class laid down under the 1908 program represented a substantial increase in size, being some 21 meters (70 feet) longer and taking displacement to 22,800 tons, making them the largest dreadnoughts up to that time.

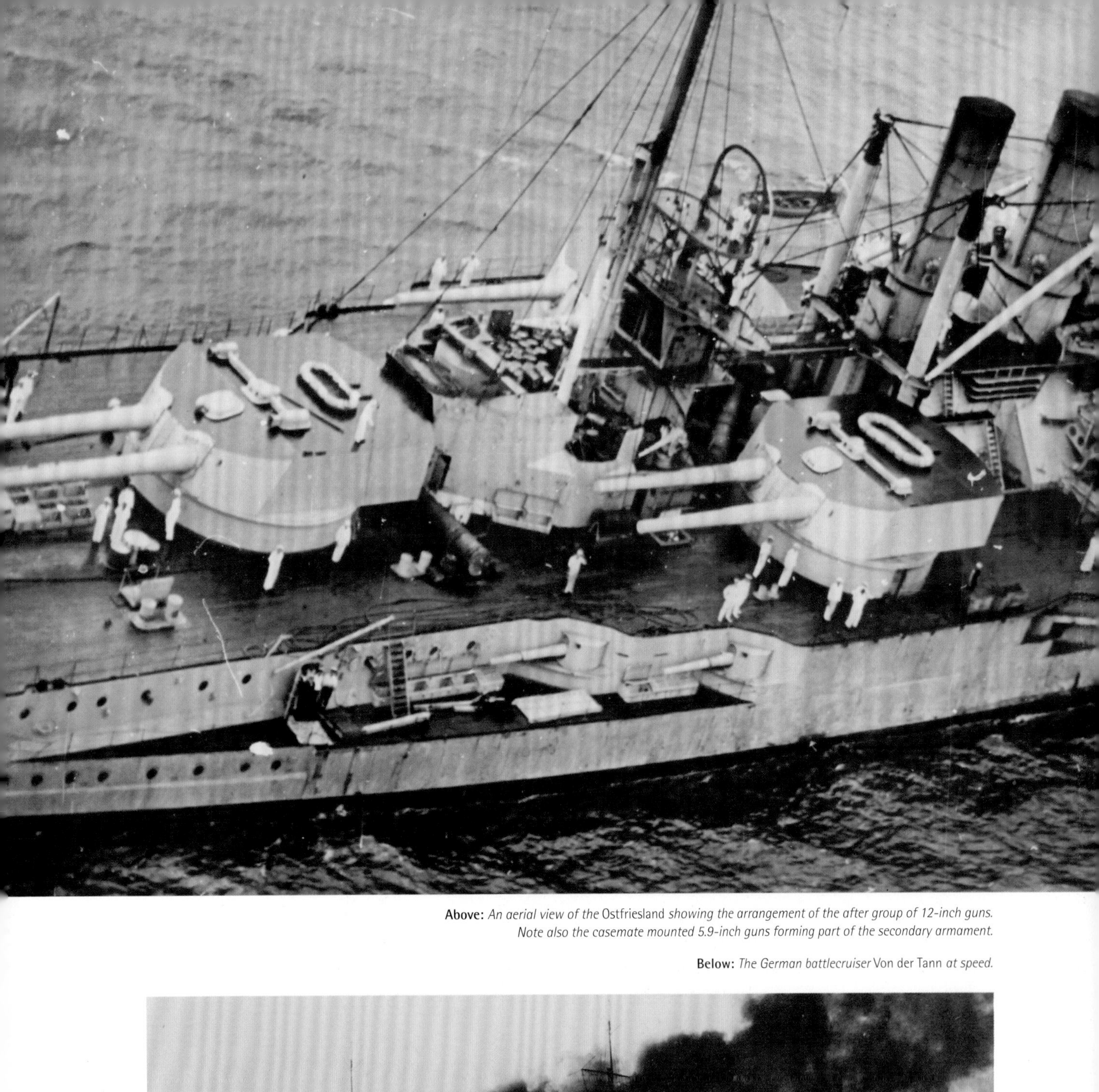

Above: *An aerial view of the* Ostfriesland *showing the arrangement of the after group of 12-inch guns. Note also the casemate mounted 5.9-inch guns forming part of the secondary armament.*

Below: *The German battlecruiser* Von der Tann *at speed.*

In addition, the caliber of the main armament guns was increased to 12-inch although the arrangement of the six twin turrets was the same as the preceding Nassau class with all the attendant disadvantages. This layout was necessary because the German ships were still using reciprocating machinery, which took up a lot of internal space, restricting the potential locations for the magazines. Output was increased by to 28,000 horsepower, good for just over 20 knots, and a three-funnel arrangement was adopted giving these ships a distinctive appearance.

At the same time, the Germans followed the British concept of the battlecruiser although their interpretation allowed for much better protection. In the *Von der Tann* (laid down March 1908), the main belt armor was 25 cm (10 inches) tapering to 10 cm (4 inches), while the turrets and barbettes had up to 27 cm (11 inches) and the conning tower 30 cm (12 inches). Between 5 and 7 cm (2–3 inches) of horizontal armor was also applied over vital compartments and there was comprehensive underwater protection including a torpedo bulkhead. Although the main armament was only eight 11-inch guns disposed as in the British ships with the wing turrets in echelon to fire on the broadside, a powerful secondary armament of ten 150-mm (5.9-inch) guns was carried in broadside casemate mounts amidships. Speed was a fraction under 25 knots using 42,000-shp steam turbines (of British design!).

Two further battlecruisers, *Moltke* and *Goeben*, were laid down in 1908–9, and although based on the *Von der Tann*, the hull was lengthened by 15 meters (50 feet) to allow for an additional 280-mm (11-inch) twin turret to be installed

A stern view of the battlecrusier Goeben *showing the super-firing after 11-inch gun turrets.*

Above: *HMS* Colossus*, completed in 1911, reverted to placing the mast aft of the fore funnel, where the spotting top was badly affected by fumes and smoke .*

in a super-firing position aft. The longer hull and an increase to 52,000-shp machinery raised speed to 25.5 knots.

In 1908, Admiral Tirpitz announced new naval laws that allowed for the laying down of four battleships or battlecruisers every year until 1911, reducing to two a year thereafter. British intelligence became convinced that an even greater rate was planned with substantial orders for lead items, such as armor plating and gun mountings being placed. German leaders insisted that these ships were needed to protect their legitimate interests in trade and colonial expansion, but it was readily apparent that most of the new ships were designed for service in the North Sea where there was only one potential adversary – Britain. Tirpitz realized that he did not have to equal the Royal Navy ship for ship in order to break Britain's monopoly of maritime power, as long as he had enough ships to threaten the Royal Navy with losing a major engagement in the North Sea. This danger was clearly seen by some in Britain, who agitated for eight new battleships in order to maintain the necessary superiority in numbers. Their slogan of 'We want eight, and we won't wait!' was taken up by the press, and public opinion began to mount. In a typical British compromise, the government agreed to the laying down of four new ships in 1909, with another four conditional on German build rates exceeding their stated numbers. In fact, the prompt came from a different direction. Approval for the additional four British ships was given when Austria and Italy (members of the so-called Triple Alliance with Germany) announced plans to build dreadnoughts.

The first of the eight new ships (*Colossus* and *Hercules*) were laid down in July 1909, and were similar to the *Neptune*, certainly in terms of disposition of the main armament. Only a single tripod foremast was fitted, and inexplicably this was stepped aft of the fore funnel where it suffered from the same problems of smoke fumes that had plagued *Dreadnought*. Another retrograde step was the discarding of an internal anti-torpedo bulkhead, which had been a feature of *Bellerophon* and subsequent ships, on the basis that the external side armor had been increased. However, the remaining ships of the 1909 program, four battleships and two battlecruisers, were a different story. The Royal Navy's philosophy had always been to ensure that as well as outnumbering a potential enemy, individual ships should carry a superior armament. Thus, when the Germans moved to the 12-inch gun in the Helgoland class, the British response was to arm their new capital ships with a 13.5-inch gun which fired a 567-kg (1,250-lb) projectile over a range of

Above: *HMS* Thunderer, *an Orion-class battleship, was the first to be completed with a central fire control director which enabled accurate shooting out to the maximum range of the guns.*

21,000 meters (23,000 yards). The first to receive this new weapon were the four Orion-class battleships laid down in 1909 and 1910, which carried ten guns in five twin turrets all arranged on the centerline of the ship. Super-firing turrets were arranged fore and aft, and the midship mounting (Q turret) was at main-deck level aft of the twin funnels. Despite problems with funnel fumes, the tripod foremast was still set aft of the fore funnel although the control positions were mounted high up. Displacing 22,500 tons and with a heavier armament, these ships were substantially more powerful than their predecessors – and the term *super-dreadnought* was coined to describe them.

As well as the heavier guns, the *Orion* also participated in a major advance in gunnery techniques. In the pre-dreadnoughts, the main guns were aimed directly from the mounting in a manner little changed from the days of sail. *Dreadnought* was fitted with the beginnings of a more advanced system, which was required to cope with the greater ranges of which the guns were capable. A control top was established on the foremast from where the target could be kept under clear view and the fall of shot observed, while separate range finders calculated the distance to the target. This and other information, such as target bearing and speed, were passed to the compartment below the armored conning tower, known as the transmitting station. An early form of analogue computer known as a Dumaresq worked out the bearing and elevations to be set on the guns, including the 'deflection' needed to allow for the motion of the target while the shells were in flight. These values were transmitted to telegraph repeaters in the turrets, which the gun-layers then applied when sighting their individual guns. The fire command was given from the control top to ensure a synchronized salvo (one gun in each turret) or broadside (both guns in each turret). Under the auspices of gunnery expert Admiral Sir Percy Scott, this system was refined and evolved into fire control by a single director. This was an armored position at the foretop that carried out all sighting and range-taking functions, information being fed to a Dreyer fire-control table in the transmitting station. This was a much more advanced computer than the Dumaresq and was electrically driven, effectively making it the earliest electronic computer although it worked on analogue rather than digital principles. The output was fed to the pointers in the turrets, which the gun-layers followed to align the guns – they did not need to be able to see the target. Salvoes and broadsides were triggered remotely from the director.

The director system considerably improved gunnery performance, and in general British ships were ahead of their German counterparts, although German range-finders were more accurate, especially at longer ranges. After successful trials aboard HMS *Bellerophon*, the first ship fitted with a director was the Orion-class battleship HMS *Thunderer*, which was completed in 1912. Directors were then incorporated in all subsequent ships and retrospectively fitted to the earlier dreadnoughts.

The adoption of the 13.5-inch gun was also applied to the two battlecruisers laid down under the 1909 program, HMS *Lion* and HMS *Princess Royal*, while a third and slightly modified ship, HMS *Queen Mary*, was subsequently laid down in 1911. These were imposing ships, over 30 meters (100 feet) longer than the Indefatigable class with a displacement of 26,350 tons. Steam turbines drove four shafts for total power output of 70,000 shp, well over twice that of the Orion-class battleships, and speed rose to over 27 knots – *Princess Royal* made 28.5 knots on trials. Belt and turret armor was increased to 23 cm (9 inches). But there was little improvement in horizontal armor. Once again the foremast was initially stepped aft of the fore funnel, this arrangement apparently instigated at the insistence of Admiral Jellicoe as it facilitated the handling of the ship's boats despite the fact that smoke and fumes were a major problem for the fire control positions, an interesting commentary on the priorities held by some officers, even at this stage. The foremast was eventually relocated forward of the funnel at a cost of £60,000 per ship. Nevertheless, the size and imposing appearance of the Lion class led to their nickname: 'Splendid Cats.'

The battlecruiser was very much the brainchild of Sir John Fisher, and the final iteration of his ideas was HMS *Tiger*, a notable ship on several counts. Probably the best of the pre-war battlecruisers, she was originally intended as the fourth ship of the Lion class, but her design was heavily influenced by the Vickers designed *Kongo* being built for the Japanese navy. The armament of eight 13.5-inch guns was retained, but the Q turret was moved aft where it had a clear field of fire, and

Below: *The Orion class introduced the 13.5-inch gun by virtue of which they were called 'super dreadnoughts.'*

Above: *HMS* Tiger *was the last pre-Jutland battlecruiser, and her design was heavily influenced by the* Kongo *being built by Vickers Armstrong for the Japanese Navy.*

the three funnels were then grouped together giving the ship a much more symmetrical appearance. All previous battlecruisers had carried a secondary battery of 4-inch QF guns, but in *Tiger* this was upgraded to 6-inch QF in broadside casemate mountings amidships. Armor protection was as in the Lions, but *Tiger* was the first British warship with an installed power in excess of 100,000 shp, which drove her at 29 knots, significantly faster than any of the German battlecruisers. She was completed in October 1914, just after the outbreak of the First World War.

By 1910, the British dreadnought-building program was now well underway in the almost certain anticipation of a major war and orders were placed for four King George V-class dreadnoughts, which were all laid down in 1911, followed by four Iron Duke class in 1912. The first group basically followed the Orion-class design except that the pole foremast was forward of the funnels, although this was subsequently strengthened with short tripod legs. The *Iron Duke's* were similar with the significant difference that the secondary anti-torpedo boat armament was increased to 6-inch caliber, and these were carried in casemate mountings sited forward at upper deck level abreast the forecastle.

While this relentless building program ensured that the Royal Navy maintained numerical superiority over Germany, the Admiralty became aware that both they and other powers were building or planning battleships with 14-inch guns or larger. It was therefore decided to arm the next group of battleships with 15-inch guns, which fired a 871-kg (1,920-lb) shell to a range of just under 22,000 meters (24,000 yards). The twin turrets protected by 33 cm (13 inches) of armor weighed around 750 tons each, so it was not surprising that the number of guns was reduced to eight in super-firing turrets fore and aft. One benefit of this arrangement was that the removal of the midship Q turret left space for additional machinery, and these ships could make just over 24 knots on 75,000 shp.

The resulting Queen Elizabeth class were laid down over a 12-month period beginning in October 1912.

Below: *HMS* Lion *leads the 1st Battlecruiser Squadron. Note the booms for anti-torpedo netting stowed against the hull sides.*

Above: *The R-class battleship HMS* Royal Sovereign *shown at anchor in 1921. The anti-torpedo bulge along the waterline is clearly visible.*

HMS King George V. *In these ships, the foremast was repositioned ahead of the fore funnel and tripod legs were added at a later date. The Short seaplane overhead is a portent of things to come.*

Original plans allowed for four ships but the Malayan States agreed to finance a fifth ship (HMS *Malaya*), and all five had joined the Royal Navy's Grand Fleet by the spring of 1916, at which time they were the most powerful battleships in the world.

The Queen Elizabeth class were also significant in that they were the first Royal Navy capital ships designed to burn oil fuel instead of coal. The advantages of oil fuel were well understood but until secure supplies could be guaranteed, the navy was reluctant to place too much reliance on it. In 1914, the British government bought a controlling share in the Anglo-Persian Oil Company so that oil-burning ships became a practical proposition in strategic terms. However, the last class of pre-war battleships, the Revenge or R class, reverted to a mix of coal and oil. This proved to be a wise decision when the German U-boat offensive in 1917 caused a shortage of oil. Unfortunately, the lower installed power output meant that the R class could only make 23 knots, and although this was quite sufficient for operations with the Grand Fleet, it made them less useful in later years. In other respects, these ships were basically repeats of the Queen Elizabeth class except for one ship, HMS *Ramilles*, which was fitted with a new form of underwater protection. In her case, the hull at and below the waterline was bulged outwards to form a cavity within the outer hull that was intended to

absorb the explosive force of a torpedo and leave the inner hull undamaged. This arrangement was widely applied to modernized ships after the First World War, but at the time *Ramilles* was unique in this respect.

The driving force behind the British dreadnought building program was, of course, the growing power of the German navy. Following on from the earlier Helgoland class, five new dreadnoughts (Kaiser class) were laid down in 1909–10 followed by another four (König class) in 1911–2. The Kaiser class were Germany's first turbine-powered battleships and had provision to burn both oil fuel and coal. The three-shaft machinery rated at 31,000 shp gave a speed of 20 knots, and it is interesting to note that the fourth ship, *Prinzregent Luitpold*, was originally intended to have steam turbines on two shafts only, with 12,000 hp diesel on the center shaft for cruising. In the event, this configuration was not fitted, but German interest in diesels for large warships persisted with dramatic results in the post-war decades. The Kaiser class were armed with ten 305-mm (12-inch) guns in five twin turrets, one on the forecastle, two in echelon amidships, and a super-firing pair aft. Use of steam turbines allowed this more efficient arrangement than in the preceding Helgoland class. With a main armor belt of 35 cm (14 inches) at its thickest point and turret armor of 30 cm (12 inches), these ships were better protected than the equivalent British dreadnoughts.

The subsequent four ships of the König class were also armed with ten 305-mm (12-inch) guns and this,

Below: *HMS* Iron Duke's *13.5-inch gun turrets. A Royal Navy staff requirement that battleships should be able to fire directly ahead with guns at zero elevation meant that there was no sheer of the forecastle deck, which was therefore often awash in heavy seas.*

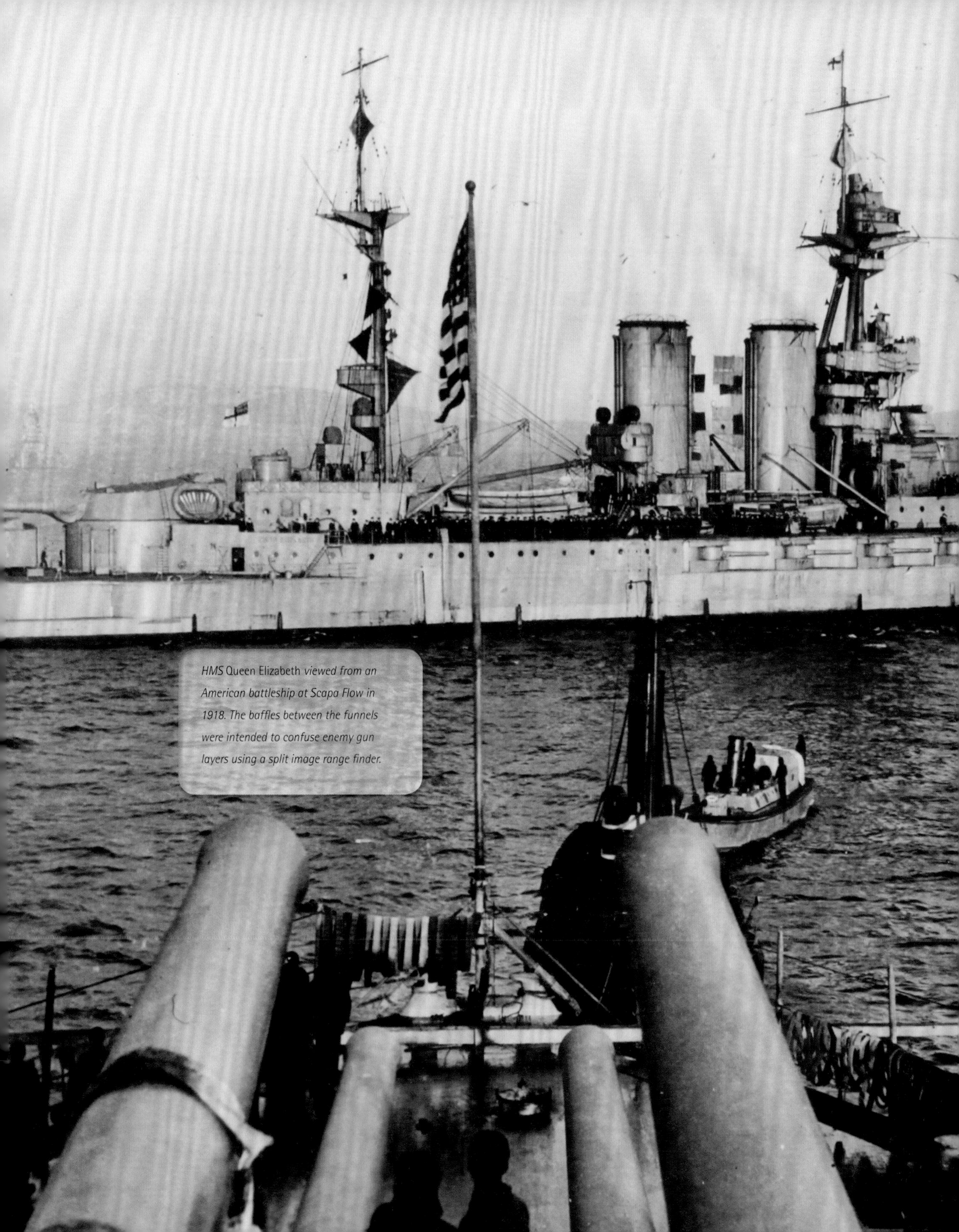

HMS Queen Elizabeth *viewed from an American battleship at Scapa Flow in 1918. The baffles between the funnels were intended to confuse enemy gun layers using a split image range finder.*

of course had already prompted the Royal Navy to move up to the 13.5-inch guns for their dreadnoughts. However, the Königs were the first German ships to mount all their main armament on the centerline, four turrets being placed fore and aft in a super-firing arrangement and Q turret being amidships between the funnels. Both the Kaiser and König classes carried a heavy secondary battery of fourteen 150-mm (5.9-inch) and eight 88-mm (3.5-inch) guns. The latter were intended for anti-aircraft (AA) use, demonstrating an early appreciation of the likely threat from the air. In passing, it should be noted that contemporary British Iron Duke-class dreadnoughts were the first Royal Navy ships to have a built in AA armament, 4-inch QF guns being carried for this purpose.

Germany's final class of dreadnoughts to be completed were the 28,600-ton Baden class laid

down 1913–15. Four ships were planned, but only the first two (*Baden* and *Bayern*) were completed by 1916, and although the other pair were launched, work was suspended in 1917. These ships resembled the British Queen Elizabeth class and, indeed, it was the fact that they were intended to carry 380-mm (15-inch) guns that had prompted the Royal Navy to adopt this caliber. As with the British ships, the main armament was reduced to eight guns in four twin turrets evenly distributed fore and aft. The ships had a distinctive profile with two tall closely spaced funnels, and they were the only German battleships to carry a tripod foremast. The uncompleted ships (*Sachsen* and *Württemburg*) were intended to have a diesel engine on the central driveshaft.

In parallel with the battleship program, Germany also continued to develop their battlecruisers. The

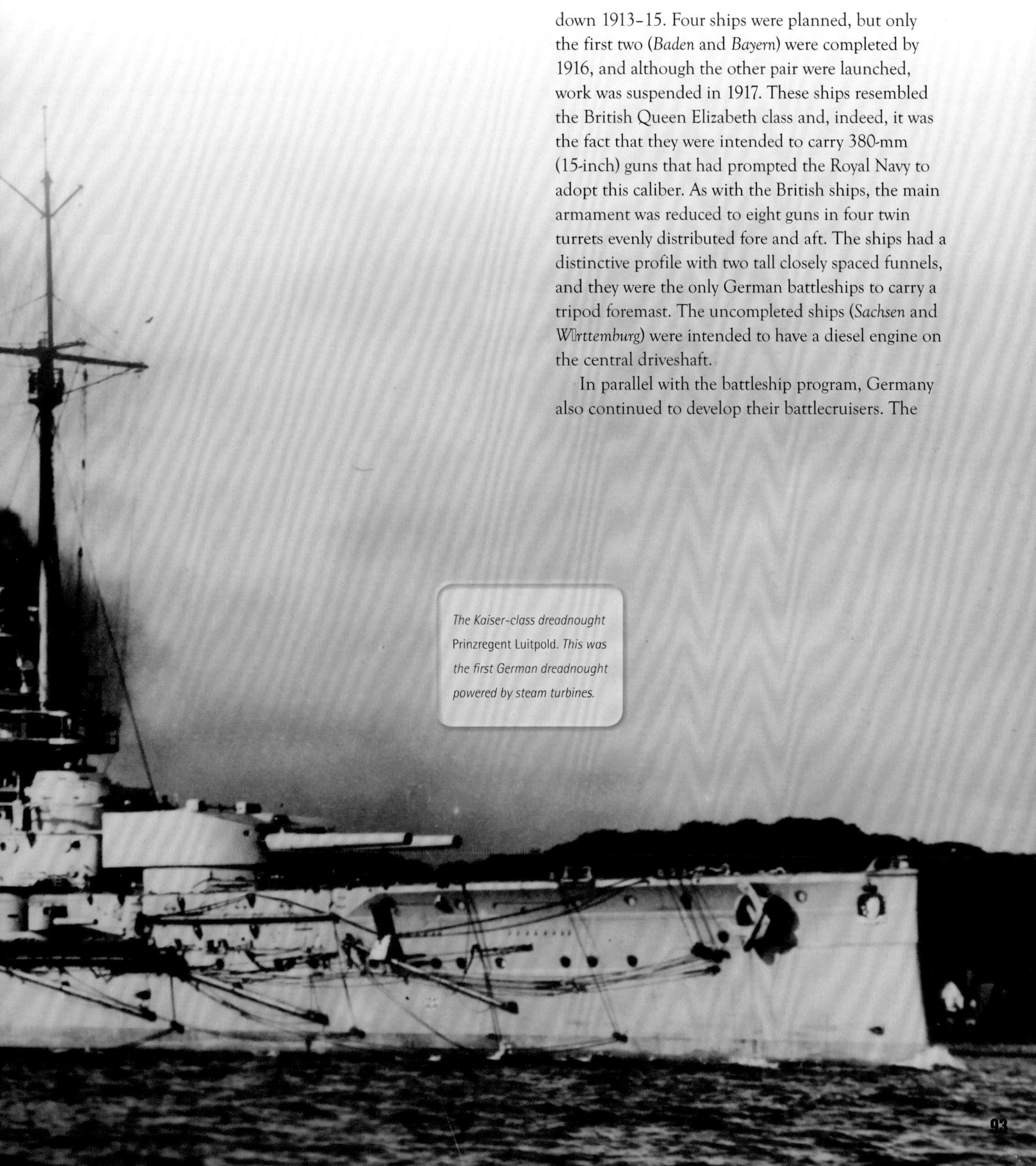

The Kaiser-class dreadnought Prinzregent Luitpold. *This was the first German dreadnought powered by steam turbines.*

Seydlitz, laid down in 1911 and completed two years later, was basically an enlargement of the preceding Moltke class. Armament remained the same but the hull was lengthened and the forecastle raised one deck level, which much improved sea-keeping qualities. An increase in installed shp from 52,000 to 67,000 raised speed to 26.5 knots. Three more battlecruisers of the Derfflinger class were laid down in 1912–3 and these adopted the 305-mm (12-inch) gun, eight being carried in four twin turrets all on the centerline, two forward and two aft. A heavy secondary armament of 150-mm (5.9-inch) and 88-mm (3.5-inch) guns was carried and armor protection was substantial for this type of ship. The main belt tapered from 30 to 10 cm (12–4 inches), the turrets and armored citadel were protected by 28-cm (11-inch) steel, the control tower received 30 cm (12 inches) and decks up to 7.5-cm (3-inch) armor plating. The last of the three, *Hindenburg*, displaced around 26,500 tons of which no less than 9,800 tons (37 per cent) was devoted to armor, compared to only

Armed with 15-inch guns, Bayern *and her sister ship* Baden *were the most powerful of the German dreadnoughts. Both were commissioned too late to take part in the Battle of Jutland.*

26 per cent on HMS *Tiger*. The ultimate German battlecruisers would have been the Mackensen class of which four were laid down in 1915, but none were ever completed. These would have been large ships armed with eight 356-mm (14-inch) guns on a displacement of 31,000 tons

While the naval arms race between Britain and Germany was the main feature of the decade leading to war in 1914, other nations were also building dreadnoughts but not in such great numbers. By 1905, when *Dreadnought* was launched, France had already ceased to rival Britain in terms of battleships and was concentrating on a system of coastal defense using fast torpedo-armed craft, together with numerous cruisers for trade protection. The last French pre-dreadnoughts were the six 18,300-ton Danton class armed with four 305-mm (12-inch) and twelve 240-mm (9.4-inch) guns, although these were not actually laid down until 1907–8 and were already obsolete when completed in 1911. The first modern dreadnoughts were the four Courbet

class (laid down 1910–1), which carried a powerful armament of twelve 305-mm (12-inch) guns in six twin turrets, two super-firing pairs fore and aft, and one on either beam amidships. A heavy secondary armament of twenty two fast-firing 138-mm (5.5-inch) guns for protection against torpedo boats was also mounted. The ships were well armored and although not quite up to British and US standards, great attention was paid to underwater protection.

The Courbet class all entered service just before the outbreak of war in 1914 by which time a further three ships of the Bretagne class were under construction. Similar to the Courbet class, they followed British and German practice by upgrading the main armament to ten 340-mm (13.4-inch) guns in five twin turrets on the centerline although the midship turret was mounted high up on the superstructure between the two funnels. *Bretagne* was completed in September 1915, and her sister ship, *Lorraine*, in July 1916. These were the last two French dreadnoughts to be commissioned as construction of three further Normandie class ships was suspended in 1918. Although not completed, these

The battlecruiser Seydlitz *in dry dock.*

ships gave some idea of future battleship development. The main armament would have comprised no less than twelve 340-mm (13.4-inch) guns but these were unusually mounted in three quadruple turrets, one forward and two aft. In this manner, displacement remained at around 26,000 tons despite a considerable increase in the weight of main armament.

France's main rival in the Mediterranean was Italy, which had already been responsible for many innovative designs in the pre-dreadnought era and did not disappoint when it came to building later ships. Her first dreadnought, *Danti Alighieri* was completed in 1913, and designer Vittorio Cuniberti created a most unusual layout. The machinery comprised Parsons turbines driving four screws, but this was arranged in separate compartments fore and aft, resulting in two pairs of funnels. The heavy main armament of twelve 305-mm (12-inch) guns was mounted in four triple turrets, the first use of this arrangement for heavy caliber guns but one which was increasingly adopted in later years by other navies. These were carried on the centerline, one forward and one aft,

Above: *The* Dante Alighieri *was Italy's first dreadnought and in the best traditions of that navy was entirely unconventional in layout. It was also the fastest battleship in the world at the time of its completion in 1913.*

and the other two amidships between the funnel pairs. Compared to contemporary dreadnoughts, this ship was comparatively lightly armored so that displacement was only around 23,000 tons.

A more conventional configuration was adopted for three Cavour class (name ship *Conte di Cavour*) that were laid down in 1911. These carried no less than thirteen 320-mm (12.6-inch) guns in three triple and two twin turrets making them among the heaviest armed battleships of the period. The turrets were arranged with a twin super-firing over a triple mounting fore and aft, and another triple mounting amidships between two tall broad funnels. All three were completed by the summer of 1915, but the third ship, *Leonardo da Vinci,* was destroyed in Taranto harbor on August 2, 1915, by an accidental magazine explosion.

Two more dreadnoughts, *Caio Duillio* and *Andrea Doria*, were completed in 1915–6 and these were basically similar. The main difference being that the secondary armament was upgraded from eighteen 120-mm (4.7-inch) QF guns to sixteen 152-mm (6-inch) QF guns, again echoing international trends.

Although Italy and France were naval rivals, they were to be allies in the First World War and their potential enemy was the Austro-Hungarian empire. Despite having a very short coastline at the northern end of the Adriatic Sea, the Austrian navy had a proud history and still proudly remembered its victory over the Italian fleet at the Battle of Lissa. An ambitious plan set out in 1911 called for the construction of up to 16 battleships but only four Tegetthoff class were ever completed. At 20,000-tons displacement they were smaller than other dreadnoughts of the period, but were armed with twelve 305-mm (12-inch) guns in four triple turrets arranged symmetrically fore and aft. Another potential enemy was Ottoman Turkey, which in 1910 ordered three powerful dreadnoughts to be built in British yards. In the event, only two were ever completed and both were requisitioned by the Royal Navy before delivery.

While the naval arms race in Europe ran its course, the US Navy was steadily building up its strength with the eventual intention of challenging the Royal Navy's pre-eminent position. The design of the South Carolina class had already been one of the factors that had prompted construction of the *Dreadnought*. The next American dreadnoughts laid down in 1907 were larger, the USS *Delaware* and USS *North Dakota* displaced 20,000 tons and carried ten 12-inch guns in five centerline turrets. The second ship was the first US battleship to have steam-turbine machinery installed although the results were not entirely successful. In place of traditional pole or tripod masts, the US dreadnoughts carried their fighting tops and searchlight platforms on distinctive lattice framework structures. These remained a feature of all US battleships until the mid 1920s. Another feature that was to be common to all US dreadnoughts and battleships was the adoption of the 5-inch QF gun as the standard secondary armament. Improved versions of this gun were being fitted right up to the end of the Second World War.

It was then US policy to authorize two new battleships in each financial year, and two Florida class were laid down in 1909. These were similar to the Delaware class and both had steam-turbine machinery, driving four instead of two shafts. Displacement rose slightly to almost 22,000 tons, but the succeeding Wyoming-class ships were much larger due to an

The four Courbet class were France's first true dreadnoughts and all were completed just before the outbreak of the First World War.

increased main armament of twelve 12-inch guns in six twin turrets, two forward and four aft. The twin funnels and two lattice masts were closely grouped amidships to give the guns clear arcs of fire. Two ships of the New York class were laid down in 1911, but these reverted to reciprocating machinery due to the problems experienced to date by the turbine installations in other ships. However, main armament was now ten 14-inch guns in five twin turrets, two forward and three aft, and these ships were well protected on a scale generally thought to be superior to Royal Navy dreadnoughts.

USS North Dakota *(BB29), a Delaware-class dreadnought completed in 1910, passes through the Panama canal. Until well after the Second World War, the size of US warships was restricted by the requirement that they be able to use the canal.*

Several changes were incorporated in the two Nevada class laid down in 1912. In particular, the concept of all-or-nothing armor protection was introduced as a result of trials carried out against old ironclad targets. Under this system, all vital areas such as machinery compartments, turrets, barbettes, magazines and control positions were given the maximum practical armor protection with the rest of the ship then being left relatively unprotected. Although the main armament remained at ten 14-inch guns, the number of turrets was reduced to four by mounting the guns in two triple and two twin turrets. Despite the weight saved by this arrangement, displacement rose to 27,500 tons, partly due to increased armor protection. Problems with machinery meant that *Nevada* had steam turbines installed

Below: *Austria–Hungary completed four Viribus Unitis-class battleships between 1912 and 1915. Although relatively small, they were heavily armed with twelve 12-inch guns.*

An impressive show of potential firepower featuring the three after 12-inch gun turrets aboard the USS Florida *(BB30).*

Above: *The USS* Nevada *(BB36) was armed with ten 14-inch guns in double and triple turrets. The armor belt along the waterline is clearly visible.*

but *Oklahoma* again reverted to reciprocating VTE machinery. Nevertheless, the power outputs were virtually identical, and both ships made the standard fleet speed of 21 knots. With plentiful domestic oil fields, the supply of such fuel did not pose the same problems as those, which caused concern to the Royal Navy, and the Nevada class were the first US dreadnoughts to be entirely oil fueled.

US battleships continued to grow steadily in size and armament. The Pennsylvania class (1913–4) were the heaviest to date, tipping the scales at over 31,000 tons, and main armament was now no less than twelve 14-inch guns in four triple turrets. The rise in displacement was a reflection of yet even heavier armor with a main belt up to 34 cm (13.5 inches), barbettes and internal bulkheads 36 cm (14 inches), and up to 46 cm (18 inches) on the turret faces. The boiler uptakes were trunked into a single funnel, a feature repeated in the subsequent New Mexico class (laid down 1915), which actually numbered three ships as the funds became available through the sale of two pre-dreadnoughts to Greece. The now standard armament of twelve 14-inch guns was retained, but *New Mexico* was powered by new turboelectric machinery in which the steam turbines drove generators, which in turn powered electric motors turning the propeller shafts. This arrangement was tried due to continuing problems experienced by US industry in producing the reduction gears required in conventional steam turbine installations. There were several disadvantages with turboelectric propulsion, not least the weight of the machinery that was over twice that of a steam turbine and gear train of comparable output. Nevertheless, the Tennessee class (1916–7) had turboelectric machinery and were otherwise similar to the New Mexico class but could be distinguished by a reversion to two tall, thin funnels and the adoption of a new clipper bow form for improved seaworthiness. The ultimate development of the US Navy dreadnought-type battleships was the mighty Colorado class, which introduced the 16-inch gun (*see* chapter 3).

Although the US Navy sought to keep pace with the Royal Navy in terms of technical expertise, if not numbers, it was also driven by the expansion of the Japanese navy. Initially, Japan built few dreadnoughts, partly because of the cost incurred in fighting the war against Russia and also because victory there had removed a major threat. However, two 21,000-ton Kawachi-class vessels were laid down in Japan in 1907. In outline they were similar to the German Nassau class, carrying an armament of 12 heavy guns in six twin turrets, one each fore and aft mounting 12-inch, 50-caliber guns, and two on either beam mounting 12-inch, 45-caliber guns. All the guns were purchased from Britain, and the machinery consisted of Parsons turbines produced under license in Japan. However, Japan's shipyards did not then possess the capacity or expertise to build larger ships, and when it was required to build large battlecruisers, the contract for the first of four ships – was given to the Vickers yard at Barrow-in-Furness, England. The design was drawn up by Vickers in response to Japanese requirements, and although based on the contemporary Lion class, the

Below: *In the Pennsylvania and New Mexico classes, the main armament was increased to twelve 14-inch guns. One of the latter, USS* Idaho *(BB42), shows the lattice masts that were a feature of all US battleships until well after the First World War.*

design was more balanced with an armament of eight 14-inch guns in twin turrets, two forward and two aft. Armor protection was increased and so marked was the improvement that the Japanese ship was taken as a model for HMS *Tiger*. The remaining three ships (*Hiei, Haruna* and *Kirishima*) were laid down and built in Japan with British technical assistance, the last pair being completed in April 1915.

Inevitably, the Japanese navy would be outnumbered by any potential adversary, particularly the United States, and so at an early stage, a decision was made to build ships that would be individually superior to their counterparts. Thus, after approving the construction of the battlecruisers, Japan moved straight to laying down four super-dreadnoughts, all of which were commissioned before the end of the First World War in 1918. The first pair, *Fuso* and *Yamashiro*, were big ships, displacing 30,600 tons and armed with twelve 14-inch guns in six twin turrets, two each fore and aft, and the other two on the centerline fore and aft of the second funnel. A secondary battery of fourteen 6-inch QF guns was carried on the broadside. In many ways, these ship were similar to the US Pennsylvania class but not as heavily armored (although 8,000 tons of armor plate was fitted). As a result of experience with mines and torpedoes in the Russian war, great attention was paid to underwater protection and compartmentation. The next two ships, *Hyuga* and *Ise*, were similar but the arrangement of the central turrets was altered so that both were in a super-firing position abaft the second funnel. This in turn released additional space for machinery and speed rose by 1 knot to 23.5 knots.

The launch of the *Dreadnought* in 1905 had led almost inevitably to a naval arms race as Britain sought to maintain its position of naval supremacy. This was

The Japanese battlecruiser Kongo *was actually built in Britain, but her three sister ships were built in Japan with British assistance.*

Right: *A deck plan showing the layout of the battleship* Fuso.

not acceptable to Germany, where a rise in national pride inspired by Bismarck, coupled with a great increase in industrial capacity meant that it saw itself as a major European power with legitimate worldwide interests. In the decade following 1905, the political tide in Europe ebbed and flowed as alliances were made and then abandoned. A frequent flashpoint was the situation in the Balkans, where various national groups attempted to gain independence from either Turkish or the Austro-Hungarian empires. Matters came to a head when the Austrian Archduke Ferdinand was assassinated in Sarajevo on June 28, 1914. A month, later Austria declared war on Serbia. This triggered Russian mobilization in support of the Serbs, which in turn led inevitably to Germany mobilizing in support of Austria. However, France was also a potential enemy as she was allied to Russia by treaty and, failing to gain assurances that she would not assist Russia, Germany prepared for war on two fronts.

In the summer of 1914, the British Admiralty ordered a test mobilization of the Reserve Fleet, which assembled at Spithead off Portsmouth alongside the Home Fleet for a royal review. Afterwards, the fleets were to disperse to their home ports, the reserve crews to stand down, and the Home Fleet crews to go on leave. However, these arrangements were cancelled in view of the events in Serbia, and Admiral Prince Louis of Battenberg, supported by Winston Churchill, then First Lord of the Admiralty, took it upon himself to order the fleet to its war stations. By the beginning of August, the whole of the Royal Navy was on a war footing – not a moment too soon. On August 4, 1914, German troops poured into Belgium, and in an immediate reaction the Royal Navy and the British Army was ordered to 'commence hostilities against Germany.' And so the dreadnoughts went to war.

The Royal Navy's Grand Fleet steams to war, led by Jellicoe's flagship HMS Iron Duke.

Armor Protection

The story of iron and steel armor for battleships begins with the first ironclad warship, the French *La Gloire* launched in 1859. Ironclads were developed as a response to the introduction of naval guns able to fire explosive shells rather than roundshot (cannonballs). Iron warships had been tried out before *La Gloire* arrived, but building ships with an iron structure or iron cladding did not of itself constitute an advance in protection. It had been found that ordinary cast iron was in fact more brittle than wood and iron frames were actually more easily distorted than wooden ones. Perhaps ironically, iron warships were more vulnerable to attack, even by roundshot, than vessels constructed of wood alone. The term *ironclad* was introduced to describe ships protected by specially manufactured armored plates of wrought iron, which could be attached to hulls that were either wooden like *La Gloire*, or iron like HMS *Warrior*.

Below: *The old pre-dreadnought USS* Indiana *(BB1) was used as a trial target in 1901. Notice that while the unarmored sections of the hull are easily holed, the armoured barbette at left and the armoured turret at right are relatively undamaged even though they show evidence of having been hit.*

Wrought iron is an alloy that has a very low carbon content but which deliberately includes impurities (generally known as slag) that give the iron greater malleability and toughness. The impurities were most commonly introduced in the 19th century by a process known as puddling. The puddled iron, having been cast into bars, had to be further improved by piling, which involved a number of bars being cut up, piled atop one another and bound together with wires, then reheated and hammered or rolled together, a process which had to be repeated several times to produce wrought iron of the best quality. In *La Gloire* and *Warrior*, 10 to 12 cm (4–5 inches) of iron armor were fitted, backed by around 46 cm (18 inches) of teak. The teak acted as a shock-absorbing layer and also helped to contain shell fragments and splinters of armor when the armor was wholly or partly penetrated. Teak or mild steel backing was used in armor throughout the period covered by this book – even the *Bismarck* had its armor backed by 5 cm (2 inches) of teak.

The first ironclads initiated a technical race to produce ever more effective armor, a process closely tied to continual developments in naval guns. The wrought iron armor of *La Gloire* was piled by hammering. The famous British engineer John Brown saw the ship in France and by 1862 was producing superior rolled iron armor. More sophisticated schemes of armor arrangement were also tried to improve protection, involving layers of armor and wood with an inner iron skin, but in general single plates tended to give the best protection.

Wrought iron armor was eventually superseded by compound and steel armor. Compound armor used a harder, more brittle, high-carbon steel layer fused to the outside face of the wrought iron. The secret of successful compound armor was the ability to fuse the two types of armor solidly together, and this was achieved independently by two British companies in 1877. Cammell Laird used a process of pouring molten steel on to the face of white-hot wrought iron, while the John Brown Company positioned the two plates closely together and joined them by pouring molten steel into the gap. The resulting plate from either process was rolled down to about half its original thickness, with the steel forming about a third of the total depth. Compound armor was around 25 and 30 per cent more effective than wrought iron, and offered a much needed improvement. By this time ordinary iron armor needed to be 57 cm (22 inches) thick to withstand hits from the most powerful contemporary naval guns.

Compound armor's competitor was steel armor, which had first been developed for warships by the French Schneider company in 1876. However, compound armor was generally found to be comparable or even better than contemporary steel armor, and it was also cheaper. The strength of compound armor was that the very hard steel face would shatter incoming projectiles, while being supported by the more malleable iron backing, which was less likely to crack. Steel armor at this time was often found in tests to be more brittle than compound armor and vulnerable to cracking right through. However, steel armor was soon to be transformed in the late 1880s and 1890s by the development of tougher nickel-steel and chromium-steel alloys, as well as the face-hardening process.

Nickel-steel is a steel alloy typically including 3 to 5 per cent nickel, and this alloy fixed the problem of the brittle nature of steel armor plate. First developed in 1889, nickel-steel plate was superseded only a few years later by yet another advance, the invention of face-hardened armor. Face hardening (or, more technically, cementation) replicated the advantages of compound armor, but in a single homogenous plate. This eradicated the main drawback of compound armor, which was the tendency of the two layers of armor to become separated when the facing layer cracked. The first face-hardening process was developed in 1891 in the United States at the Washington Navy Yard, and was named after its inventor H.A. Harvey. Steel plate was kept at a high temperature with one face in contact with a layer of charcoal. After two weeks, the heated surface had absorbed the carbon from the charcoal to a significant depth (around 2.5 cm; 1 inch). The plate then had to go through a regulated cooling process. The Harvey armor thus produced was now about twice as effective as wrought iron armor, and 15 to 20 per cent better than plain nickel steel armor.

Above: *The thickness of armor in later battleships is illustrated here where the armored mantle of a turret aboard USS* Maryland *(BB46) is being removed to facilitate the changing of worn-out gun barrels.*

The application of face hardening to nickel steel armor plate produced excellent results, but a further advance was introduced almost immediately. In 1893, Krupp in Germany patented a process that added 1 to 2 per cent of chromium to nickel steel. The chromium added further to the hardness of the steel and also enabled the steel plate to absorb carbon to a greater depth. Tiny amounts (less than 1 per cent) of manganese and molybdenum could also be added to this type of armor to further improve its properties. Along with the significant Krupp improvements to the face-hardening process, this resulted in an armor (usually called Krupp Cemented, or KC, plate) which was on average 2.5 times as tough as wrought iron. Krupp Cemented armor completed the headlong series of developments in armor plate that took place during the late 19th century. Its production was licensed to other countries developing battleships, notably Britain and the United States. Although a number of companies (including Krupp) in various countries developed slightly different processes designed to enhance the qualities of KC plate, improvements were generally minor. KC plate was to be the type of armor used in the battleships of both world wars, until the last battleship ever built, HMS *Vanguard*, was completed in 1946.

Machinery

The transition from sail to steam really got under way in the 1840s, although successful demonstrations of both screw and paddlewheel-driven ships had occurred prior to that time. However, the paddlewheel was never seriously considered for seagoing warships as it was vulnerable to battle damage and reduced the length of gun decks for broadside fire. The first Royal Navy steam warship was HMS *Rattler*, which displaced 867-tons and had a 200-horsepower (hp) four-cylinder reciprocating steam machinery driving one two-bladed

Below: *A set of three Yarrow water tube boilers being readied for installation in the Chilean battleship* Almirante Latorre *under construction in Britain. Eventually completed for the Royal Navy as HMS* Canada, *this ship had a total of 21 boilers installed.*

Before the adoption of oil fuel, the operation of coaling a ship was a dirty and tedious job that had to be repeated at regular intervals, as often as two days if the ship had been steaming hard.

screw. She commenced trials in 1843, and two years later these culminated in a famous tug of war between *Rattler* and the *Alecto*, a ship of similar size and power but driven by paddlewheels. *Rattler* was the convincing winner, but by then the Admiralty was already convinced of the potential for steam-driven screw ships. It had ordered several wooden screw frigates and was about to order screw-powered battleships. The first of these, HMS *Ajax*, sailed in September 1846, the world's first seagoing steam battleship.

Until the early 20th century, steamships were driven by reciprocating machinery in which the steam acted on a piston that in turn drove a crankshaft. Early steam engines had pistons and cylinders arranged horizontally, but vertical cylinders quickly became the norm as this made the machinery more easily accessible and took up less deck space. Initially, engines were of the simple expansion type in which steam is only cycled through one stroke of the piston, but this method was extremely inefficient. It was improved by the adoption of compound engines. In this system, steam is cycled through one or more additional cylinders, each at a successively lower pressure so that more of the energy in the steam was harnessed. Such engines produced significant gains in efficiency, which in turn gave a substantial increase in cruising range for a given tonnage of coal.

Double-compound engines came into service from the mid 1870s, but in the following decade triple expansion engines became virtually standard for large warships. Some idea of the progress made can be seen by comparing the machinery of HMS *Warrior* in 1860 with that of the Duncan-class pre-dreadnoughts laid down in 1898. The former had a single twin-cylinder horizontal-acting single-expansion engine producing 5,250 hp, while the Duncans had two sets of four vertical cylinders in a triple-expansion system with a total output of 18,000 hp.

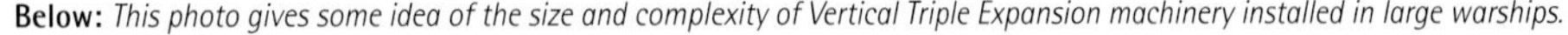

Below: *This photo gives some idea of the size and complexity of Vertical Triple Expansion machinery installed in large warships.*

However, reciprocating machinery was large and complex and there were practical limits to further development. An alternative steam turbine system was invented by the English engineer Charles Parsons in 1884. Initially intended as a means of generating electricity, Parsons quickly realized its potential as a marine system. He commissioned the building of a demonstration vessel, *Turbinia*, which was launched in 1894. On trials she achieved speeds in excess of 34 knots, and in 1897 Parsons arranged a spectacular publicity stunt in which *Turbinia* steamed at high speed through the ranks of warships anchored for Queen Victoria's Jubilee review at Spithead. She easily outpaced naval craft sent to intercept her. Parsons' turbine operated by directing high-pressure steam through a series of rotors made up of wing-shaped blades arranged as circular fans. An alternative system was developed in America by the Curtiss company in

Below: *The engine control room, one of four aboard an Iowa-class battleship in the Second World War .*

which steam jets drove bucket-shaped rotor blades. Steam turbines were significantly smaller and lighter than reciprocating machinery and were capable of producing considerably more power. HMS *Dreadnought* in 1905 had four Parsons turbines each producing just under 8,000 hp, while the US Navy's *Iowa* class of the Second World War had four turbine sets each giving more than 50,000 hp.

Turbine machinery was lighter, offered the advantage of much smoother operation, less complexity and was much more reliable in service. During the First World War era, most battleships had turbines connected directly to the propeller shafts, but the faster battleships of the Second World War had single or double reduction gears. Some battleships also had low-powered cruising turbines that were connected to the driveshafts by auxiliary gearing. However, American industry experienced problems in producing reliable reduction gear systems, and this led them to adopted turboelectric machinery in which the steam turbines drove electrical generators, which in turn powered electric motors driving the propeller shafts. The first battleship with this system was the USS *New Mexico* launched in 1917, and the subsequent Tennessee and Colorado classes also had turboelectric propulsion. Although turboelectric systems offered many advantages in terms of flexibility of use, they were significantly heavier and took up more deck space than conventional steam turbines. For example, HMS *Hood's* (1918) machinery developed more than twice as much power per ton of machinery than the USS *Tennessee*, while the latter's machinery occupied three times the amount of space. When battleship construction resumed in 1937, the US Navy reverted to geared turbines.

By definition all steam-operated machinery requires a supply of steam in order to function. A typical marine boiler in the 19th century used the fire-tube system in which a coal-fired furnace fed hot air into a series of tubes that ran through a water tank. Usually known as a Scotch boiler, it was simple to build and operate but took a long time to raise a head of steam, and could not produce steam at the higher temperatures and pressures required by more powerful engines. These disadvantages were overcome by the introduction of water-tube boilers in which water held in drums at the lower sides of the boiler was fed upwards through narrow tubes heated by the combustion process at the base of the boiler to a central steam drum at the top. The steam can then be recirculated through more tubes to produce high-pressure superheated steam, typically around 25 atmospheres (375 pounds per square inch) at 340 °C (650 °F) during the Second World War period. Although early boilers used seawater, corrosion problems at higher temperatures required the use of fresh water, which was contained in feed tanks. This was heated into steam, passed through the engines and then condensed back into water to be recycled through the boilers. In theory this was a closed system, but ships were also equipped with distillation plants to purify additional fresh water when required. The efficiency of boilers was also improved by the adoption of oil fuel instead of coal.

Although almost all battleships were exclusively steam powered, Germany did experiment with marine diesels. Towards the end of the First World War, she was building a battleship (*Sachsen*) that would have had steam turbines on the outer shafts, and a 12,000-hp diesel engine on the center shaft. She was never completed, but the three Deutschland-class *Panzerschiffe* built in the 1930s were diesel powered. Diesels offer great economy for cruising, but in general such machinery producing the power output required by battleships would have been significantly heavier than an equivalent steam-powered engine.

THE FIRST WORLD WAR

The German High Seas Fleet prepares for war.

The First World War

Even before the British ultimatum demanding that Germany respect Belgian neutrality expired at midnight on August 4, 1914, the Royal Navy was already steaming to its war stations. But while the Grand Fleet converged on its base at Scapa Flow in the Orkney Islands, events of which were to have a major effect on the course of the war were already taking place in the Mediterranean. Here the Royal Navy's Mediterranean Fleet commanded by Admiral Sir Berkeley Milne included a squadron of battlecruisers armed with 12-inch guns *Inflexible, Indefatigable, Indomitable* together with the 1st Cruiser Squadron made up of the armored cruisers *Defence, Black Prince, Duke of Edinburgh* and *Warrior* armed with 9.2-inch and 7.5-inch guns and capable of 23 knots. Potentially, the fleet faced a total of six powerful dreadnoughts belonging to the Italian and Austro-Hungarian navies, while a question mark hung over the status of Turkey where German officers were helping to train the army. A major complication was that Germany had detached the battlecruiser *Goeben* to the Mediterranean,

Left: *Admiral Sir Berkeley Milne, Commander in Chief of the Royal Navy's Mediterranean Fleet in August 1914.*

Below: *The battlecruiser* Goeben *flies the Turkish flag after evading the Royal Navy and reaching Istanbul.*

supported by the light cruiser *Breslau*. Milne could expect little direct support from the French navy, which at that time had only one modern dreadnought available at Toulon.

At the time of the assassination of Archduke Ferdinand in June 1914, the German ships were undergoing repairs at the Austrian port of Pola – currently known as Pula, Croatia. Their commander, Rear-Admiral Souchon, did not want to be trapped in the Adriatic Sea if war broke out and sailed in mid-July. At the end of the month, Milne received signals from the British Admiralty that instructed him that in the event of war he should assist in the protection of French forces being transported from North Africa. If possible, he should also engage the German ships although avoiding action with a 'superior force.' At dawn on August 4, with France and Germany already at war, the German ships appeared off the North African coast and bombarded the French Algerian ports of Bône and Philippeville, before heading for Istanbul, Turkey. In order to reach Turkey, Milne's ships needed to call in at Messina, a port on the Italian island of Sicily, to take on coal. As the Germans set course for the Sicilian port, they were spotted by the battlecruisers *Indomitable* and *Inflexible*, who turned to shadow them. As Germany and Britain were not actually at war at this point, the British ships could not open fire. A stern chase then developed in which *Goeben* gradually pulled ahead, and eventually contact was lost. Concerned that the Germans would again attempt to turn west to attack the French convoys, Milne ordered his ships to patrol west of Sicily, although this move was partly prompted by the news that Italy had decided to remain neutral and would not be a belligerent alongside Austria and Germany. However, as a neutral, she would not allow belligerent warships within 10 km (6 miles) of her coastline. While the British respected this, Souchon had no compunctions about continuing to Sicily where full facilities were made available to him. Sailing again on the morning of August 6, he was spotted and shadowed by the cruiser HMS *Gloucester*.

The British battlecruisers west of Sicily were too far away to intervene and in any case had to proceed to Malta for coaling before taking up the chase. The only substantial force in a position to intercept was

Due to a signal error, British battlecruisers were fatally delayed in their pursuit of the Goeben *and* Breslau*.*

Above: *The German light cruiser* Breslau *was armed with twelve 105-mm (4.1 inch) guns and could make 28 knots.*

Rear-Admiral Troubridge's 1st Cruiser Squadron then off Corfu, Greece. After some initial confusion, he set course towards Cape Matapan where he hoped to meet the German ships at dawn. However, during the night he allowed his flag captain to convince him that Admiralty orders not to engage a superior force applied in this case and with a heavy heart he turned away. *Gloucester's* captain was made of sterner stuff and although his single ship was completely outgunned by the *Goeben*, he caught up with and engaged the *Breslau*. As expected, the *Goeben* turned back to support the smaller ship, thus delaying her eastward progress. Unfortunately, *Gloucester's* low coal supplies meant that she had to abandon the attack and again the Germans pulled away. A final chance to catch the German ships arose on August 8, when they stopped at the Aegean island of Denusa to take on more coal, not leaving there until the morning of the August 10. In the meantime, the British battlecruisers had left Malta early on August 8, but a signal sent in error from the Admiralty had them diverted northwards to face a possible emerging threat from the Austrian fleet. By the time it was realized that this was a false alarm, the chances of catching the *Goeben* and *Breslau* had evaporated once again, and the two ships entered the heavily fortified narrow sea passage through the Dardanelles on the evening of August 10, reaching Istanbul a few hours later.

The whole event was a great embarrassment for the Royal Navy, which through a series of misjudgments had failed to stop the two ships. Needless to say there was considerable disquiet at home. Troubridge came in for heavy criticism in particular for his decision not to engage the *Goeben* and was brought back for a court martial at Portland. However, due to the ambiguity of his orders and instructions he was found not guilty of charges of failing to engage the enemy, although he was not subsequently offered any seagoing commands.

Technically, Turkey was still neutral but when Britain insisted that the German ships should only be allowed to stay for 24 hours, it was found that they had been handed over to Turkey and now flew the Turkish flag. Nevertheless, Winston Churchill, as First Sea Lord of the Admiralty, ordered a squadron to be formed under Vice-Admiral S.H. Carden with the purpose of blockading the entrance to the Dardanelles and engaging the *Goeben* and *Breslau* if they attempted to break out – even if flying the Turkish flag. However, on October 30, 1914, Souchon led his ships, together with the Turkish cruiser *Hamideh*, northwards into the Black Sea to bombard the Russian ports in the Crimea. This act immediately led Britain and Russia to declare war on Turkey, which now became part of the German-led alliance. Carden was ordered to bombard the outer forts of the Dardanelles seaway to test the effect of modern guns against land fortifications. On November 3, 1914, the battlecruisers *Indefatigable* and *Indomitable*, supported by the French pre-dreadnoughts *Suffren* and *Verité*, which carried four 305-mm (12-inch) guns, fired a total of 76 shells. A fortunate hit caused one of the fort's magazines to explode after which the ships withdrew. The whole exercise had served little purpose except to alert the Turks to the need to reinforce their coastal defenses and wrongly gave the impression that battleships could be successful in any future bombardments.

With the enthusiastic backing of Churchill, Carden was ordered to prepare plans to force a passage through the Dardanelles with a strong naval force, the ultimate objective being the capture of Istanbul, and the destruction of the Turkish fleet, including the *Goeben*. For this task he was given a powerful bombarding force that included the new 15-inch-gun battleship HMS *Queen Elizabeth*, the battlecruiser *Inflexible*, and no less than 12 British and four French pre-dreadnoughts. Despite strong objections by Admiral Fisher, the First Sea Lord, the operation went ahead on February 19, 1915, although bad weather caused delays and it was

Winston Churchill was appointed First Lord of the Admiralty in 1911 but resigned after the catastrophic failure of the Dardenelles Campaign.

Above: *HMS* Lord Nelson *was one of the battleships involved in the attempt to silence the Dardenelles forts on March 18, 1915.*

not until March 1 that Carden could report that the outer forts had been demolished. However, attempts to silence the forts located further up at the Narrows met with considerable resistance from both the forts and mobile artillery batteries, and the ships were eventually forced to withdraw.

Carden was replaced by Rear-Admiral John de Robeck who was instructed to take a less cautious approach and attempt to neutralize the forts and batteries by an overwhelming concentration of firepower. On March 18, the *Queen Elizabeth, Inflexible, Lord Nelson* and *Agamemnon* moved into the Dardanelles and began to lay down heavy fire on the forts at the Narrows while pre-dreadnoughts *Majestic, Prince George, Swiftsure* and *Triumph* moved closer to the shore to engage the mobile batteries. The four French pre-dreadnoughts under Admiral Guépratte then moved to within 7,300 meters (8,000 yards) of the Narrows forts and almost succeeded in silencing them, as a further six British pre-dreadnoughts were moving into position to complete this work. It was at this point that things began to go wrong. The French *Bouvet* was hit by a heavy-caliber shell, which caused a magazine

Above: *The French pre-dreadnought* Bouvet *was lost when a Turkish shell caused her magazine to explode.*

to explode, sinking the ship and taking all 700 of her crew with her. For a time the engagement continued, but just over two hours later, the battlecruiser *Inflexible* struck a mine, which caused severe flooding and killed 29 of her crew. A few minutes later the pre-dreadnought HMS *Irresistible* repeated the same fate and had to be abandoned, although all her crew were taken off. Following this, de Robeck ordered his ships to withdraw but as they did so another pre-dreadnought, HMS *Ocean*, struck a mine and subsequently sank. At the end of the day, the attempt to force the Dardanelles was a failure with the loss of three ships and another three including the *Inflexible* seriously damaged. Plans for a further naval assault where subsequently abandoned in favor of a combined operation involving the landing of more than 80,000 troops, mainly from Australia and New Zealand. This eventually went ahead on April 25, 1915, but by that time the forewarned Turks had been given plenty of time to prepare their defenses, and the assault was bogged down from the very start. Despite severe casualties, no real progress was made over the next few months, and Allied troops were eventually evacuated by the navy at the end of the year. A strong force of battleships continued to provide fire support during the fighting, but three were lost, all in May 1915. HMS *Goliath* was torpedoed by a Turkish destroyer, and both *Triumph* and *Majestic* were torpedoed by the German submarine *U-21*. It is relevant to the story of the battleship to note that, apart from the French *Bouvet*, all of the pre-dreadnoughts lost at Gallipoli were sunk as a result of underwater damage from mines or torpedoes. Very little damage was done to the heavily armored ships by gunfire from the shore batteries.

In the meantime, the battlecruiser *Goeben*, which had initiated this whole series of events, made only one abortive sortie into the Dardanelle's, and until 1917 was only occasionally in action against Russian ships in the Black Sea. In January 1918, the *Goeben* and *Breslau*, now under the command of Vice-Admiral von Rebeur-Paschwitz made a brief sortie into the Aegean Sea, sinking two British monitors at Kusu Bay. However, the German ships then ran into a British minefield in which the *Breslau* sank after detonating no less than five mines in succession, while *Goeben* herself struck three and was barely able to make her way back, running aground at the entrance to the Sea of Marmara. Here, she was stuck for a week before being towed to Istanbul for repairs, which kept her out of action for the rest of the war.

HMS Goliath *fell prey to torpedo fired from a Turkish destroyer.*

The escape of the *Goeben* and *Breslau* was not the only setback suffered by the Royal Navy in the opening stages of the war. When war broke out at the beginning of August 1914, a substantial German cruiser squadron under Vice-Admiral Maximilian Count von Spee was at large in the Pacific Ocean. Making its way eastward, it was intercepted off the Chilean port of Coronel by a British force under Rear-Admiral Sir Christopher Craddock in the late afternoon of November 1, 1914. Von Spee's force comprised two 11,600-ton armored cruisers, *Scharnhorst* and *Gneisenau,* both armed with eight 210-mm (8.2-inch) and six 150-mm (5.9-inch) guns, supported by three 3,200-ton light cruisers *Leipzig, Dresden* and *Nürnburg* armed with ten 105-mm (4.1-inch) guns. The British squadron also included two armored cruisers: *Good Hope* which carried two 9.2-inch and sixteen 6-inch guns, and the slightly smaller *Monmouth,* which only carried 6-inch guns. Both ships were relatively old and had only recently been commissioned with reservist crews who had been given little chance to practice their gunnery skills. In company was HMS *Glasgow*, a fast and modern light cruiser armed with two 6-inch and ten 4-inch guns, and the *Otranto*, a converted 12,000-ton passenger liner armed with eight 4.7-inch guns.

Although Craddock unhesitatingly altered course to engage Von Spee when they were sighted – perhaps with thoughts of Troubridge's fate in mind – he was aware that his scratch force was no match for the German ships, and the battle quickly became a one-sided affair. Silhouetted against the setting sun, the British ships were an easy target for the *Scharnhorst's* and *Gneisenau's* well-trained gunners. Within an hour, the *Good Hope* was sunk and the *Monmouth*, burning fiercely, was eventually finished off by the light cruiser *Nürnburg*. Only *Glasgow* and *Otranto* managed to escape, but the outcome was a disastrous defeat for the Royal Navy. When the news reached the Admiralty in London, Fisher and Churchill reacted by concentrating all available ships off the east coast of South America to protect the vital shipping trade around the River Plate in case Von Spee was to round Cape Horn and foray into the Atlantic. More dramatically, the Grand Fleet at Scapa Flow was ordered to release two battlecruisers, *Invincible* and *Inflexible*, for service in the South Atlantic. After calling at Plymouth to take on stores

Below: *Admiral von Spee photographed with a group of his officers at Valpariso, Chile.*

Above: *HMS* Inflexible *was one of a pair of battlecruisers dramatically dispatched to the South Atlantic to avenge the defeat at Coronel.*

Below: *Vice Admiral Sir Doveton Sturdee RN.*

and coal, the two ships left on November 11, 1914, under the command of Vice-Admiral Sir Doveton Sturdee. Despite the urgency of the situation Sturdee did not rush, instead maintaining a slow cruising speed to reduce coal consumption and diverting off course to search for enemy ships. Consequently, he did not reach the Falklands until December 7, where he joined the cruisers *Bristol, Glasgow, Carnarvon* and *Cornwall* as well as the AMC *Macedonia* (AMC stood for armed merchant cruiser). Also present was the pre-dreadnought *Canopus,* which had been beached within Port Stanley harbor to act as a coast defense fort. The battlecruisers proceeded to the inner harbor, where coaling commenced and this was still in progress when, just before 8 a.m. on the morning of the December 8, a land-based lookout spotted the smoke of ships approaching from the southeast.

Sturdee's ships were potentially in a difficult position. It would take some time for his ships to clear decks and raise steam, and if Von Spee pressed on he would be able to bombard the static British

Above: *Von Spee's ships race to escape from Sturdee's powerful battlecruisers.*

ships, which would be fighting at a considerable disadvantage. By 8:45, the light cruiser *Kent* had steam up and was leaving harbor, but it would still be at least an hour before any of the others were able to move. Sturdee ordered *Canopus* to open fire as soon as the enemy were within range, and in an amazing feat of gunnery she scored a hit on the *Gneisenau* with her first salvo. Although no great damage was done, it was enough to cause Von Spee to order his ships to turn away to the east with the object of escaping from the British force which, at that stage, he believed to consist of two pre-dreadnought battleships that he could easily out-distance. It was not until 11 o'clock, when all Sturdee's ships had finally cleared harbor that Von Spee realized the true nature of his opponents. For his part, Sturdee acted with admirable calmness, even slowing down to allow some of his cruisers to catch up and ordering his ship's companies to lunch while the chase continued. With preparations complete, his battlecruisers worked up to 26 knots, rapidly overhauling the German ships, and at 12:47 p.m., the order to engage was given.

Von Spee realized that the odds were stacked against him and ordering his light cruisers to break off and attempt to escape, he gallantly turned his two armored cruisers towards the advancing *Invincible* and *Inflexible*. Despite the disparity in weight of fire, the engagement was not one sided as smoke from British battlecruisers obscured their observation of fall of shot due to the following wind, and Sturdee had to alter course several times in an effort to gain the more advantageous lee position. Although the battlecruisers were hit a few times, no serious damage was done, and the British gunnery gradually took effect. Even as the *Scharnhorst* and *Gneisenau* began to take heavy punishment, putting several of their guns out of action, both ships continued to fight right to the end. The former did not sink until 4:17, almost three and a half hours from the start of the action, taking Von Spee and most of her crew with her. The *Gneisenau* fought on for another hour, even scoring a hit on *Invincible*, but by 5:50 the British ships were ordered to cease fire as she was sinking fast. A total of 190 survivors were picked up.

While the main action was being played out, the British cruisers were endeavoring to catch and destroy the German light cruisers attempting to escape. The *Leipzig* was eventually brought to bay by *Glasgow* and *Cornwall* and was sunk after a brave fight, only 18 survivors being picked up. The 6-inch-gun cruiser *Kent* caught and destroyed the *Nürnburg* after a running fight, but only 12 survivors were found. The *Dresden* managed to escape at the time, but was eventually run down at the island of Mas a Fuera off the Chilean

Despite events elsewhere, the Royal Navy's overriding priority was the destruction of the High Seas Fleet, a squadron of which is shown here led by the pre-dreadnought Preussen

Above: *The battleship HMS* Canada *was originally being built for Turkey as the* Reshadieh *but was requisitioned by the Royal Navy at the outbreak of war in 1914.*

coast on March 14, 1915. When approaching British warships opened fire, her captain hoisted a white flag, evacuated his crew ashore and destroyed the ship with scuttling charges.

The destruction of Von Spee's squadron was exactly the sort of action for which the battlecruisers had been designed, and Sturdee had skillfully exploited their advantages to achieve his well-deserved victory. The fact that it was accomplished within a reasonably short time meant that his ships could return to the Grand Fleet, where they were sorely needed in the most important theater of the naval war. Almost up to the outbreak of war, the Royal Navy planned a blockade of Germany along traditional lines, with squadrons of warships standing close off the ports and harbors ready to intercept any ships attempting to break out. However, Fisher realized that developments in military airplanes and submarines would make such a strategy unsustainable, and a policy of distant blockade was adopted. While torpedo boats and squadrons of pre-dreadnoughts guarded the English Channel, the Grand Fleet consisting of the most modern dreadnoughts supported by the battlecruisers, cruiser squadrons and destroyer flotillas was sent to the remote anchorage of Scapa Flow off the north coast of Scotland. From here, they could patrol the exits from the North Sea preventing the German High Seas Fleet or individual commerce raiders breaking out into the Atlantic and, just as importantly, preventing enemy or neutral merchant vessels reaching Germany with valuable food and war materials.

On paper, the Royal Navy held a substantial advantage with a total of 29 completed dreadnoughts and battlecruisers in commission with another

Below: *HMS* Agincourt *was the only battleship ever built with seven main armament gun turrets and was also requisitioned from Turkey in 1914.*

13 under construction, while the equivalent German figures were 18 and nine respectively. The difference was even greater when it is considered that five of the British ships then nearing completion were the new Queen Elizabeth class with 15-inch guns. The Grand Fleet was further bolstered by three dreadnoughts under construction in British yards for foreign navies that were requisitioned just before the outbreak of war. Two of them, the Turkish *Reshadieh* and Chilean *Admiralte Latorre* were similar to the Royal Navy's Iron Duke class, although the former mounted 14-inch instead of 13.5-inch guns, and were commissioned as HMS *Canada* and HMS *Erin* respectively. The third dreadnought, originally ordered by Brazil but subsequently purchased by Turkey while under construction, was the *Sultan Osman I* which was requisitioned on August 2, 1914, days before the outbreak of war. This ship represented the extreme development of the dreadnought concept, and at the time was the largest battleship in the world: 204 meters (671 feet) long and displacing 27,500 tons. However, her most remarkable feature was a main armament of no less than fourteen 12-inch guns in seven twin turrets all on the centerline. Fitting this number of mountings required some ingenuity; on the fore deck was a super-firing pair, two more were carried amidships between the funnels, and no less than three on the quarterdeck, one each facing fore and aft and a raised super-firing turret between them. Commissioned as HMS *Agincourt*, the ships internal design was an uneasy compromise between the positioning of the machinery spaces and the need to locate the magazines below the turret mountings, and several of the turrets suffered from restricted arcs.

Despite its numerical superiority, the Grand Fleet faced calls for its ships to be deployed out of UK waters, whereas the High Seas Fleet remained concentrated at Wilhelmshaven so that the overall margin was not as great as its commander, Admiral Sir John Jellicoe, might have wished. Also the High Seas Fleet commander, Admiral von Ingenohl, held the initiative as no major battle could be fought unless he chose to take his ships to sea, something he was reluctant to do on any significant scale. In both fleets,

Above: *Admiral Sir David Beatty, best known as the dashing commander of the battlecruiser squadrons.*

Right: *Admiral Franz von Hipper commanded the German battlecruisers with great distinction.*

the battlecruisers were organized into independent squadrons, whose main function was to scout ahead and then draw an enemy fleet towards their own battle squadrons for a decisive engagement. Both sides had battlecruiser commanders of significant personal standing although different styles of leadership. Vice-Admiral Sir David Beatty was the archetypal inspirational naval officer always ready to engage the enemy whatever the odds, believing passionately in the power of his great ships and their crews. On the German side Admiral Franz von Hipper was perhaps more thoughtful, relying on a high standard of training for all his ships and commanders with a particular emphasis on accurate gunnery.

In the absence of any immediate prospect of the German battle fleet emerging, Commodore Tyrwhitt commanding the Harwich-based destroyer flotillas decided to take the offensive and sailed with a force of destroyers and light cruisers to attack German light forces in the Helgoland Bight, in the North Sea, at dawn on August 28, 1914. It was also hoped that such action would draw out at least part of the High Seas Fleet, which would then be attacked by a line of waiting British submarines. Jellicoe detached the battlecruiser squadron under Beatty, as well as a light-cruiser squadron, to support this operation.

In an initial engagement between Tyrwhitt's force and German light cruisers and torpedo boats, one of the latter was sunk but the British then found themselves hard pressed, as a German light cruiser squadron emerged from the Jade estuary. It was at this point that Beatty took the courageous decision to bring his battlecruiser right into the thick of the action despite the risk of mines or submarine attack. His initiative was amply rewarded as two German cruisers, *Köln* and *Ariadne*, were sighted and blown out of the water, but subsequently the deteriorating visibility caused contact to be lost. Beatty ordered all British forces to withdraw to the west. Nevertheless, it was a significant victory. In all, three German cruisers and a torpedo boat were sunk at the cost of repairable damage to one British cruiser and three destroyers. Nevertheless, the whole operation was adjudged to have been extremely risky and was never repeated in the same form.

Unbeknown to Jellicoe and Beatty, the German admirals were operating under severe restrictions on the use of the battle fleet imposed by Kaiser Wilhelm, who was anxious not to see his navy destroyed. However, he allowed Ingenohl enough discretion to order sorties by Von Hipper's battlecruisers, and the first of these took place on November 3, 1914, when

Below: *The German battlecruiser* Seydlitz *fires a broadside.*

Above: *During the Battle of Dogger Bank one of* Seydlitz*' after turrets was hit by a 13.5-inch shell. Only prompt action saved the ship and important lessons were learnt.*

Below: *The weakly armed* Blucher *was easily outgunned by the British battlecruisers at Dogger Bank.*

ships of the 1st Scouting Group (1st SG) bombarded the British coastal town of Great Yarmouth. Although not intercepted by British forces, Von Hipper lost the armored cruiser *Yorck* to a German minefield off the Jade estuary. However, this action resulted in Beatty's battlecruisers being detached southwards to Cromarty, and a squadron of King Edward VII-class dreadnoughts to Rosyth, where they would be better placed to intercept such raids in future.

An opportunity occurred when Von Hipper's battlecruisers sortied again on December 15 to bombard the northeast ports of Scarborough, Whitby and Hartlepool, at dawn the next day. Hartlepool was particularly heavily damaged before the German ships turned for home. Despite being sighted by British cruisers and even by HMS *Orion*, a battleship of the 2nd battle squadron (BS), Von Hipper got away due to a combination of circumstances including British signal errors, a reluctance for some officers to act on their own initiative and the winter weather.

It was not long before Von Hipper tried again, although in the meantime Beatty had moved even further south to Rosyth. On January 23, 1915, Von Hipper left the Jade with the modern battlecruisers *Seydlitz* (flag), *Moltke* and *Derflinger*, as well as the older 15,600-ton *Blücher*. His objective was to raid the British fishing fleet, and their accompanying naval patrols off the Dogger Bank in the middle of the North Sea. However, through

wireless (radio) and telegraph intercepts, Admiralty code breakers in the famous Room 40 got wind of the plan. Beatty was ordered to sea with two squadrons of battlecruisers as well as Trywhitt's cruisers and destroyers. The German force was successfully intercepted at dawn on January 24, and Von Hipper turned onto a southeasterly course, heading for the Jade estuary, confident he could outrun what he took to be a squadron of battleships. In the meantime, Beatty's battlecruisers led by his flagship *Lion* worked up to 27 knots and began to close on Von Hipper, opening fire at long range. It was not long before *Seydlitz*, Von Hipper's flagship took a hit from one of *Lion's* 13.5-inch shells, which pierced the barbette of the after turret and ignited charges in the working chamber. This in turn ignited charges being sent up to the guns, and also flashed downwards to the magazines of both after turrets and from there up into the other after turret. All the gun crews and ammunition handlers were killed, and had the fires been unchecked it would only have been a matter of minutes before the whole magazine would have blown up, destroying the ship. Only prompt action to flood the magazines prevented such a catastrophe, but with half her main armament out of action and speed reduced, the ship was in a bad way. An even worse fate befell the last ship in the line, the armored cruiser *Blücher*, which was hit several times by 12-inch shells from the *Indomitable* and *New Zealand* and with speed reduced to 17 knots, she quickly fell behind the other German ships. With *Seydlitz* badly damaged and five British battlecruisers in pursuit, Von Hipper had no option but to attempt to escape and abandon the *Blücher* to her fate. In the meantime, Beatty's flagship *Lion* was hit, damaging the port boiler feed tanks and causing her to lose speed. As the battle drew away from him, Beatty attempted to control his fleet by flag signals, but these were misunderstood and instead of pursuing and possibly destroying all of the enemy battlecruisers, they concentrated on the unfortunate *Blücher*, which soon sank. However, by that time Von Hipper's ships had drawn out of sight and contact was lost.

Although the Battle of Dogger Bank was an undoubted victory, it was the Germans who were to gain most from the lessons to be learned. The near loss of the *Seydlitz* prompted a review of the method of transferring ammunition from the magazines to the guns. Shell and cartridge hoists were provided with doors which closed automatically after the carrying cages had passed. Flameproof containers for

Above: *Commander of the High Seas Fleet. Admiral von Ingenhol.*

As the Blucher *capsizes, her crew struggle for survival. Only 189 were eventually picked up by British destroyers out of a complement of 888.*

propellant charges were introduced and connecting doors between magazines were kept locked in action. Unfortunately, the British were unaware of the potential design problems with their own ammunition handling methods and would only learn of them the hard way several months in the future.

As a result of the Dogger Bank action, Admiral von Ingenohl was replaced by Admiral von Pohl, but in January 1916, Von Pohl was in turn replaced as commander of the High Seas Fleet by Admiral Reinhold Scheer, who was anxious to adopt a more offensive attitude. In April 1916, Scheer launched another bombardment mission with Von Hipper's battlecruisers, this time against the port of Lowestoft, in which over 200 houses were destroyed. Although intercepted by Trywhitt's light cruisers, Von Hipper emerged unscathed when the British chasing forces were called off by the Admiralty before they ran into the High Seas Fleet under Scheer. In early May, Jellicoe made a sweep with the Grand Fleet to support a seaplane raid on Tondern, but this failed to draw out the German battle fleet. However, towards the end of May, Scheer launched another operation in an attempt to draw out the British battlecruisers into a trap. Leaving the Jade estuary on the evening of the May 30, 1916, he headed northwards with the intention of attacking merchant shipping west of the Skagerrak, the sea channel between Denmark and Norway. Leading the fleet were Von Hipper's battlecruisers of the 1st SG accompanied by four light cruisers and 30 torpedo boats. Some 100 km (60 miles) astern was Scheer's High Seas Fleet consisting of 1st and 3rd BS with a total of 15 dreadnoughts as well as the 2nd BS with five pre-dreadnoughts, all accompanied by six light cruisers and 32 torpedo boats.

In the meantime, alerted by wireless intelligence from Room 40, the Admiralty became aware of the fact that some of the High Seas Fleet was preparing to leave harbor and ordered Jellicoe and Beatty to sea. Although having no knowledge of the German

Part of the High Seas Fleet at Wilhelmshaven with Hipper's battlecruisers in the foreground.

intentions, by a singular coincidence, Jellicoe ordered Beatty to rendezvous with him to the west of the Skagerrak, and the stage was finally set for the much-awaited decisive battle. Beatty's battlecruiser fleet comprised no less than five battlecruisers, fourteen light cruisers and 27 destroyers, as well as the seaplane carrier HMS *Engadine*. In addition, he also had the 5th BS commanded by Rear-Admiral Evan-Thomas with four of the powerful Queen Elizabeth-class battleships.

As Beatty approached the appointed rendezvous on a southeasterly heading, Jellicoe was 105 km (65 miles) north of him heading south with the rest of the Grand Fleet. This consisted of 24 dreadnoughts sailing in six columns of four ships, with Jellicoe flying his flag in HMS *Iron Duke* leading the third column in from the port wing of the fleet. Attached were three battlecruisers of the 3rd battlecruiser squadron (BCS), seven armored cruisers, twelve light cruisers and 49 destroyers. At 14:15 on the afternoon of May 31, Beatty ordered his battlecruisers to turn north to close the distance between the two British forces. As he did so one of his light cruisers, *Galatea,* broke off to the east to investigate a merchant ship and almost immediately spotted German warships – two torpedo boats that had been detached from Von Hipper's fleet for the same purpose. As soon as Beatty received this news, he turned back onto a course of south-southeast, but due to signaling confusion, the 5th BS did not turn immediately and eventually ended up some 16 km (10 miles) behind the battlecruisers. It is interesting to note that at this point the *Engadine*

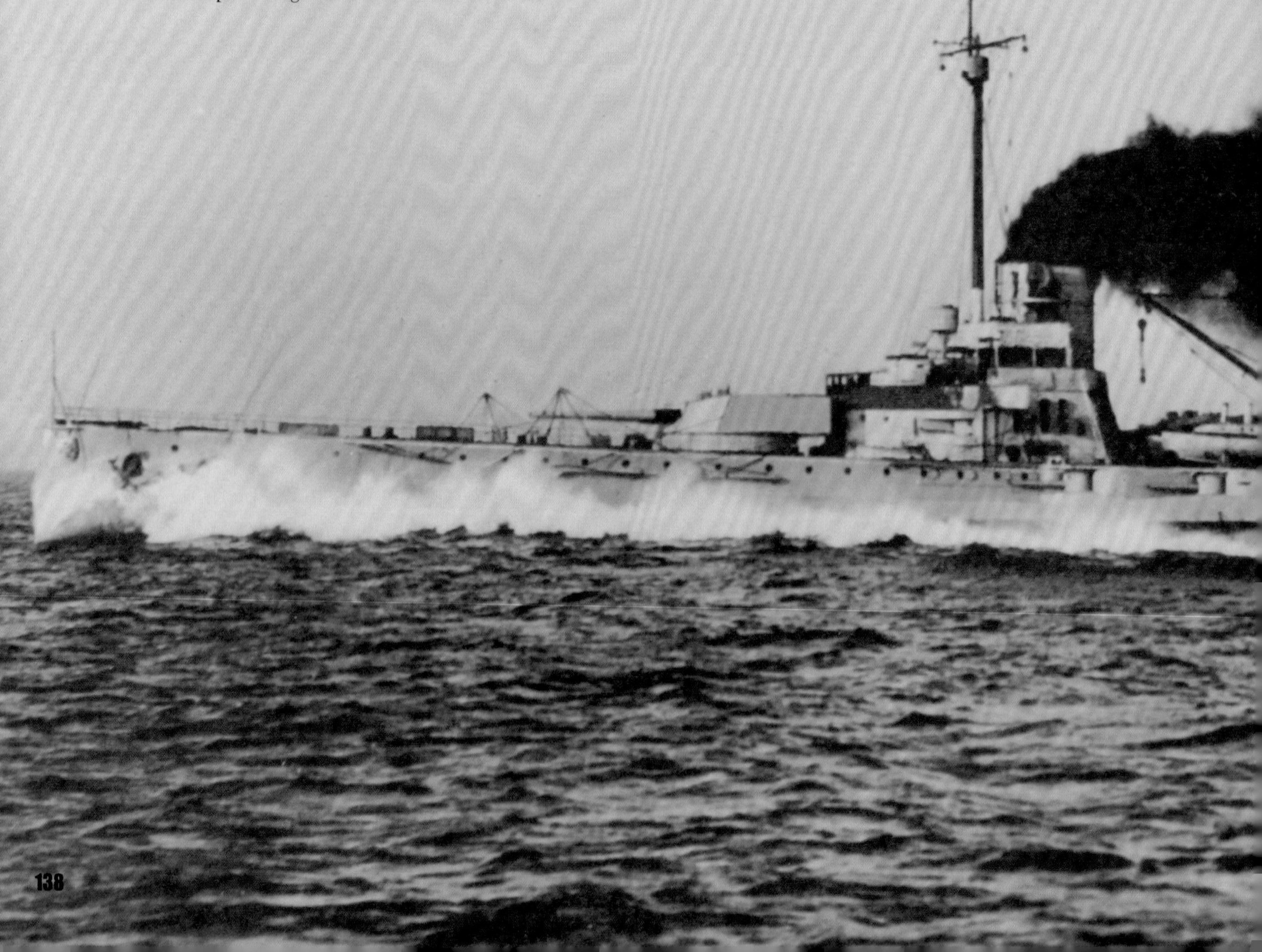

The German battlecruiser Moltke *at speed. She was hit by four heavy shells during the fighting at Jutland but not seriously damaged.*

stopped and launched a seaplane whose observer spotted some of Von Hipper's force and sent back radio reports to its parent ship. Unfortunately, for technical reasons, the *Engadine* was unable to forward this intelligence to Beatty or Jellicoe, although that would have undoubtedly had a significant impact on the course of the subsequent battle.

In the meantime, the opposing battlecruisers forces had sighted each other, and Beatty realized that with Von Hipper's ships to the east-northeast, he was in a position to cut off their return home. A turn onto an easterly course allowed the 5th BS to make up some of the lost ground, while Von Hipper turned on to SE so that the distance between the two battlecruiser fleets began to reduce rapidly. At this point neither

Von Hipper or Beatty realized that the other's whole battle fleet was also at sea. Von Hipper's zeppelins, a fleet of gas-filled, non rigid airships had been unable to patrol due to strong winds, and the Room 40 intelligence to Jellicoe had suggested that only some of the High Seas Fleet had sortied, with Scheer's flagship still in the Jade estuary. As they tore into the battle, Beatty's battlecruisers presented a stirring sight, working up to full speed with smoke pouring from their funnels and battle ensigns flying. In the lead was Beatty's flagship *Lion* followed by *Princess Royal, Queen Mary, Tiger, New Zealand* and *Indefatigable*. The German line was led by *Lützow* (flag) with *Derflinger, Seydlitz, Moltke* and *Von der Tann*, and as the range fell to 13,700 meters (15,000 yards) they were the first to open fire. Closing further to 11,000 meters (12,000 yards) both sides took hits and almost simultaneously Beatty and Von Hipper altered course to open the range. At 4 p.m. a shell penetrated the roof of *Lion's* midships turret and exploded inside, setting fire to

'There seems to be something wrong with our bloody ships today!' A pall of smoke marks the destruction of HMS Queen Mary.

cordite charges in the hoists. A quick-thinking officer, Major F. Harvey RMLI, ordered the magazine doors to be closed thus saving the ship but losing his own life in the process, an action that brought the award of a posthumous Victoria Cross. However, only four minutes later, the *Von der Tann* scored a hit on *Indefatigable's* fore turret with similar results only in this case there was no one to close the magazine doors. Within seconds the great ship was rent apart by an enormous explosion and sank immediately leaving only two survivors – later picked up by a passing German torpedo boat.

As the range opened, firing reduced but at this point the 5th BS finally came into action and

Above: *Despite taking heavy punishment, the German light cruiser* Weisbaden *managed to hit the British battleship* Marlborough *with a torpedo before finally sinking.*

opened fire at 17,300 meters (19,000 yards). Almost immediately *Barham* scored hits on the *Von der Tann,* and with these reinforcements in action Beatty turned back towards Von Hipper. While *Lion* slugged it out with the *Lützow*, the *Queen Mary* was shooting at the *Derflinger* with great accuracy, firing rapid eight-gun broadsides. Despite being hit, *Derflinger* responded in kind, and at 16:26, the *Queen Mary* suddenly erupted in flame and was torn apart by several explosions. Only 17 survivors were rescued after the ship had disappeared. With remarkable understatement, Beatty commented, 'There seems to be something wrong with our bloody ships today!' At this point, the opposing destroyers were released and a dramatic mêlée resulted. Two destroyers on each side were sunk and one torpedo hit the *Seydlitz*. However, even as this was being fought out, a dramatic signal came from the *Southampton,* one of the scouting cruisers ahead of Beatty, 'Battleships southeast'. It was Scheer's High Seas Fleet.

Beatty immediately turned his battlecruisers onto a course of north-northwest so that he could fall back on Jellicoe's advancing Grand Fleet, but again signaling difficulties resulted in a delay before the 5th BS complied. The result was that Evan-Thomas's ships came within range of Scheer's leading ships as they turned, as well as still being engaged by Von Hipper's battlecruisers, and experienced a hot time before they were able to draw away. Beatty now brought his ships around to northeast, which brought him back into action with Von Hipper's battlecruisers, but also helped to hide the advancing Grand Fleet from German observers. At the same time, Von Hipper became aware of other ships approaching him from the northeast. These were the battlecruisers *Invincible, Inflexible* and *Indomitable* that had been detached ahead of the Grand Fleet, and had run into the German cruiser screen, heavily damaging the *Weisbaden,* which later sank. In reaction to this, Von Hipper fell back on Scheer's advancing battle fleet and took up position at the

head of the line.

Here he ran into the British 1st Cruiser Squadron, also advancing ahead of the Grand Fleet. The unfortunate armored cruisers took a hail of fire from the German battlecruisers and dreadnoughts with the result that three of them (*Defence, Warrior* and *Black Prince*) were heavily damaged and subsequently sank. Behind were the battleships of the 5th BS, which turned away to open the range but for a while came under devastating fire from the High Seas Fleet. At this point, *Warspite's* steering jammed and she completed a full circle before pulling away, during which time she was hit several times. This perilous part of the battlefield became known as 'Windy Corner.'

In the meantime, Jellicoe was frustrated by the deluge of conflicting signals, which made it difficult to establish the precise location of the enemy ships in relation to his own force. He needed to deploy his dreadnoughts from the cruising column formation into a line of battle so that his firepower could be concentrated. The crucial decision was whether to do this by turning the columns to port or starboard. The wrong decision could lose him the battle. Eventually

An incredible picture showing the battlecruiser Invincible *hit by fire from* Derflinger. *Seconds later a magazine explosion ripped the ship apart - the third British battlecruiser casualty at Jutland.*

Beatty, who by this time had also put himself ahead of the advancing Grand Fleet signaled Jellicoe: 'Sighted enemy's battle fleet south-southwest.' This was the last piece in the jigsaw, and Jellicoe ordered deployment on the port column that was heading southeast. This meant that all the other columns turned 90 degrees to port and then, in turn, 90 degrees to starboard as they fell in line astern of the port column. In the meantime Von Hipper continued northeast, visibility obscured by haze and gun smoke. He came within almost 8,200 meters (9,000 yards) of the British battle line before he became aware of his predicament. The horizon ahead of him erupted in gun flashes as far as he could see on either side. His battlecruisers and Scheer's leading ships came under heavy fire and all thoughts of finishing off the crippled British cruisers were lost as they executed a practiced maneuver known as a 'battle turn-away.' Nevertheless, the *Lützow* and *Derflinger*

Above: *A German battlecruiser opens fire.*

Left: Derflinger *had both of her after turrets put out of action at Jultand.*

were heavily damaged, and three of the German dreadnoughts were also hit. However, Von Hipper scored one more major success as almost the last shell fired from *Derflinger* hit *Invincible's* Q turret, with the now inevitable consequence, flames flashed down to the magazine, and the resulting explosion split the ship in two as she sank leaving only six survivors.

Nevertheless, Jellicoe now held a commanding position. Except for *Moltke*, all of Von Hipper's remaining battlecruisers were badly damaged, and the German fleet was cut off from its route home. Unfortunately, due to the poor visibility Jellicoe did not immediately realize that Scheer had turned away and continued on a south-southeast course, as the Germans pulled away to the west. Eventually, Scheer ordered another about turn hoping to pass to the rear of the British line so that he could return home under cover of the approaching darkness. However, this was misjudged and his fleet, led by the battlecruisers that had already borne the brunt of the action, again ran headlong into the British line. Another battle turn-away was ordered, but not before the *Lützow* received fatal damage and subsequently sank. Some of the dreadnoughts also sustained major damage, including the *König*, *Grosser Kurfürst* and *Markgraf*, and this inspired Scheer to order his battlecruisers to attempt to ram the British dreadnoughts. This order was shortly rescinded but not before the *Derflinger*, *Seydlitz* and *Von der Tann* had sustained severe damage. This brave action, supported by destroyers launching torpedoes from cover of a smokescreen, allowed the High Seas Fleet to complete its turn away unhindered

Below: Pommern, *a Deutschland-class pre-dreadnought was sunk in a night attack by British destroyers. There were no survivors.*

and, more importantly, caused Jellicoe to alter course away to the southeast to avoid torpedoes.

Effectively, this was the end of the battle as the main battle fleets lost contact with each other in the gathering gloom and darkness. There were subsequently some intermittent sightings, skirmishes involving Beatty's battlecruisers and some spirited destroyer actions. During one of the latter, destroyers of the 12th flotilla carried out a successful torpedo attack on the German pre-dreadnought *Pommern,* which sank with the loss of all her crew. However, during the night, Scheer was able to take his ships across the rear of the British line and make for the safety of the German minefields in the Helgoland Bight. When dawn broke on June 1, 1916, the Grand

Seydlitz *took a dreadful battering at Jutland and would probably have sunk had she not run aground. She was subsequently refloated and towed to Wilhelmshaven for extensive repairs.*

Fleet was intact and ready for battle, but the High Seas Fleet was riding at anchor, licking its wounds with no immediate intention of renewing the battle.

Since that time, there has been endless controversy over who, if anyone, could claim victory. The Germans, certainly, were quick to announce a great victory, and could back this up with listing the ships lost on either side, which was definitely in their favor. While the British had lost three large battlecruisers, three large armored cruisers and eight destroyers, the German fleet had lost a battlecruisers, four light

cruisers, a pre-dreadnought battleship and five destroyers. The Admiralty was slow to make an announcement, and the British press gleaned their first information from German sources and subsequent claims of a British victory did not ring true. Indeed, Beatty's battlecruisers were subjected to booing and jeering when they returned to Rosyth. As time passed, it became apparent that a strategic victory had been won as the High Seas Fleet never again mounted a serious challenge to the Grand Fleet, which quickly replaced its losses with new construction, and was further reinforced by a US battle squadron

The United States' entry into the war in April 1917 brought a squadron of US Navy battleships to Scapa Flow where they formed the 6th Battle Squadron of the Grand Fleet.

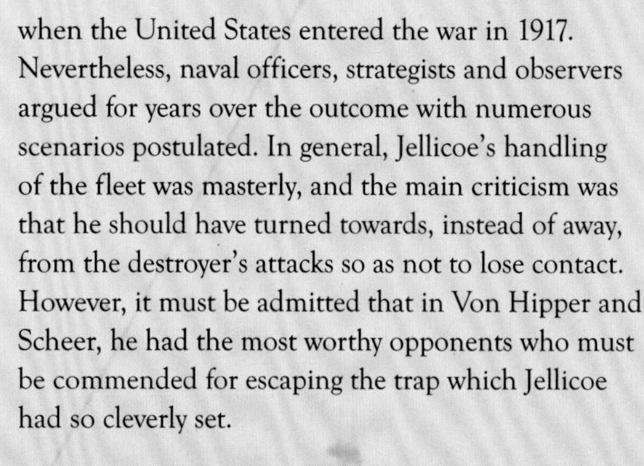

when the United States entered the war in 1917. Nevertheless, naval officers, strategists and observers argued for years over the outcome with numerous scenarios postulated. In general, Jellicoe's handling of the fleet was masterly, and the main criticism was that he should have turned towards, instead of away, from the destroyer's attacks so as not to lose contact. However, it must be admitted that in Von Hipper and Scheer, he had the most worthy opponents who must be commended for escaping the trap which Jellicoe had so cleverly set.

Above: *The new battlecruiser HMS* Repulse *at speed. She and her sister ship* Renown *were armed with 15-inch guns.*

Even while the Battle of Jutland was being fought, the Royal Navy was building more battlecruisers, and two of these, *Renown* and *Repulse*, joined the Grand Fleet in September 1916. Originally intended as R-class battleships, the design was recast in the light of the success of *Invincible* and *Inflexible* off the Falklands in November 1914. The hull was lengthened by 50 meters (170 feet) and armament was reduced from eight to six 15-inch guns in three twin turrets, two forward and one aft. The space gained was used to install steam turbines driving four shafts. Total power output was 120,000 shp, three times that of the R class, and Renown achieved 32.68 knots on trials making her the fastest of all British battlecruisers. The secondary

HMS *Courageous*. *Although sometimes referred to as battlecruisers, this ship was very lightly armoured. Note the aircraft on a flying off platform over the forward gun turret.*

Above: *HMS* Furious *as completed with a flight deck forward and a single 18-inch gun aft.*

anti-torpedo boat armament comprised a total of seventeen 4-inch QF carried in five triple and two single mountings. Although, intended to facilitate a high rate of fire, the triple 4-inch mountings were not successful, and each required a crew of 32 in action. As with the earlier battlecruisers, the scale of protection was minimal with 15-cm (6-inch) main belts and 18 cm (7 inches) on the turrets and barbettes. At the last moment an additional 500 tons of armor was added around the magazines as a result of the catastrophic experiences at Jutland.

While *Renown* and *Repulse* were being completed, the first of four even larger Admiral-class battlecruisers was being laid down. Intended as a response to the projected German Mackensen class, these were going to be the largest capital ships ever built with a length of 243 meters (800 feet) and a displacement of 36,000 tons. Armament was set at eight 15-inch guns in four twin turrets and a speed of 33 knots was projected. The secondary armament was intended to be sixteen 5.5-inch guns of a new design offering a faster rate of fire than the standard 6-inch gun. However, when the lessons of Jutland were fully appreciated, it was decided to substantially increase armor protection by generally increasing armor thickness by 50 per cent, adding 5,000 tons to the displacement, which now rose to 41,200 tons. This had the effect of reducing speed to 31 knots. Only the lead ship, HMS *Hood*, was laid down although she was not completed until 1920, and the others were all cancelled. However, during the inter-war years *Hood* was the largest warship afloat and the pride of the Royal Navy.

While by the standards of the time HMS *Hood* was adequately armored, she was pre-dated by another class of battlecruiser that had only the flimsiest protection of any major warship. These were the three Courageous class which were actually classified as large light cruisers and were the brainchild of Admiral Fisher who, encouraged by Winston Churchill, envisaged a plan to invade northern Germany through the Baltic Sea. In 1915, orders were placed for an armada of shallow draft warships that would be required to carry out this operation. The list included three large cruisers armed with four 15-inch guns in twin turrets fore and aft as well as eighteen 4-inch QF in triple mountings. With a draft of only 6.7 meters (22 feet), displacement was limited to around 19,000 tons, which precluded the fitting of armor protection on any meaningful scale. Although the turrets and barbettes were protected by 17.5 cm (7 inches) of armor, the main belt was only 7.5 cm (3 inches) thick and deck armor generally only around 2.5 cm (1 inch) thick. Two ships, *Courageous* and *Glorious*, were completed as designed and entered service in January 1917 but the third ship, HMS *Furious*, had a more interesting career. Instead of the twin 15-inch gun turrets, the projected armament was two single 18-inch guns, the heaviest naval artillery ever mounted in a British warship, although in the event only the after turret was fitted. On the forecastle, a take-off deck was erected over a hangar that replaced the forward turret. After the ship was commissioned in mid-1917, flying trials took place during which Squadron Commander Edwin Dunning became the first pilot

Below: *Before the end of the war, HMS* Furious *was further modified with an after flight deck and hangar replacing the 18-inch-gun mounting.*

to land an aircraft on a moving ship. However, his technique of side-slipping around the central bridge structure was inherently dangerous, and he was killed while making a second attempt. As a result, the after turret was removed and replaced by a stern landing deck in March 1918. This arrangement was still not satisfactory, and eventually in 1922 the ship was converted into an aircraft carrier with a full-length flush deck. Both *Courageous* and *Glorious* were also converted into aircraft carriers after the war although

The battleship Bayern *sinking after being scuttled at Scapa Flow on June 21, 1919.*

their conversions were better planned with the result that they could stow more aircraft.

There were no more major fleet actions after Jutland, but elements of the High Seas Fleet occasionally sortied. A typical action occurred on November 17, 1917, when Scheer dispatched a pair of dreadnoughts to cover minesweeping operations supported by a squadron of light cruisers and some destroyers. Alerted by the Room 40 code breakers, a force of British battlecruisers including the new *Renown* and *Repulse*, as well as *Courageous* and *Glorious*, was dispatched to intercept. In support was Admiral Madden's 1st BS with eight dreadnoughts. The German force scattered when the British battlecruisers were spotted, but these were called off when the chase led towards the German minefields. However, Admiral Phillimore in *Repulse* ignored the order and continued eastwards until the German dreadnoughts were sighted

and opened fire. He reversed course hoping to lead them towards Madden's waiting battleships, but the German ships refused to leave the protection of their own minefields despite the fact that reinforcements including the new battlecruiser *Hindenburg* were not far away. Scheer did make another major sortie up the Norwegian coast with the High Seas Fleet in April 1918, but returned to port when the battlecruiser *Moltke* lost a propeller. By the time the Admiralty learned of this operation it was too late to catch them. At the end of October 1918, Scheer ordered his fleet to sea for a last desperate battle, but many crews refused to sail, a belated acceptance of the true outcome of Jutland. The next time British ships sighted the whole German High Seas Fleet was on November 21, 1918, when they sailed in accordance with the instructions of the Armistice Commission to be interned at Scapa Flow under the guns of the Royal Navy. Here, they lay at anchor while the armistice negotiations dragged on. Immediately prior to the signing of the Treaty of Versailles, which provided for the surrender of the German ships, their crews acting in accordance with orders from their commander Rear-Admiral von Reuter set about scuttling the whole fleet on 21 June, 1919. Having made earlier preparations, they were almost completely successful and only one battleship (*Baden*), and a few cruisers and destroyers were saved.

Thus, the cycle that had begun at the end of the 19th century was finally played out. The German challenge had been met and conquered, and the Royal Navy still reigned supreme on the world's oceans, confident in the strength of its battle fleet. However, in the next few years there were to be dramatic changes of fortune, and the paramount position of both the battleship and the Royal Navy itself was about to be severely challenged.

The end: funnels and masts are all that are visible as the scuttled battlecruiser Hindenburg *settles on the seabed at Scapa Flow.*

Admirals of the First World War

Above: *Admiral J Fisher in his cabin on HMS Renown*

Admiral of the Fleet John 'Jackie' Fisher RN (1841–1920)
John Fisher was a great reforming admiral, creating the navy that confronted Germany in the First World War. He is often considered the second most important figure in Royal Naval history after Nelson.

Early in his career, Fisher specialized in gunnery and torpedoes, becoming Director of Naval Ordnance from 1886–1890. Fisher introduced destroyers to the navy as Third Sea Lord (1892–1897), then after commanding the Mediterranean Fleet (1899–1902) he became Second Sea Lord and dramatically reformed officer selection and training. Promoted to First Sea Lord in 1904, he ruthlessly dispensed with over 150 obsolete ships, and was the driving force behind the creation of the dreadnought class and the new battlecruisers. He created the Home Fleet, converted the navy from coal to oil fuel and encouraged the introduction of submarines. Retiring in 1911, he was recalled as First Sea Lord in 1914 aged 73 but resigned in 1915 over his opposition to the Gallipoli campaign.

Admiral of the Fleet John Jellicoe RN (1859–1935)
John Jellicoe took command of the Grand Fleet at the start of the First World War, and went on to become First Sea Lord. Popular, and concerned with the well-being of his crews, he was a dedicated and highly knowledgeable officer (being Director of Naval Ordnance from 1905 to 1907), and worked closely with Fisher. He had survived the infamous sinking of the *Victoria* in 1893.

Commanding the fleet at Jutland in May, 1916, Jellicoe was criticized at the time for failing to deliver a decisive victory, but subsequent analysis has confirmed that overall he did well and acted in accordance with his strategic task of confining the German fleet to port.

Jellicoe became First Sea Lord in November 1916, but was dismissed at the end of 1917 due to exhaustion and his perceived pessimism over Britain's prospects of winning the protracted and bloody war.

Below: *A rare view of Admirals Jellicoe* **(right)** *and Beatty* **(left)** *together. Between them these men were responsible for the overall conduct of the struggle against the German High Seas Fleet.*

Above: *Admiral Beatty on HMS* Queen Elizabeth

Admiral of the Fleet David Beatty RN(1871–1936)
In 1910, aged 38, David Beatty became the youngest Royal Navy admiral since Horatio Nelson. He commanded the battlecruisers at Jutland and is remembered for his remark, 'There seems to be something wrong with our bloody ships today!' when two of his battlecruisers exploded and sank within 20 minutes during the battle.

Before Jutland, Beatty's battlecruisers scored minor victories at the actions of Heligoland Bight (1914) and the Dogger Bank (1915). His dashing and aggressive character contrasted with Jellicoe's more sober approach, leading to disagreements during and after the war over Jellicoe's conduct at Jutland. However, when Beatty took over as commander of the Grand Fleet in November 1916, he nevertheless continued Jellicoe's cautious strategy.

Beatty took the surrender of the German High Seas Fleet in 1918, stage-managing the event to ensure the Germans were humiliated. After the war he served a lengthy term as First Sea Lord from 1919 to 1927.

Admiral of the Fleet Frederick Doveton Sturdee RN (1859–1925)
Frederick Sturdee is remembered as the victor of the Battle of the Falkland Islands in December 1914. He also commanded the Fourth Battle Squadron at the Battle of Jutland.

In late 1914, Sturdee was a vice-admiral and Chief-of-Staff at the Admiralty, but had clashed with his superior, John Fisher. Following the British defeat at Coronel, Fisher took the opportunity to relieve himself of Sturdee's presence by sending him away to the South Atlantic to exact revenge.

Sturdee's battlecruiser and cruiser force was heavier, faster and numerically superior that of his opponent, Von Spee. At the subsequent action, only one of the five German cruisers escaped being sunk, there being no British losses. The scale of the victory earned Sturdee considerable credit.

Sturdee later criticized Jellicoe's conduct at Jutland and was expected to succeed him as commander of the Grand Fleet, but Beatty was chosen instead. Thereafter, Sturdee received no further notable wartime advancement.

Grand Admiral Alfred von Tirpitz (1849–1930)
Alfred von Tirpitz is regarded as the founder of the Imperial German Navy. He was a statesman as much as an admiral, and saw naval strength as a fundamental step towards status as a great power.

Von Tirpitz (then a rear-admiral) was appointed Secretary of State for the Imperial Navy Department in 1897. His views on building a battleship fleet big enough to challenge the British were already well known. Working closely with the kaiser, he used his political talents to create an effective High Seas Fleet, which remained roughly 40 per cent smaller than the British Grand Fleet. Realizing Germany could never match Britain's surface fleet, he became a supporter of unrestricted submarine warfare, despite its risks. The continuing restrictions on submarine use caused him to resign in 1916, and he remained in retirement for the rest of the war.

Above: *Admiral Reinhard Scheer*

Admiral Reinhard Scheer (1863–1928)
Reinhard Scheer commanded the High Seas Fleet at the Battle of Jutland, and in August 1918 was promoted to Chief of the Naval Staff. He was known as a strict disciplinarian and an aggressive commander.

Scheer had already served in the High Seas Fleet as its chief-of-staff, and as a battleship squadron commander before assuming overall charge in January 1916. His performance at the Battle of Jutland is generally assessed as good.

Scheer was another strong advocate of unrestricted submarine warfare, being one of the main German strategists of their use. Together with Von Hipper, Scheer planned a final, probably suicidal attack on the British fleet in October 1918, but was thwarted by the naval mutiny at Kiel. Scheer was then dismissed by the kaiser just before the war ended.

Admiral Franz von Hipper (1863–1932)
As commander of the High Seas Fleet Scouting Forces from 1913, Franz von Hipper was in charge of the German battlecruisers at Jutland. Of the four main admirals at the battle (Jellicoe, Beatty, Scheer and Hipper), his performance is usually assessed as the most accomplished.

Earlier in the war, Von Hipper had led his battlecruisers on raids against the British coast, notably at Scarborough (1914) and the Dogger Bank (1915). Civilian deaths at these actions caused him to be dubbed the 'baby killer' by the British press. At Jutland, his battlecruisers succeeded in sinking three British battlecruisers (*Indefatigable*, *Queen Mary* and *Inflexible*), and also led a bold charge against the Grand Fleet, which allowed the Germans to escape. Von Hipper succeeded Scheer as C-in-C of the High Seas Fleet in August 1918. Only a few months later he was forced to lead it on its final voyage of surrender to Scapa Flow.

Inside a Gun Turret

Above: *The ammunition handling room below the forward 12-inch turret aboard the pre-dreadnought USS* New Hampshire *(BB25). Here shells and propellent charges are transferred from the magazines through the flash proof scuttles to turret hoists.*

The *raison d'être* of a battleship is to mount and fire a battery of heavy guns. These weapons were carried in heavily armored turrets, the basic elements of which were established with the introduction of the Dreadnought-class battleships.

The structure where the guns are mounted and are loaded, aimed, fired and cleaned out is known as the gunhouse. Directly under the gunhouse – and rotating with it – there is a working chamber or handling room, (sometimes more than one), usually wholly or partly below deck level. Here ammunition is transferred from the hoists leading from the magazines onto the hoists that take the shells and cartridges to the guns. Also below the gunhouse is the gun pit where the gun layers work and below this a central trunk or shaft containing the magazine hoists, which descend into the ship. This shaft also rotates with the gunhouse, which itself rests on a bed of rotating rollers set around the top of a circular housing known as the barbette. The gunhouse is heavily armored, as is the barbette down to the level of the main armored deck, which is usually well below the level of the upper deck of the ship. The barbette therefore provides the armor protection for the working chambers, hoist shafts and turret-turning machinery.

The shells or projectiles are always stored separately from the charges that propel them to their target, a basic safety feature going back to the earliest turreted warships. Another fundamental safety feature is that the various hatches and openings between magazine and gun are designed so that there is never an open path for an explosive flash to pass down into the

Above: *A 16-inch shell is rammed into the gun breech.*

magazine from the turret in the event of an accidental explosion or a hit during action. (This was a lesson learned the hard way by the Royal Navy during the Battle of Jutland.) Extensive machinery was needed to handle ammunition of the size and weight used in battleships, but turrets also needed crew members at every level. The turret crew of a British dreadnought numbered around 35, but the US Navy's last group of battleship, the Iowa class, had 47-man turret crews. Conditions were tough. In 1999, the *Navy Times* had this to say in an article about life aboard the *Iowa*.

A coal miner or even a steelworker on an open hearth blast furnace had better working conditions than a gun-turret crew... It was hot, grimy, hazardous and cramped. The turret decks were slippery, coated with hydraulic fluid and oil. A tumbling shell could pulverize a man. One misstep in the gunhouse, and a sailor could plunge into the pit, where he might be crushed to death by moving machinery... Friction and static electricity were a constant source of worry. A spark could trigger an explosion.

The following is a description of the operation of the 14-inch guns aboard the USS *Texas*, a dreadnought-type battleship launched in 1912, which saw service in both world wars: Separate projectile and powder magazines were located deep in the ship, below the barbette, fore and aft of the turret's central column. The 14-inch projectiles (weighing between 544 and 680 kg [1200–1500 pounds] each depending on type) were stored nose down and were lifted by hooking them to an overhead monorail using rings attached to their bases. Crew members slid them along the monorail from the magazine to the lower handling room, in the middle of which was the central shaft containing the hoists. The projectiles were transferred to the electric chain hoist, which lifted them to the upper handling room (or shell deck) within the barbette. Up to 30 shells could be stored here, and from here they were transferred via another overhead monorail to the upper projectile hoist. Arriving in the gunhouse, the shells were tipped back by the loaders through an opening in the rear of the hoist into the transfer tray, from where the loaders pushed them into the loading tray aligned with the gun's breech. From here, an electrical rammer pushed the shell into the breech.

Meanwhile, powder bags (weighing 47 kg [105 pounds] each and stored in two bag cans) were manually transferred from the powder magazine, through a flash-proof rotating scuttle into the lower handling room. From here, they traveled up on their own hoist to the powder flat, just above the upper handling room. They were then lifted by hand-operated hoists to one of the two powder-transfer rooms, one below the breech of each gun. Once again, they were manually handled through flash proof scuttles into the gun pit below the gun trunnions, and then lifted by hand onto the loading tray ready to be hand-rammed into the breech behind the projectile, using a 3-meter (10-foot) wooden pole.

The gun captains (one to each gun) now closed the breech and inserted a firing cartridge into the firing lock. The gun was then laid (positioned) by the gun layers working in the gunpit, who normally responded

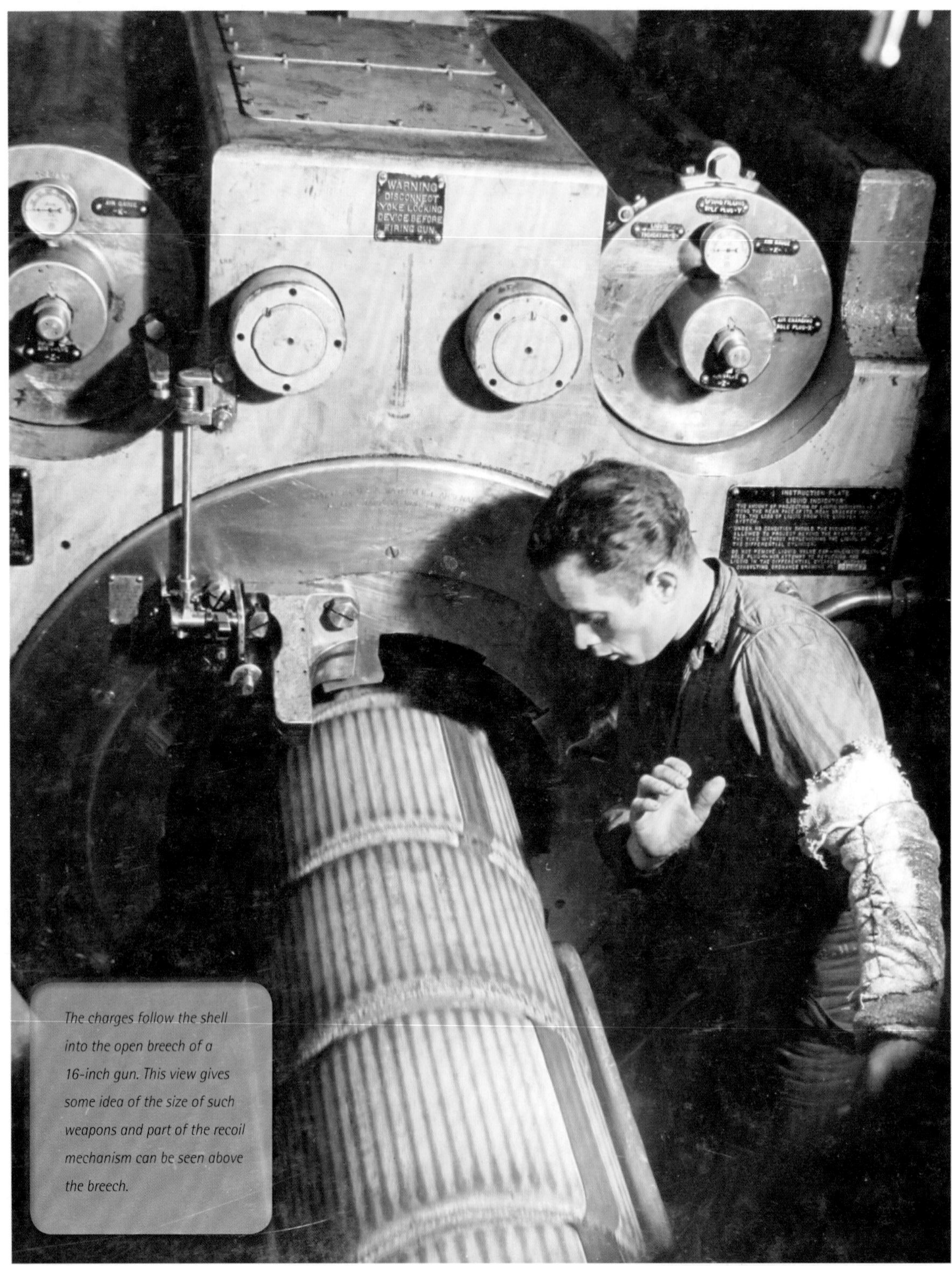

The charges follow the shell into the open breech of a 16-inch gun. This view gives some idea of the size of such weapons and part of the recoil mechanism can be seen above the breech.

to data received from the gun-control position on the mast above the ship. Guns could also be aimed under 'local control,' using optical equipment within the turret. The turret crew stood clear and braced themselves, conveying their ready status by means of light indicators. A warning bell was rung, and the guns were then fired electrically from the central control position. The immense guns had a recoil of more than a meter (40 inches).

Overall operation of the turret was controlled by officers located in booths at the rear of the gunhouse. After firing, they directed the gun layers to level the guns so that they once again lined up with the loading trays. The gun captains then opened the breeches and compressed air was blown into the chambers to expel any smoldering remnants of powder out through the gun muzzles. The loading cycle was then repeated. Rate of fire would vary with a number of factors, such as crew fatigue, sea state and training levels, but was one round every 90 seconds, on average. In the case of electrical failure, gun equipment and turret rotation could be operated manually using chain falls located under the gun pit, though this would slow the rate of fire. The turrets of the *Texas* were labor intensive: 45 men worked in the magazines and lower handling room plus 25 men in the turret crew – a total of 70 men assigned to each turret. With five turrets and the fire control team included, over 400 men were involved in keeping the guns in action, almost a third of the ship's total crew.

Below: *The operation of the turret is monitored from the control position at the rear. The sailor in the background is viewing the target through a periscope sight and guns could be engaged under local control from this position if the central control system should be put out of action.*

BETWEEN THE WARS: THE TREATY BATTLESHIPS

USS California *was completed in October 1921, before the Washington Treaty introduced limitations on the building of battleships.*

Between The Wars: The Treaty Battleships

Despite the end of hostilities in November 1918, there was no immediate pause in the battleship construction plans of the victorious nations. In particular, the United States pressed ahead with the construction of four new Maryland class, which had been ordered in December 1916, although only the name ship had been laid down by the end of 1918. However, *Colorado* and *Washington* were laid down during 1919 followed by *West Virginia* in 1920. Displacing over 32,000 tons, these ships were heavily armored and were based on the preceding Tennessee class (which themselves were not completed until 1921), but the main armament was now eight 16-inch guns. The same Navy Act which had authorized the Maryland class, also authorized six even larger South Dakota-class battleships and six Lexington-class battlecruisers. The battleships were real monsters with a standard displacement in excess of 42,000 tons and an armament of twelve 16-inch guns

By 1920, the US Navy had four Maryland-class battleships armed with 16-inch guns under construction.

Above: *The projected South Dakota-class battleships would have been armed with no less than twelve 16-inch guns.*

in four triple turrets. In fact, original design studies had shown ships of up to 80,000 tons and capable of speeds up 35 knots, armed with no less than fifteen 18-inch guns. However, more practical considerations prevailed, including the need to restrict size so that ships could transit the Panama Canal, and the final South Dakota design would only be good for 23 knots – still 2 knots faster than existing US ships. All six ships of the class (*South Dakota, Indiana, Montana, North Carolina, Iowa, Massachusetts*) were laid down in 1920, except for the last which followed in April 1921.

The battlecruisers also went through several design iterations and construction was also delayed to allow all the lessons from the Battle of Jutland to be incorporated. Inevitably this resulted in a substantial increase in armor protection, and as a result of this and other changes displacement rose from around 35,000 tons to 43,500 tons. The armament was originally to have comprised ten 14-inch guns but this was changed to eight 16-inch guns in four twin turrets. A unique feature of the original design was no less than seven funnels to serve a total of 24 boilers, which provided steam for four turbines. These were coupled to 40,000 kW generators driving the propellers by means of two 16,500 kW electric motors on each shaft. The funnels were arranged in a 1-2-1-2-1 configuration so that when viewed from the side they appeared as five funnels. In the final design a more conventional two funnel arrangement was adopted. Four ships (*Constellation, Saratoga, Constitution, United States*) were laid down in 1920 with *Lexington* and *Ranger* following in 1921.

This North American activity was mostly prompted by construction in Japan, which in 1916 had approved the so-called '8 by 8' program, which allowed for the construction of eight new battleships and eight battlecruisers. In November 1918, the first two battleships, *Nagato* and *Mutsu*, were already under construction. These were the first battleships laid down to be armed with 16-inch guns and preceded the similarly sized US Maryland class. Two further ships (*Tosa, Kaga*) were laid down in 1920, these having a planned displacement of just under 40,000 tons and an additional twin 16-inch mounting was added aft on a lengthened hull. Design speed was 26.5 knots, slightly greater than the Mutsu class, but both groups were fast for their time and only matched by the British Queen Elizabeth class, which was only armed with 15-inch guns.

Although the 16-inch shell was not much heavier (1,020 kg [2,250 lbs] as against 880 kg [1,938 lbs] for the 15-inch gun), the Japanese gun had a range of up to 38,400 meters (42,000 yards), which was more than 9,100 meters (10,000 yards) greater than anything the British gun could manage and this conferred obvious tactical advantages.

Also in 1920, the first pair of battlecruisers (*Akagi, Amagi*) were laid down followed by another two (*Atago, Takao*) in 1921, and orders for a further four were confirmed at the same time. These were also to be armed with ten 16-inch guns and on a displacement of 41,200 tons were intended to make 30 knots.

To complete the 8 by 8 program it was planned to lay down four more Japanese battleships (provisionally known only as numbers 13 to 16) in 1922. These would have been the largest and most powerful battleships in the world at that time, displacing 47,400 tons and armed with eight enormous 18-inch guns, upping the stakes yet again in the race to possess the heaviest armaments.

Below: *In 1918, Japan had started work on two Nagato-class battleships and had plans to build another 14 capital ships.*

Faced with such competition from America and Japan, the Royal Navy had no choice but to follow suit if it was to remain the world's pre-eminent maritime power. At the end of 1918, the only major warship still under construction was the 41,000 ton battlecruiser *Hood*, which had been laid down in 1916. The orders for three more sister ships were cancelled in 1917 when it became apparent that German battlecruiser construction had virtually ground to a halt. Although the Royal Navy had two other modern battlecruisers (*Renown* and *Repulse)* in commission, as well as the five Queen Elizabeth-class fast battleships, none of these were a match for the new US and Japanese ships and so work commenced on four new battlecruisers at the end of 1921. The allocated names were *Invincible* and *Inflexible* to commemorate those lost at Jutland, as well as *Indomitable* and *Indefatigable*. These ships were of an entirely new design – coded as G3 – that owed much to the experience at Jutland. The main armament of nine 16-inch guns was carried in three triple turrets, two forward and one amidships immediately behind the bridge superstructure. This arrangement allowed the maximum possible armor protection to be applied to the central citadel containing the guns and their magazines. Aft of that were the machinery spaces, surmounted by two closely spaced funnels, and these were also well protected. In fact, although termed battlecruisers, the overall armor protection was a least as good as contemporary battleships and in recognition of the growing threat from the air, an 20-cm (8-inch) armored deck covered the magazines and machinery spaces. Secondary armament was sixteen 6-inch guns in eight twin turrets, four grouped around the bridge tower and four right aft. The final G3 design had a projected displacement of over 48,000 tons and with four shaft-geared

Below: *The battlecruiser HMS* Hood *was the only one of four similar ships to be completed, commissioning in March 1920.*

Above: *HMS* Renown, *one of a pair of battlecruisers armed with six 15-inch guns completed in 1916.*

turbines producing 160,00 horsepower, a speed of up to 32 knots was expected. Also planned were four battleships, provisionally named the St. Andrew class or otherwise known as design N3. These were based on the G3 battlecruisers but had a smaller engine reducing speed to 23 knots. That allowed for the main armament to be upgraded to nine 18-inch guns in three triple mountings. Displacement was substantially unaltered although the main armor belt was increased from by 2.5 cm (1 inch) to 38 cm (15 inches). Construction of these immense ships were scheduled to begin in 1922 but in the event, no orders were actually placed.

Thus by 1921, it was apparent that the world's major maritime nations were engaged in a significant and very expensive arms race that showed every sign of spiraling out of control. Having just come out of a long and costly war (in both human and financial terms), Britain was reluctant to fund the construction of these large warships. A revulsion to the suffering experienced in World War I inevitably fueled, strong understandably pacifist sentiments, feelings that were echoed in North America. However, the US Navy was now strongly pressing for parity with the Royal Navy and realized that America's industrial muscle was quite capable of building the necessary ships. America was also drifting towards a strong isolationist policy, having rejected the Treaty of Versailles and any involvement in the newly formed League of Nations. Nevertheless, even they balked at the cost of their own projected naval construction program.

When President Harding replaced President Wilson in 1920, the new administration was keen to show its credentials as a force for peace and disarmament. Harding proposed a conference to be held in Washington, D.C., with the object of agreeing to limitations on naval construction, as well as looking at some broader issues affecting the balance of power in the Pacific and Far East. The invited participants were to be the United States, Britain, Japan, France and Italy and each side prepared to present its case at the conference. On the American side, the US Navy was adamant that it would not reduce its building program until parity with the Royal Navy had been reached. However, this could hardly be presented as a case for general disarmament, and a more innovative approach was required.

The conference was opened by the US Secretary of State Charles Hughes, who put forward some breathtaking proposals of which the following were particularly relevant to the future of capital ships:
i) All projected or approved capital ship construction programs should be immediately abandoned.
ii) Existing capital ship strengths should be reduced by scrapping many older ships.
iii) After the above proposals had been implemented, the relative strengths of the naval powers at that time would then be maintained.
iv) The measure of naval strength should be set at the total tonnage of capital ships (not numbers) and tonnage of other types of warships (e.g. cruisers or destroyers) should be held at the same proportion.

Needless to say, such wide-ranging proposals came as a great surprise, but after some consideration the delegates welcomed them in principle, although there was then considerable discussion and bargaining over the detail and method of implementation. More detailed proposals relating to capital ships restricted the maximum standard displacement to 35,000 tons and proposed that no work on new capital ships could be commenced for at least ten years. Also that existing ships could only be replaced when they were at least 20 years old. In terms of scrapping older ships, the US Navy proposed to scrap fifteen ships then planned or under construction, as well fifteen older pre-dreadnoughts. It was suggested that similar action

Below: *The USS* South Carolina *(BB26) launched in 1908 was one of several battleships scrapped as a result of the Washington Treaty.*

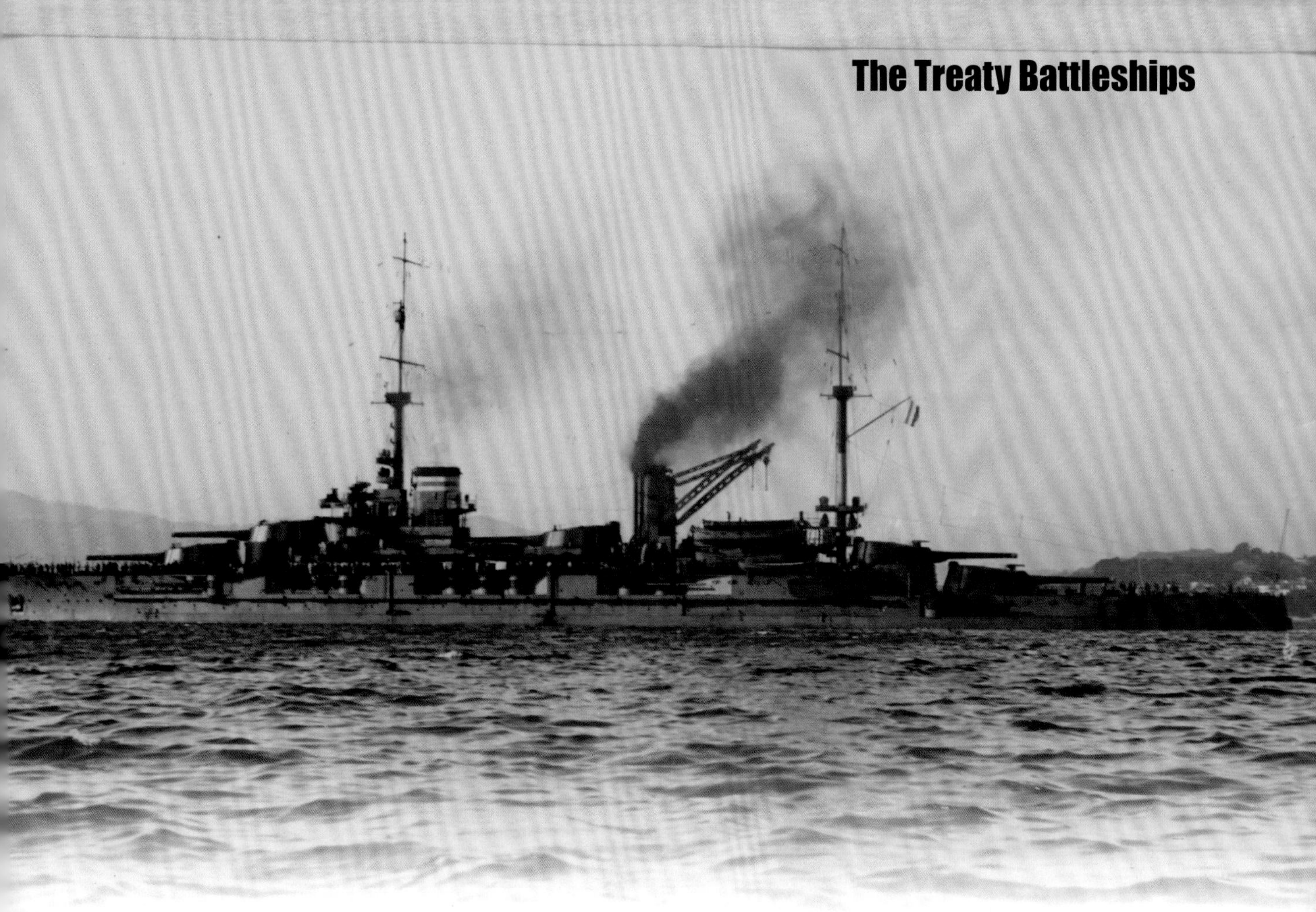

Above: *The Bretagne-class battleship* Lorraine *was one of only seven dreadnoughts built in France before the end of the First World War.*

was taken by Britain and Japan. The result would be that Britain would have 22 capital ships (totaling 604,000 tons), the United States 18 (501,000 tons) and Japan ten (300,00 tons). As older ships were retired or replaced, the intention was that Britain's total would fall to 500,000 tons in line with the US total, and this then set the relative strength of the British, US and Japanese fleets at 5:5:3. On this scale, France and Italy were set at 1.75, which aroused a furious Gallic protest as France was effectively relegated to third-class status, at least as far as naval strength was concerned. This reflected the fact that the French navy had built few dreadnought battleships during the First World War due to the overwhelming requirements to produce armaments for her embattled army. Italy raised no protest as they were content to match French strength in the Mediterranean.

Eventually, all of these proposals were accepted after a considerable amount of negotiation. Britain was concerned that as Japan was permitted to complete the two Mutsu class armed with 16-inch guns and the Americans to complete three of the four Maryland class, also armed with similar guns, they would have no comparable ships. It was therefore agreed that despite the ban on new construction, Britain would be permitted to lay down two new battleships also armed with 16-inch guns. As a side issue, it was agreed that any vessel displacing more than 10,000 tons or armed with guns greater than 8-inch caliber would be included in the capital ship tonnage total. Inadvertently, this triggered a substantial building program of 8-inch armed heavy cruisers, but that is a separate story.

The Washington Treaty that encapsulated all these proposals was finally signed in February 1922, and immediately halted all the projected construction programs including the British G3 and N3 projects, the American South Dakota and Lexington classes

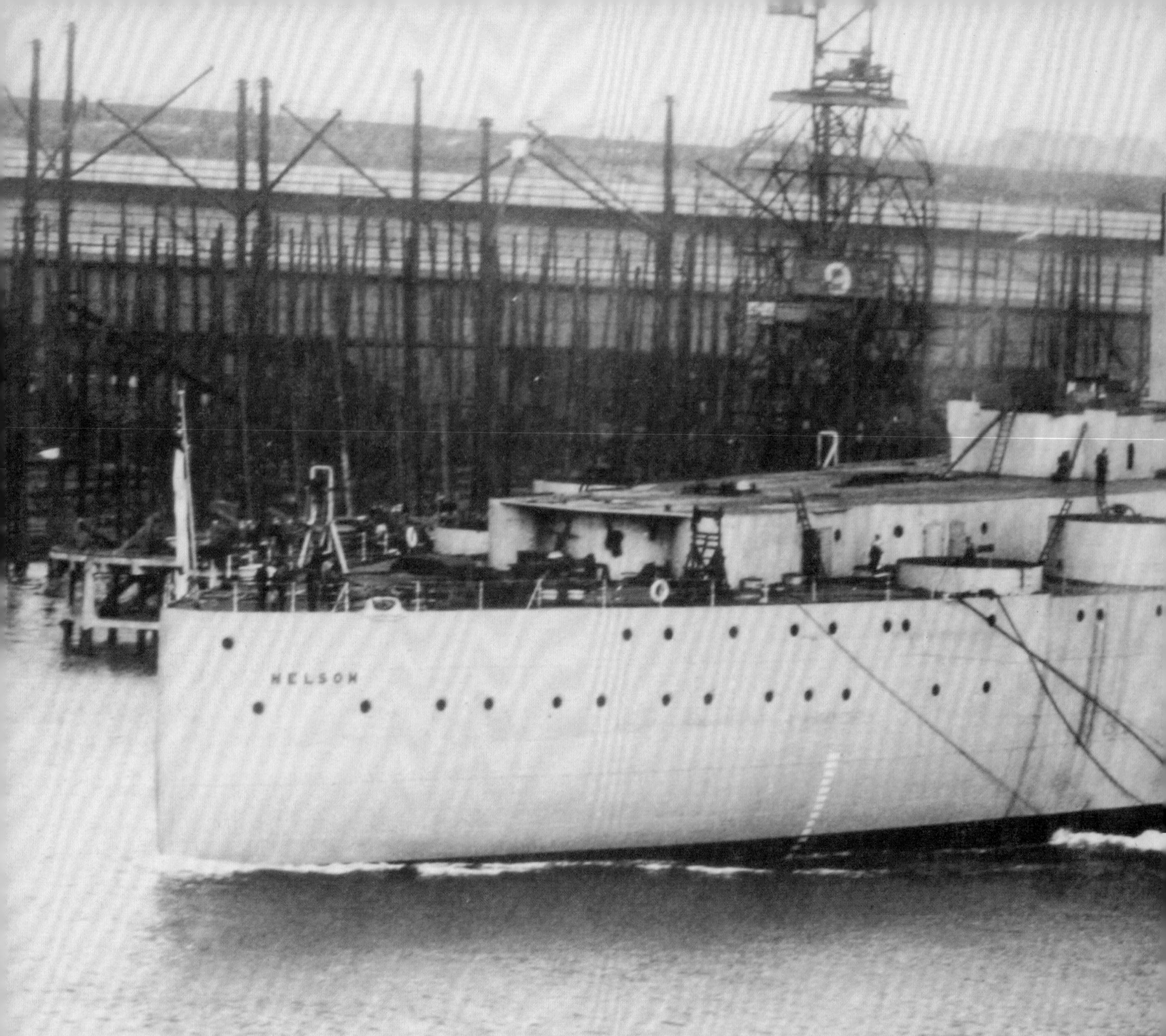

and the Japanese Toga, Akagi and Project 13 classes. Interestingly, some of these ships actually survived in another form as the treaty had laid down no restriction on size or numbers of aircraft carriers, and some of the battlecruiser hulls proved ideal for conversion. Britain converted three existing battlecruisers (*Furious, Courageous* and *Glorious*), while the US Navy converted the *Lexington* and *Saratoga*. Similarly Japan earmarked the *Amagi* and *Akagi* for conversion, but the former was wrecked in an earthquake in 1923, and the hull of the battleship *Kaga* was used instead.

In retrospect, the treaty agreements brought mixed benefits. All the major participants were spared the cost of major naval shipbuilding programs, but the most significant beneficiary was the US Navy which, at a stroke, had gained the long sought after parity with the Royal Navy. However, Japan was not happy with the restrictions placed upon her future naval expansion and had used this to extract some concessions over bases and territorial gains that were to work to her advantage. On the British side, there was relief that the country was spared the expense of the projected building program but, nevertheless plans moved rapidly ahead to lay down the two new 16-inch gun battleships permitted by the treaty. These would also be the first battleships designed to conform with the 35,000-ton limit, and this immediately forced compromises. Basically, the new Nelson-class

HMS Nelson, *launched September 2, 1925, was the first battleship constructed in accordance with the restrictions of the Washington Treaty.*

The Nelson class had a distinctive profile with the main armament of nine 16-inch guns concentrated on the foredeck in order to reduce the amount of armor protection required.

battleships were scaled down versions of the G3 battlecruisers, and the main armament of nine 16-inch guns in three triple mountings was retained although they were now all sited forward of the bridge tower. This reduced the area that required the maximum armor protection and was one way to keep within the weight limits. The main belt was between 28 and 35 cm (11–14 inches) thick, barbettes were 38 cm (15 inches) thick, turrets 40 cm (16 inches) on the faces and 23 cm (9 inches) on the crowns, conning tower 34 cm (13.5 inches) thick and horizontal protection over magazines and machinery spaces was 16.5 cm (6.5 inches). With the main armament all forward, the tall bridge tower was set well aft and its design allowed for the incorporation of the various range finders, directors and spotting positions required by the main and secondary armaments. This aspect of the design proved to be very successful and with modifications was incorporated into future British battleships. In order to place the funnels as far aft as possible so that smoke fumes would not affect the bridge positions, the machinery arrangement was transposed from normal practice with the boilers being placed aft, and the turbines installed amidships. The secondary armament of twelve 6-inch guns in six twin turrets was grouped aft. A unique feature of the Nelson class was that they were the only British warships to carry the 24-inch torpedo, fired from fixed underwater tubes in the forward section of the hull. In fact, all the First World War battleships had provision for firing torpedoes but these were the standard 21-inch weapon and in practice were rarely used. By the start of the Second World War, the practice of battleships carrying torpedoes had been discarded by most navies, and the 24-inch torpedoes in the Nelson class were removed by 1939.

Nelson and her sister ship *Rodney* were laid down in December 1922 and were completed in 1927. In terms of main armament, they were the most powerful British battleships ever built but in order to carry the 16-inch guns and provide effective armor protection it was necessary to compromise on the issue of speed, and these ships were only capable of 23 knots – slower than the Japanese Mutsu class, or even the earlier British Queen Elizabeth class.

As a result of the 10-year building holiday included in the treaty agreement, no other new battleships could be laid down until 1931, and the subsequent

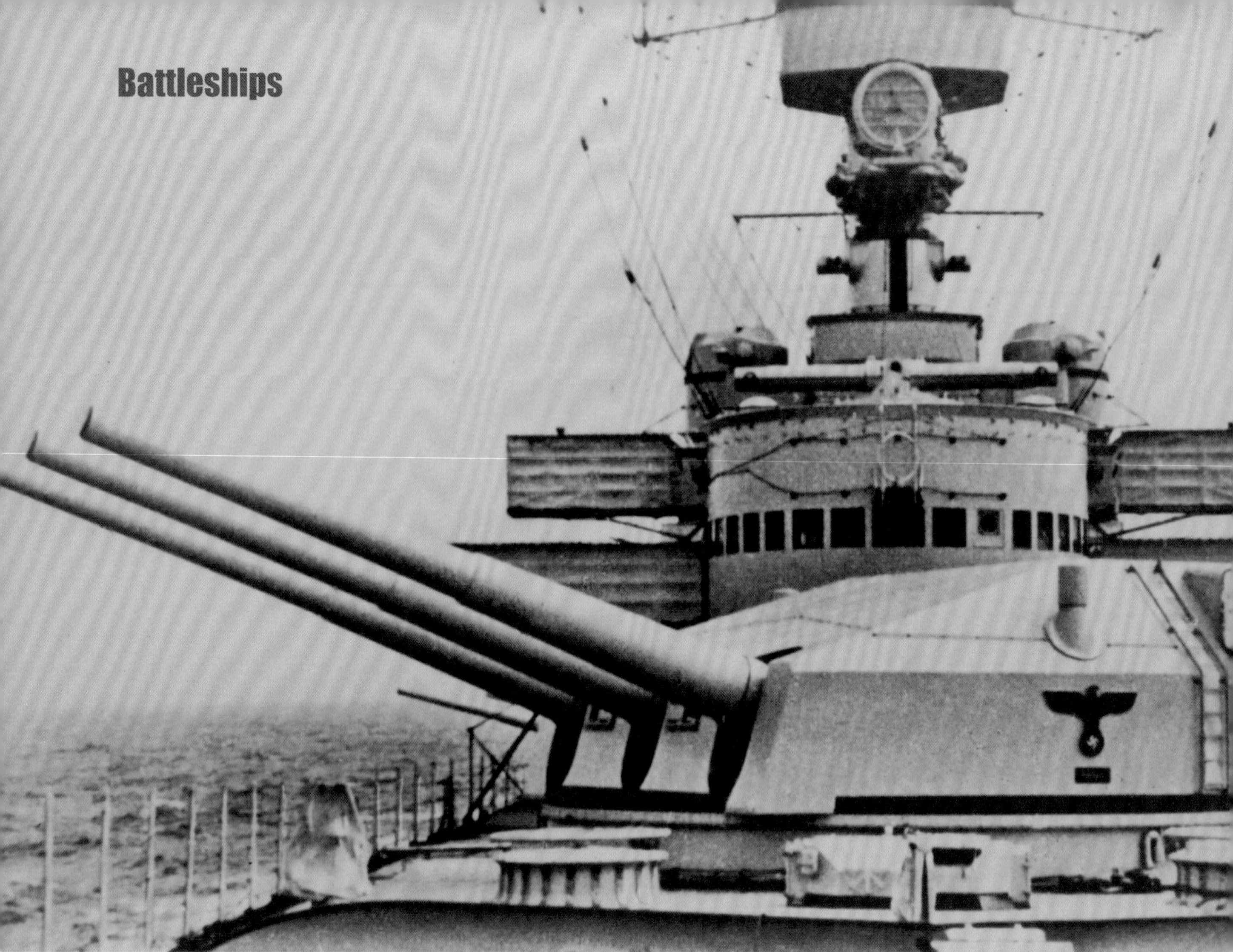

Above: *Despite a nominal displacement of only 10,000 tons, the Deutschland class packed a heavy punch of six 280-mm guns in two triple mountings.*

1930 London Naval Treaty led to America, Britain and Japan agreeing to defer any such construction until 1937, although France and Italy were not bound by this arrangement. However, none of this applied to Germany, which was not a signatory of the Washington Treaty although she was bound by the provisions of the 1919 Versailles Treaty. This laid down severe restrictions on the size and composition of the remaining fleet of which only six pre-dreadnought battleships, six light cruisers, twelve destroyers and twelve torpedo boats were permitted to be active. Significantly, no submarines or aircraft were permitted; an indication of how such weapons were even then seen to be the most potent threats. However, Germany was permitted to replace the elderly pre-dreadnoughts after ten years, and so in 1929 laid down the first of three new vessels termed *Panzerschiffe* (armored ship). Its specification appeared to conform with the stipulated 10,000-ton limit and an armament 11-inch guns, which corresponded to the older ships it was replacing. However, when she was commissioned in 1933 as the *Deutschland*, it was immediately apparent that the German naval staff had come up with an ingenious design which, while remaining within the treaty limitations, was actually a completely new type of warship, which the contemporary press immediately labeled as a 'pocket battleship.' Within a nominal 10,000-tons displacement (the actual standard displacement was nearer 12,000 tons), the ship carried six 11-inch guns in two triple turrets and also a powerful secondary battery of 5.9-inch and 3.5-inch guns, as well as mounting 21-inch torpedo tubes and carrying two seaplanes. Armor protection was light by capital ship standards, but this saved weight and the use of diesel machinery gave a speed of 26 knots. More significant was the resulting range of 16,000 km (10,000 miles), which clearly indicated the main role intended for these ships – commerce raiding on the world's oceans. As such, these ships were almost impossible to counter at that time as they outgunned any cruiser that could catch them, and could outrun virtually every other major capital ship.

The other ships, *Admiral Scheer* and *Admiral Graf Spee*, were laid down in 1931–1932, and the threat posed by these unique warships was directly responsible for France deciding to lay down two 26,000-ton ships in 1932 and 1934, *Dunkerque* and *Strasbourg*. France had not agreed to the 1930 London Treaty that postponed capital ship construction, and therefore was free to build these vessels, which otherwise complied with the various treaty specifications. As designed, they displaced 26,500 tons and carried eight 13-inch guns in two quadruple turrets forward, the overall arrangement owing something to the earlier British Nelson class although a more balanced profile was achieved. Within each turret, the four guns were mounted in independent pairs. Although often referred to as battlecruisers,

Below: *A close-up view of the* Graf Spee *showing the secondary armament of single 150-mm and twin 105-mm guns.*

Above: *The French Dunkerque class concentrated the main armament of eight 330-mm guns in two forward-mounted quadruple turrets.*

these ships made few concessions in respect of armor protection and with a speed of just over 29 knots they were the first of the new breed of fast battleships. They were also the first battleships to carry a dual-purpose (DP) secondary armament which comprised sixteen 130-mm (5.1-inch) guns capable of high angles of elevation and a high rate of fire so that they could be used against both
air and surface targets.

Subsequently, France laid down two more slightly larger battleships in 1935 and 1935, *Richelieu* and *Jean Bart*. These were of similar design to the Dunkerque class but displaced the full 35,000 tons allowed by the Washington Naval Treaty and were armed with 380-mm (15-inch) guns, still carried in quadruple turrets forward of the bridge. The original intention was that the secondary battery would consist of a uniform battery of fifteen 152-mm (6-inch) DP guns in five triple mountings capable of 90-degree elevation for anti-aircraft (AA) fire. However, loading difficulties resulted in elevation being restricted to 75 degrees so the number of guns was reduced to nine in three triple mountings and the AA battery supplemented by twelve 100-mm (3.9-inch) guns in six twin mountings. As with the Dunkerque class, a hangar and catapult for aircraft operations was sited at the stern with up to three Loire 130 seaplanes embarked. Two further ships were planned and a third, *Clemenceau* was actually laid down in January 1939, but the fourth ship, *Gascogne*, was not started. The latter would have featured a major revision in the disposition of the main armament with

The disposition of the main armament before the bridge tower was repeated in the two Richelieu-class battleships.

the two quadruple turrets sited fore and aft, resulting in a more balanced profile. In the event, neither *Richelieu* or *Jean Bart* were completed before war broke out in 1939, and both had very checkered careers. *Clemenceau* was never completed.

The decision to build the Richelieu class was influenced by an earlier decision of Mussolini's Italy to lay down new battleships. Like the French, the Italian government had not accepted the provisions of the 1930 London Treaty, and therefore laid down two Littorio-class battleships in 1934. Armed with nine 380-mm (15-inch) guns they were nominally within the 35,000-ton limit but in war, trim standard displacement rose to in excess of 40,000 tons. They were handsome and powerful ships and a further two (*Roma, Impero*) were laid down in 1938 although the latter was never completed. Both French and Italian ships were designed for speeds of 30 knots, which was now regarded as the standard for major capital ships. The Littorios carried main armament of nine 380-mm (15-inch) guns in three triple mountings, two forward and one aft. Like the French ships, the secondary armament was a mixed battery of twelve 152-mm (6-inch) and twelve 90-mm (3.7-inch) AA guns, the former in six twin mountings but the latter unusually in evenly spaced single mountings, six on each broadside. The main belt armor had a maximum thickness of 35 cm (15 inches) and similar protection was applied to the barbettes and turret faces. For protection against torpedoes, a novel Pugliese system (named for its inventor) was incorporated below the waterline. The lower hull was slightly bulged, but inside its double skin were two concentric cylinders running the full length of the armored citadel. The outer cylinder was filled with oil fuel, while the inner was an empty void. It was intended that the force of an exploding torpedo head would be absorbed by the compression of the inner cylinder so that the shock would not be transmitted to the inner longitudinal bulkheads. While none of these ships

The Vittorio Veneto *and her sisters were fast and powerful ships armed with nine 380-mm guns.*

Above: *The* Scharnhorst *and her sister ship* Gneisenau *were among the most successful of the German capital ships.*

had been completed by September 1939, both *Littorio* and *Vittorio Veneto* were ready for service when Italy entered the war in June 1940, although *Roma* did not commission until mid-1942.

In the meantime, Germany had not been idle. Following the successful introduction of the pocket battleship, two more were completed but construction of a fourth was cancelled in favor of a new 26,000-ton battlecruiser design of which two were laid down in 1934 and 1935 respectively. These were the *Scharnhorst* and *Gneisenau,* which on an announced displacement of 26,000 tons were much larger than the Deutschland class and were armed with nine 11-inch guns in three triple turrets. Substantial secondary and anti-aircraft batteries were also shipped, and there was provision for no less than four aircraft. In size and concept, they were very similar to the French Dunkerque class although, as with many Axis warships, the actual standard displacement was much greater than the announced figure – in this case it was around 32,000 tons. In 1936, Germany laid down two battleships which were to become the *Bismarck* and *Tirpitz* although they were not completed until August 1940 and February 1941 respectively. Armed with eight 380-mm (15-inch) guns on an announced displacement of 35,000 tons, they appeared to conform with the Washington Treaty and also to an Anglo-German Treaty of 1935. In fact, as is now well known, they were considerably larger, and the final displacement was in excess of 50,000 tons at full load. Secondary armament comprised twelve 150-mm (5.9-inch) guns disposed in twin turrets and – for the time – a heavy AA armament of no less than eight twin 105-mm (4.1-inch) high-angle guns backed up by a sophisticated fire-control system. Although imposing vessels that were to cause the Allies significant problems in the Second World War, the basic design had evolved from the Bayern-class battleships of the First World War and had a number of weak points. The most significant was that much of the wiring system for gunnery communications was not below the armored deck and therefore vulnerable to battle damage. The mixed secondary armament was not as efficient as a single DP battery favored by Allied battleships, particularly in regard to the weight of AA fire.

Thus by the start of 1937, two of the future Axis powers in the Second World War were already busily engaged in the construction of new and powerful capital ships. Curiously, Japan had made no attempt to enter the race despite having withdrawn from the 1935 London Naval Conference, and was therefore not bound by the requirement to defer new construction until 1937. However, when they did finally go ahead later in the year, they did so in no uncertain style, laying down two monster 64,000-ton battleships armed with nine 460-mm (18.1-inch) guns in three

Below: *The battleship* Tirpitz *was launched on 1 April 1939.*

9月20日
844
1號艦

The two Yamato-class battleships were the largest ever built. In terms of displacement they were almost twice the size of contemporary British and American battleships.

triple turrets backed up by twelve 155-mm (6.1-inch) and twelve 127-mm (5-inch) DP guns. During the Second World War, this armament was boosted by the addition of around 100 light AA guns while Yamato's AA battery eventually included no less than twenty-four 127-mm (5-inch) guns. Due to Japan's island geography and effective exclusion of foreigners, details of these ships only became available to the Allied powers after the outbreak of war.

All this construction activity could not be ignored by Britain and the United States, and as soon as they were permitted under the terms of the 1930 London Treaty, they began laying down new battleships. In fact, Britain began with almost indecent haste, officially commencing work on two new King George V-class battleships on January 2, 1937, and by the end of that year had no less than five under construction. In practice some preliminary work had already been started prior to that date, including the manufacture of the all-important main armament guns and their mountings. Some indication of the scale of this work is indicated by the fact that a Mark III quadruple 14-inch mounting weighed in at 1,550 tons, and even the Mark II twin mounting was almost 900 tons. Production of guns and their mountings was the most complex aspect of battleship construction, and it was necessary to order them well in advance of the ship being laid down. The choice of the 14-inch gun was the result of attempts by the British government at the 1935 London Naval Conference to have this adopted as the limit for subsequent battleship construction. This was actually accepted but there was a proviso that if the Japanese did not ratify the treaty by April 1, 1937, (which it did not) then the upper limit would revert to the previous 16-inch gun. By then Britain had already begun construction of the ships and their armament in order that they would be ready for any outbreak of hostilities, an occurrence that was now becoming alarmingly likely within a relatively short time. In fact, over the next few years, the British and other European governments made every effort to avoid a war with a Germany that was now actively re-arming. This was partly because of a natural desire to avoid a repeat of the bloodshed of the first war as well as the more prosaic fact that their armed forces were not yet

To save weight (over 600 tons) in the King George V-class battleships the superfiring 14-inch guns were reduced from a quadruple to a twin mounting.

adequately prepared. In hindsight, however, neither were those of Germany.

The five King George V class were built strictly to the 35,000-ton limit and for this reason the main armament comprised only ten 14-inch guns in two quadruple and one twin turret, instead of the original intention to carry twelve guns in three turrets. However, in contrast to the French, Italian and German ships (as well as previous British practice) the use of separate batteries of low-angle guns for defense against small surface ships and high angle-guns for AA defense was abandoned in favor of a single battery of sixteen dual-purpose 5.25-inch guns. These were supplemented by four eight-barreled 2-pounder AA mountings, otherwise referred to as 'Chicago Pianos.' Although thinking along the right lines, the Royal Navy was unfortunate in the choice of the standard Vickers 2-pounder, a weapon of limited effectiveness and much inferior to the Swedish Bofors 40-mm (1.6-inch) gun, which was eventually put into wide use by all the Allied navies.

Naturally there was considerable criticism of the relatively light main armament of these ships. In a bid to counter this, it was officially stated that the new 14-inch gun had a longer range than contemporary 15-inch and 16-inch guns. In fact, this was not true as the British gun had a maximum effective range of around 33,000 meters (36,200 yards) compared to 35,500 meters (38,800 yards) of the *Bismarck's* 15-inch guns and 38,400 meters (42,000 yards) for the 16-inch guns carried by the Japanese Nagato class. Despite this, the ships were well protected with armor accounting for just over a third of the total displacement. For torpedo protection, the machinery and magazines were protected by an armored bulkhead, and the space between that and the hull side was divided into three watertight spaces by longitudinal bulkheads. The center space was filled with a liquid (either fuel oil or seawater) and together these were calculated to be able to absorb the explosion of a 450-kg (1,000-pound) torpedo warhead.

Despite the early start on construction work, none of the King George V class were ready by the outbreak of war in September 1939. The name ship was

Below: *HMS* Anson *as completed in June 1942.*

HMS Duke of York *was completed in November 1941 and became famous as the ship that sank the* Scharnhorst.

Above: *The US Navy retained the 16-inch gun in the North Carolina and subsequent classes.*

commissioned in October 1940, followed by the *Prince of Wales* and *Duke of York* in March and November 1941 respectively. The last pair, *Anson* and *Howe* were completed in the summer of 1942. These were originally to have been named Jellicoe and Beatty but the controversy over the Battle of Jutland still raged 20 years on, and the names of less controversial admirals were eventually chosen.

During the 1930s, the United States was determined to keep out of any potential European war but was concerned about Japanese expansionism and she also wished to keep pace with the technical developments of other nations. They therefore began work on two North Carolina-class battleships in October 1937 and June 1938. The slight delay in starting this program allowed the inclusion of the 16-inch gun in the design of these 35,000-ton fast battleships, which were probably the best all-round examples of their type to see action in the Second World War. Although the US Navy initially favored the 14-inch gun in order to save weight, the actions of Japan in not releasing details of any new construction led to the assumption that their ships would be armed with at least 16-inch guns, and inevitably the Americans had to follow suit. The standard Mark V1 16-inch gun was a reliable and effective weapon that could fire a 1,125 kg (2,700 lbs) shell to a range of 33,740 meters (36,900 yards). Like their British counterparts, the US Navy decided to adopt a single-caliber DP secondary armament, in this case no less than twenty of the excellent 5-inch, 38-caliber gun, which had a rapid rate of fire and proved reliable in action. In fact, the US Navy achieved a commendable standardization with this weapon, the twin mounting also equipping all new cruisers while single and twin mounts were standard throughout the destroyer flotillas. In contrast, British battleships were variously equipped with 4-inch, 4.5-inch or 5.25-inch guns, while destroyers slowly transitioned from low-angle 4.7-inch guns to dual-purpose 4.5-inch guns.

Again considerable attention was paid to underwater protection. The hull was bulged externally below the waterline, and several anti-torpedo bulkheads were incorporated, as well as a triple-hull bottom. In practice, this seemed to work well, the *North Carolina* surviving a hit from a Japanese submarine torpedo in September 1942. Other armor protection was on a generous scale so that it accounted

Above: *The North Carolina class (USS* Washington *shown here) were built to the same limitations as the British King George V but carried a heavier armament of nine 16-inch guns.*

for almost 40 per cent of the total displacement. The arrangement of the machinery spaces meant that the maximum hull beam was carried well aft although the long bow with noticeable sheer allowed a finely tapered entry. Machinery consisted of steam turbines driving four shafts and a total output of 121,000 hp resulted in a speed of 28 knots, the slowest of all the treaty battleships.

America possessed one great advantage compared with any of the other combatant powers in the Second World War – its immense industrial capacity. Consequently it was to build more battleships in the Second World War than any other nation, and after laying down the *North Carolina* and *Washington* in 1937 and 1938, a further four South Dakota class were authorized in 1939, and three (*South Dakota, Indiana, Massachusetts*) were laid down in the same year with a fourth (*Alabama*) in early 1940. The design of these ship was based on that of the *North Carolina,* but a re-arrangement of the machinery spaces resulted in overall length being reduced by almost 18 m (60 feet). The most noticeable effect was a single instead of twin funnels, and the concentration of the superstructure and secondary armament amidships. (*South Dakota* carried only sixteen 5-inch guns but the others all received the full complement of twenty.) Total construction time for each of the four ships was less than 36 months, an illustration of the efficiency of the US shipbuilding industry, and all were in commission by mid-1942.

A second London Treaty had been negotiated in 1935, but by 1937 all nations were building new battleships, and Japan had completely withdrawn from all treaty restrictions. Although Germany had not been represented at the various negotiations due to the restrictions imposed at Versailles, Britain had negotiated a separate treaty with her in 1935, which restricted the size of the German navy to 35 per cent of that of the Royal Navy. This was really a *de facto* recognition of the fact that Allied powers seemed unwilling to take any positive action to prevent German re-armament. Finally, in 1938, the original participants in the London Treaty negotiations, apart from Japan agreed that the limit on capital ship displacement be raised to 45,000 tons, and that they could be armed with 16-inch guns. This was despite earlier British efforts to have the 14-inch gun adopted as the maximum permitted. However, these relaxations allowed both Britain and the United States to plan new larger battleships armed with 16-inch guns, and these will be described in the following chapter.

Although considerable effort was put into the design and construction of new battleships, there were never going to be enough of these to meet naval requirements as the prospect of world war became more and more likely throughout the 1930s. Consequently, most navies instituted schemes to modernize many of their older battleships. One of these most imaginative projects was the updating of the Italian battleships of the Conte de Cavour and Caio Duillio classes. By 1933, all earlier Italian battleships had been scrapped, but these four ships were substantially altered and updated between 1933 and 1940. In the case of the two Cavour class, the superstructure was completely razed, and the central 300-mm (12-inch) twin turret removed. The hull was lengthened by 10 meters (33 feet) and entirely new and more powerful propelling machinery was

Below: *USS* South Dakota *(BB57), name ship of a class of four. Although retaining the same armament as the North Carolinas, the shorter hull necessitated a more compact superstructure and single funnel.*

The modernising of the Cavour and Duillio-class battleships resulted in ships that were a considerable improvement on the original designs.

After World War II, the transatlantic passenger ship entered its last golden age. But the heyday was short-lived. By the late fifties, fast and comfortable jet airplane travel attracted an increasing share of the transatlantic trade. The loss of the *Andrea Doria* off Nantucket in the summer of 1956 seems in retrospect to have sounded the death knell of a whole way of traveling.

QUEEN ELIZABETH

installed, driving two instead of four shafts. The remaining ten 300-mm (12-inch) main armament guns were bored out to a new 320-mm (12.6-inch) caliber. A new secondary armament of twelve 120-mm (4.7-inch) DP guns in six twin turrets and eight 100-mm (3.9-inch) AA guns, also in twin mountings, was added. A combination of increased power and a longer hull brought the speed up to 28 knots, in line with new construction battleships and an impressive improvement on the original 22 knots.

Changes to the two Duillio-class ships were along similar lines. The main difference was that a more powerful secondary armament was fitted. This comprised twelve 135-mm (5.2-inch) DP guns in four triple turrets arranged either side of the bridge superstructure, and ten single 90-mm (3.5-inch) AA guns positioned on either beam abreast the two funnels. Unlike other contemporary battleships, none of the Italian modernized ships had provision to carry aircraft, the assumption being that in the confines of the Mediterranean Sea land-based air cover would always be available – although in practice the support was not always provided.

By contrast, changes to the French Courbet and Bretagne classes were much more limited consisting mainly of installing improved machinery, changing to oil fuel, increasing the elevation of the main armament guns and augmenting the AA armament by the addition of a few 75-mm (3-inch) AA guns. During the 1920s, they all had the original pole masts replaced by strong tripod structures to carry new gunnery control systems. The only ship to have more extensive alterations was *Lorraine,* which between 1932–5 had the midship 340-mm (13.4-inch) gun turret removed, and the space used to construct a hangar for four aircraft. A catapult was fitted atop the hangar.

Japan made substantial improvements to all her battleships during the interwar period. The oldest ships were the four Kongo-class battlecruisers of which one, *Hiei*, had actually been partially disarmed and used as training ship under the terms of the Washington Treaty. However, by the mid-1930s as a result of a series of refits and modernizations, these ships were effectively classed as fast battleships. Protection was improved and anti-torpedo bulges added. Initially this reduced speed, but following the fitting of lighter but more powerful machinery, the final speed was 30 knots, which was faster than their original 27 knots. The elevation of the main armament was increased so that maximum range was 35,000 meters (38,000 yards), and AA armament was boosted. Facilities for carrying seaplanes were also incorporated but no catapult was fitted, the seaplanes being lifted out and recovered by crane.

The remaining six ships of the Fuso, Ise and Nagato classes were all updated between the wars, mainly by the installation of improved machinery that resulted in the previous twin funnels be replaced by a single broader funnel amidships in all cases. A notable feature was the replacement of pole and tripod masts by a high pagoda-like forward superstructure, which carried the multitude of fire control and spotting equipment required by a heavily armed battleship. These very tall structures became a unique recognition feature of all Japanese battleships. As with the Kongo class, main armament elevation was increased and aircraft facilities installed, although these later ships were all fitted with a catapult.

As war approached, the Royal Navy's capital ship fleet had shrunk to a total of only 12 battleships (five Queen Elizabeth class, five R class, two Nelson class) and three battlecruisers (*Hood, Renown* and *Repulse*). The older *Iron Duke* and *Centurion* were disarmed and became training and target ships respectively. As the fastest battleships, the Queen Elizabeths were earmarked for modernization, and various schemes were progressively applied. In the mid 1920s, all five had their funnels trunked into a single uptake and had anti-torpedo bulges fitted that increased beam and reduced speed by one knot. In 1930, work began on updating *Barham*, which had additional 4-inch AA guns fitted as well as two of the new multiple 2-pounder AA mountings, which were sited on platforms attached to the after side of the funnel casing. A tripod mainmast was installed to carry an after high-angle director control tower (DCT) with similar equipment at the base of the foremast, and finally an aircraft catapult was added atop X turret.

Next to be modified was *Malaya* (1934–6), and again the AA armament was improved, this time by the addition of eight 4-inch AA guns in four twin mountings, as well as the multiple 2-pounders abreast the funnel. However, the aircraft handling arrangements introduced a system that was standardized on later British capital ships. This consisted of a catapult fixed sideways between the funnel and the after superstructure, and hangars were provided either side of the funnel base (the roofs proving to be a suitable spot to mount the light AA guns). Two large cranes were fitted to facilitate the handling of the aircraft and the ship's boats.

Above: *Although originally built as a Kongo-class battlecruiser, the various modernization programs effectively turned the* Haruna *into a well-armoured fast battleship.*

The French battleship Lorraine *in 1935. The tripod foremast was fitted in a 1921 refit while in 1938 the midships gun turret visible in this photo was replaced by an aircraft hangar and catapult.*

Warspite was the next in line and between 1934 and 1937 underwent a more substantial conversion that involved the entire midship section being rebuilt. The original machinery was removed and replaced by a lighter and more powerful installation that brought speed back to the original 25 knots despite the bulged hull. A completely new bridge structure, modeled on that of the Nelson class, was erected forward and this was able to carry all the directors for the main secondary and AA armaments. The aircraft handling

This view of HMS Warspite *in 1938 clearly shows the new bridge tower that was a feature of the Royal Navy's modernized capital ships.*

arrangements introduced on *Malaya* were installed, and as with the other ships the secondary battery of 6-inch guns in casemate mountings was retained, although in this case the forward and after guns were removed leaving a total of four on each broadside.

Finally *Queen Elizabeth* and *Valiant* were taken in hand in 1937 although their conversions were not completed until after war had broken out and their modernization was taken a stage further. Basically they repeated work carried out in *Warspite* except that the entire secondary armament of 6-inch and 4-inch guns was removed and replaced by a battery of no less than twenty 4.5-inch DP guns mounted in ten countersunk twin turrets. These were grouped on either beam, three forward and two aft so that the overlapping arcs of fire gave excellent coverage, and each group of two or three guns had its own high-angle DCT. Backed up by four eight-barreled multiple 2-pounder mountings, this was probably the most effective AA armament anywhere in the world at the time.

Left: *Between the wars, the US Navy devoted considerable effort to equipping battleships with aircraft. Shown here is a Vought O2U Corsair on a catapult mounted on the roof of X turret aboard the USS* West Virginia *(BB48).*

Lack of money and the priority accorded to the new King George V-class battleships meant that the slower R class received only the most basic modernization. Between the wars, they were fitted with anti-torpedo bulges, and the AA armament was enhanced by the addition of single and then twin 4-inch AA guns as well as multiple 2-pounder mountings. Aircraft catapults were fitted in some, but by September 1939 only *Resolution* and *Royal Oak* retained this equipment.

Of the battlecruisers, *Renown* was modernized along the lines of *Queen Elizabeth* including the addition of the new 4.5-inch DP gun batteries, but there was neither the time or money to modernize *Repulse* to the same extent although the central catapult and aircraft hangars were fitted. Some of the low-angle triple 4-inch mountings were removed and six single high-angle 4-inch AA guns installed in their place. For a ship of her size, the AA armament was to prove woefully inadequate. HMS *Hood*, the pride of the Royal Navy received even less attention although a full modernization planned for 1939 was overtaken by the outbreak of war. Apart from the addition of eight 4-inch AA in twin mountings and three multiple 2 pounder mountings, she was little altered.

In 1939, the US Navy had 17 battleships in commission (of which *Utah* was acting as a training

An aerial view of HMS Queen Elizabeth *following her refit completed in 1941. The disposition of the ten twin 4.5-inch AA mountings is clearly shown, as well as the catapult track amidships.*

vessel) with a further six under construction. During the interwar years, the older ships were continually updated, the most noticeable change being the removal of the distinctive lattice masts and their replacement by tripods or pole masts. The newest ships of the Tennessee and Maryland classes were otherwise substantially unaltered up to America's entry into the war in 1941. Most of the remaining battleships had new machinery installed, anti-torpedo bulges fitted, some additions made to the light AA armament, and in most cases the secondary 5-inch low-angle battery was raised one deck in order to improve its effectiveness in heavy weather. The US Navy was certainly air-minded, and great efforts were made to equip battleships to carry up to four aircraft, although these were stowed in the open and operated from catapults mounted on the stern or atop X turret. However, none of the ships received major modernizations along the lines of the Italian Cavour or British Queen Elizabeth classes. Apart from the inevitable question of cost, another reason for this situation was that the US Navy was beginning to see the aircraft carrier as the future capital ship, and by 1940 had embarked on a substantial construction program of these ships

By the time World War II broke out in 1939, the battleship was still seen as the backbone of any navy, but there were clear indications that its position would be challenged in the conflict. It was already realized that the submarine was a potent threat that would restrict the activities of surface fleets, but the unknown quantity was the effectiveness of air attack. During the interwar years, significant steps had been taken to improve the ability of battleships to defend themselves against air attack by the provision of new AA guns of various calibers, together with dedicated fire-control facilities. Most, especially the newer ships, had extensive deck armor that was thought to be proof against the type of attack likely to be launched in 1939. In general, naval opinion held that the threat from aircraft could be contained, and that the battleship would retain its place as the arbiter of sea power. The advocates of naval air power had yet to prove their case, although they would soon be given the opportunity to do so.

USS North Carolina *(BB55) steams to war.*

A Second Life: Conversion to Aircraft Carriers

The Washington Naval Treaty of 1922 sent dozens of older battleships to the shipbreakers and halted construction on many new and larger ships. The treaty also set out a tonnage allowance for aircraft carriers and stated that individual ships should not exceed 33,000 tons. This allowed some of the new ships, particularly the fast battlecruisers, to be converted and completed in this new role.

In fact, the Royal Navy had already begun the process during the First World War when the battlecruiser *Furious* had been adapted to carry aircraft. Initial modifications, while the ship was still under construction in 1917, had consisted of removing the forward 18-inch gun and replacing it with a large hangar on the foredeck. A take-off deck was then built over the hangar and bows although there were no facility at this stage for aircraft to land back aboard the ship. However, Squadron Commander Edwin Dunning of the Royal Naval Air Service (RNAS) succeeded in taking off in a Sopwith Pup and then landing back aboard by jinking his aircraft around the superstructure to alight on the foredeck. Such a maneuver was extremely dangerous, and Dunning was killed when making a further attempt. As a result, *Furious* was again modified by the removal of the after gun mounting and the erection of a further hangar and landing deck. This was not entirely successful as aircraft still had to contend with air turbulence from the superstructure and funnel. Consequently, the

Above: *The converted battlecruiser HMS* Furious *as she appeared in 1918 with flying-off decks fore and aft.*

Below: *HMS* Furious *as she appeared in 1927 after full conversion to an aircraft carrier.*

Above: *HMS* Eagle *was built on the hull of the ex-Chilean* Almirante Cochrane, *and the lines of the battleship can be clearly seen.* Eagle *was commissioned as a carrier in February 1924.*

ship was rebuilt between 1922 and 1925 as an aircraft carrier with a full-length, unobstructed flight deck built over a hangar capable of carrying 33 aircraft. Originally, there was no projecting superstructure, and the ship was conned from a retractable compass platform. *Furious* played an active part in the Second World War before being placed in reserve in September 1944 and was scrapped in 1948.

Following the signing of the Washington Treaty, it was decided to convert the sister ships *Courageous* and *Glorious* to aircraft carriers, the work being carried out between 1924 and 1930. Once completed, these ships could carry 48 aircraft and a now conventional island superstructure was positioned on the starboard side of the flight deck. At the outbreak of war in 1939, these two ships formed the backbone of the Fleet Air Arm, but *Courageous* was lost almost immediately by a U-boat torpedo, and *Glorious* followed in questionable circumstances off Norway in June 1940, sunk by gunfire from German battlecruisers. The Royal Navy had also obtained another carrier by purchasing and converting the uncompleted Chilean battleship *Almirante Cochrane* in 1918, although with a speed of 24 knots, she was slower than the battlecruiser conversions. Commissioned as HMS *Eagle* in 1924, she was unique in being the only carrier with two funnels (until the current Royal Navy Invincible class). She had an active service career until being hit by four torpedoes fired from U-73 while involved in the Malta relief action, Operation Pedestal, in August 1942.

During the First World War, the US Navy had gained little experience of aircraft operations from ships, but was then eager to have its own aircraft carriers. The only battlecruiser hulls available were the six Lexington class then under construction. When the treaty was signed, the two most advanced (*Lexington* and *Saratoga)* were selected for conversion, while the others were broken up. When completed in

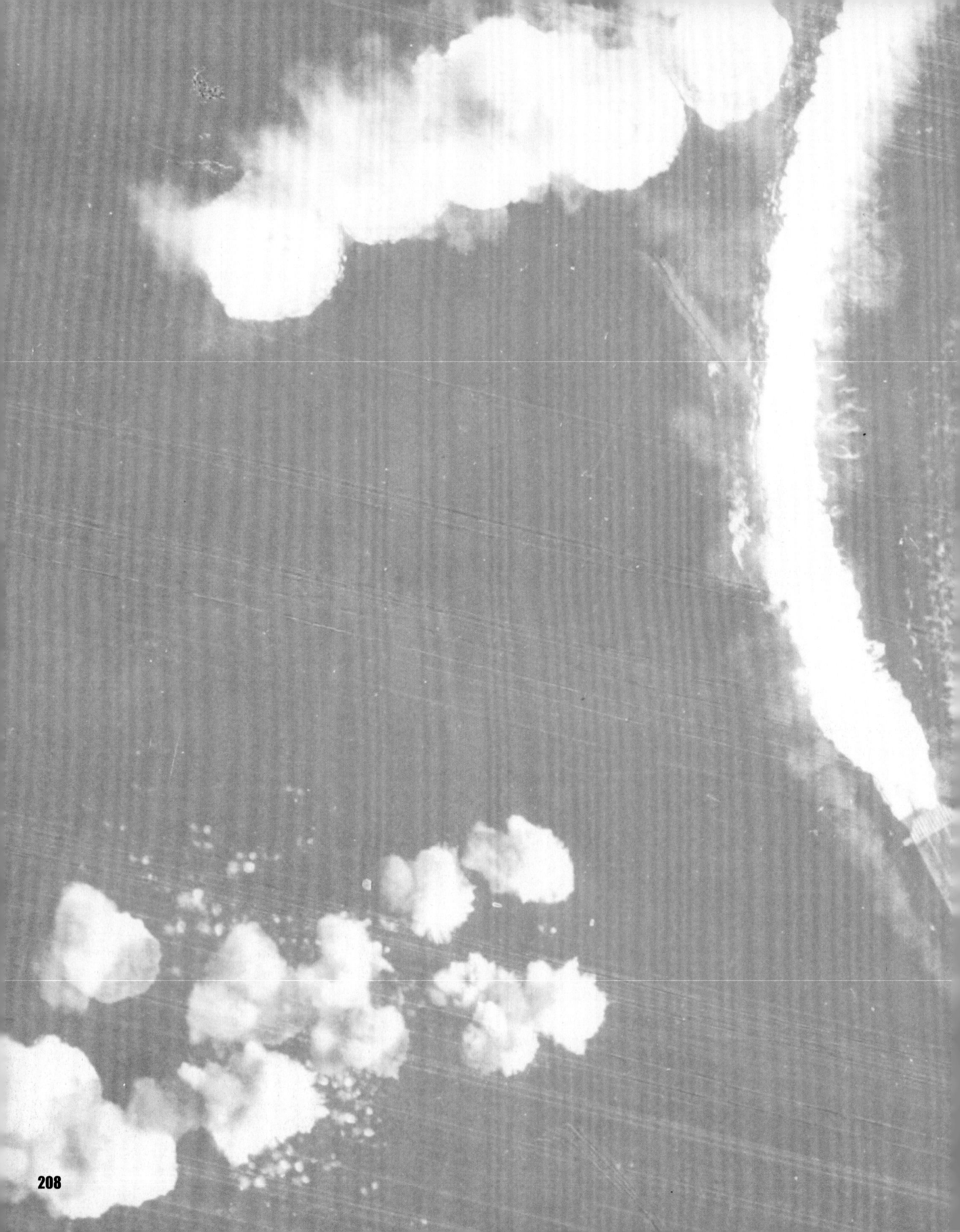

1927, these two ships were the largest aircraft carriers in the world, and remained as such until overtaken by the Midway class at the end of the Second World War. With a speed of 34 knots, they were also the fastest and could carry up to 80 aircraft, almost double the capacity of the British conversions. Using these carriers, the US Navy was able to develop aircraft and tactics that were to stand it in good stead during the Second World War, although *Lexington* was an early casualty, being sunk at the Battle of the Coral Sea on May 8, 1942. *Saratoga* survived the war.

Japan had also been impressed with Royal Navy efforts to take aircraft to sea and quickly took steps to form a naval air arm. Like the other major powers, she had battlecruiser hulls available as a result of the Washington Treaty. These were the 41,000-ton *Akagi* and *Amagi*, which had been laid down in 1920. However, as conversion work began in 1922, the Yokosuka shipyard was hit by a strong earthquake, and *Amagi* was wrecked beyond repair. To replace her it was decided to convert the battleship *Kaga*, which was the most advanced of the other laid-up capital ships. The conversion in both cases proceeded along similar lines with a two-story hangar capable of housing up to 60 aircraft over which the flight deck was constructed. Initially this did not run the full length of the ship but ended some way short of the bows so that auxiliary flying-off decks could be positioned ahead of the hangar decks. This gave the ships a stepped appearance, although by the outbreak of war the flight deck had been extended to the full length of the ship, and aircraft capacity increased to 90 in *Akagi* and 72 in *Kaga*. Neither ship was originally fitted with any superstructure, and in *Akagi* the funnel gases were vented out of a unique downward-angled funnel on the starboard side, while *Kaga* had ducts running down either side of the ship below the flight deck leading to exhaust vents at the stern. Eventually, *Akagi* was fitted with a small bridge on the port side of the flight deck, the only carrier ever to have it in this position, and *Kaga* had a more conventional starboard island erected in 1934. Both ships formed part of Admiral Nagumo's task force that attacked Pearl Harbor. Both were sunk six months later at the Battle of Midway in June 1942.

Despite having a relatively small fleet, France was also determined to develop naval aviation and had available the five Normandie-class battleships laid down before the start of the First World War but never completed. Of these the *Bearn* was selected for conversion, which was finally completed in 1927. The design was influenced by the conversion of HMS *Eagle*, and the two ships were similar in size although the French ship's unusual combination of steam turbines and reciprocating machinery was good for only 21 knots – too slow for fleet carrier work. Consequently, by the time war broke out in 1939 she was employed mainly as an aircraft transport. Interned in Martinique between 1940 and 1944, she was laid up in 1948 but not scrapped until 1967.

The Akagi *was one of two battlecruisers converted to carriers by the Imperial Japanese Navy. She is shown here attempting to avoid air attack during the Battle of Midway where she was sunk on June 4, 1942.*

Anti-Aircraft Defenses

Although no major warships were sunk by air attack during the First World War, the obvious potential of the airplane resulted in a considerable effort to improve the anti-aircraft (AA) defenses of fleets. Even by 1918, some battleships had been fitted with quick-firing (QF) 3-inch or 4-inch guns on specially developed mountings capable of the necessary high angles of elevation. These were supplementary to existing guns of similar calibers carried for defense against torpedo boats, which could not be elevated enough to engage aerial targets. The logical development was to introduce dual-purpose (DP) mountings that could engage both surface targets and aircraft, but initially this process was slow and only accelerated under the threat of war in the late 1930s.

Below: *Royal Marine gunners service a 5.25-inch dual-purpose gun mounting aboard the battleship HMS* King George V. *Traditionally, a proportion of the gun turrets on a battleship were manned by marines.*

Initially, the Royal Navy favored the 4-inch gun on single mountings capable of 85-degree elevation, but by the 1930s these were being replaced aboard many capital ships by the twin Mark XIX mounting, which remained in widespread service throughout the Second World War. A 4.7-inch gun on single high-angle (HA) mountings had been fitted to the two Nelson-class battleships, but this was their only application and in each case 6-inch guns were retained as a secondary armament for surface actions. In 1935, a new DP twin 4.5-inch mounting was introduced, and although it was originally intended for aircraft carriers, it was also put into those ships that were modernized before 1940. The *Queen Elizabeth*, *Valiant* and *Renown* all received ten twin mountings, entirely replacing the mix of 6-inch and 4-inch guns in the battleships, and the unwieldy triple 4-inch mountings in the battlecruiser. The new King George V-class battleships laid down in 1937 went a step further and introduced a new 5.25-inch DP gun of which 16 guns were carried in eight twin turrets, four on either beam. At maximum elevation, this gun could engage targets at altitudes up to 13,000 meters (45,000 feet), and rate of fire was around eight rounds per minute.

While these medium-caliber guns could reach out a considerable distance from the ship, they could not be used effectively without an adequate fire-control system. Consequently, in battleships they were arranged in groups of two or three mountings, each group controlled by a high-angle director. The problems in plotting an effective fire control solution against an aircraft moving in three dimensions were substantially greater than plotting a surface target. The most important element was setting the correct fuse interval so that the shell would explode adjacent to the target at a preset altitude. Rather than track and follow an individual target, the concept of barrage fire was also used. In this system, the whole group of guns fired together with the shells set to explode in the path of

Above: *The Mark.2 Quadruple 40mm AA mounting was extensively carried by US battleships from 1942 onwards. Here the gun crew take the opportunity to relax between actions.*

the approaching aircraft. The accuracy of fire control systems was considerably improved by the addition of range-finding radars.

While the Royal Navy adopted a mix of calibers for the AA role, the US Navy had long since standardized on the 5-inch, 38-caliber DP gun as the standard secondary armament for all battleships built after 1937, and it was retrospectively fitted to most older battleships. Although nominally only capable of firing up to 11,000 meters (37,000 feet), this was well above the height of any likely attackers and its rate of fire was around 20 rounds per minute. It was also very reliable and extensively used throughout the US Navy, so that the logistic support was very good. During the 1930s, the US Navy developed the Mark 37 Director which, requiring a crew of seven, was acknowledged to be the best HA control system during the Second World War. It was eventually adopted by the Royal Navy.

Similar developments took place within the Axis navies, who generally did not develop a suitable DP

weapon and retained separate batteries for AA and surface engagements. Thus, the Japanese navy favored the 4.7-inch gun for AA work, Germany the 105-mm (4.1-inch), and Italy the 100-mm (3.9-inch).

The medium-caliber gun systems were mainly intended for use against enemy bombers approaching in level flight but were much less effective against fast-moving fighters, dive bombers or low-flying torpedo bombers. To combat such attacks rapid-firing light-caliber weapons were required. The Royal Navy was forward thinking in this case, and in the 1920s worked on an AA mounting fitted with no less than eight Vickers 2-pounder fast-firing guns universally known as a 'pom-pom.' The first sea trials were carried out aboard the battlecruiser *Tiger* in 1928, and during the 1930s it was progressively fitted to all battleships and battlecruisers. By 1945 some carried as many as eight

Left: *The simple 20-mm Oerlikon. Some US Navy battleships carried more than sixty of these weapons.*

Below: *This view aboard the USS* Iowa *illustrates the variety of AA weapons carried including the a twin 5-inch, 38-caliber mounting, a Mark 2 quadruple 40-mm, and several single 20-mm AA guns.*

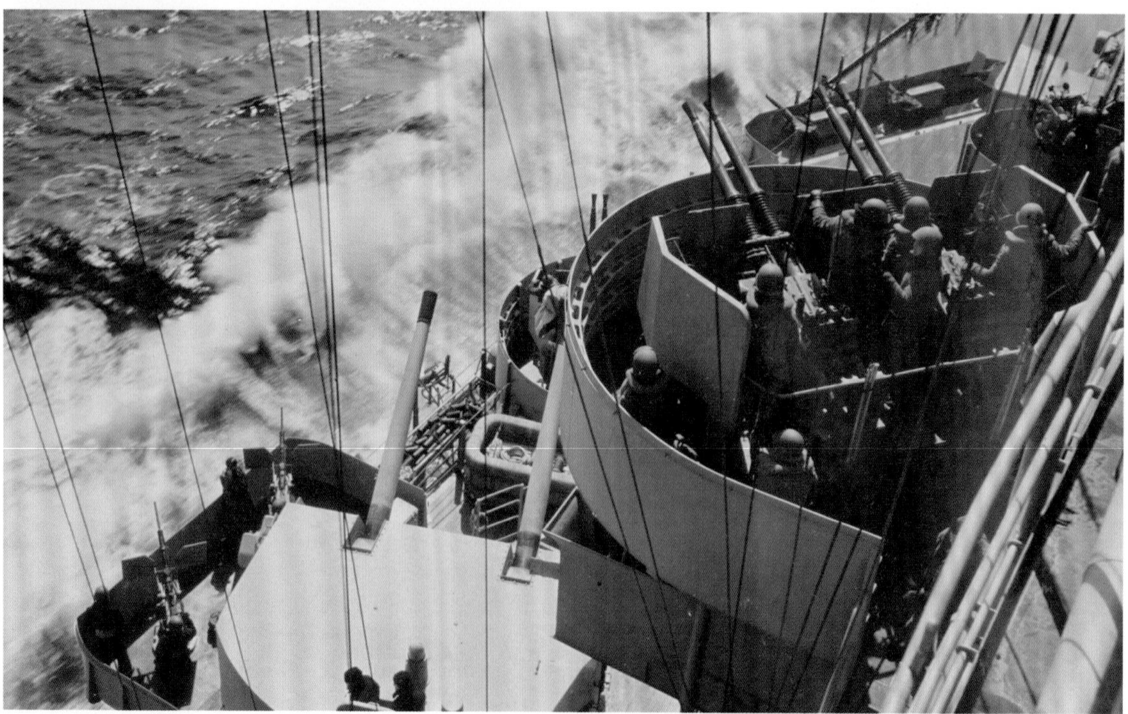

pom-pom mountings. Each individual gun fired at a rate of around 100 rounds per minute, so an eight-barreled Mark VI mounting, sometimes nicknamed as the 'Chicago Piano' for the tuneless bangs it produced, could put up a tremendous barrage, especially when later in the war it was controlled by it its own radar-equipped director.

However, the 2-pounder gun suffered from a relatively low-muzzle velocity so engagement ranges were generally limited to 4,500 meters (5,000 yards) or less. However, a much better weapon in the shape of the Swedish Bofors 40-mm (1.5-inch) gun became available at the start of the Second World War. Initially procured for army use, its attributes were quickly recognized by the Royal Navy. With a maximum range of almost 9,100 meters (10,000 yards), the gun was reliable and easy to service. Although produced in great numbers, it did not entirely replace the 2-pounder.

The US Navy had originally developed a 1.1-inch AA gun, which was always carried in a quadruple mounting. This was widely fitted up to 1941 but proved ineffective in action and was rapidly replaced by the Swedish designed 40-mm Bofors, as already adopted by the Royal Navy. The Allied navies also used another foreign-made design, the Swiss Oerlikon 20-mm (0.75-inch), which was fitted in large numbers. Essentially a short-ranged weapon, it had a very high rate of fire (480 rpm) and was normally in single, manually operated mountings, but twin and quadruple powered mountings were also produced. For example, when completed, the battleship USS *New Jersey* carried no less than sixty 20-mm in addition to sixty-four 40-mm – a formidable AA battery by any standards.

The appearance of *kamikaze* attacks in the later stages of the Pacific War increased the requirement for accurate AA fire. In this case, it was essential to destroy the target, as just damaging it would not deflect the pilot from his intended target. The device that did more than anything else to counter these attacks and improve AA fire in general was the proximity fuse. This caused the shell to explode if it passed within a preset distance from the target. The principle of the device was relatively straightforward, but the breakthrough was designing a mechanism that would survive the shock of being fired from a gun.

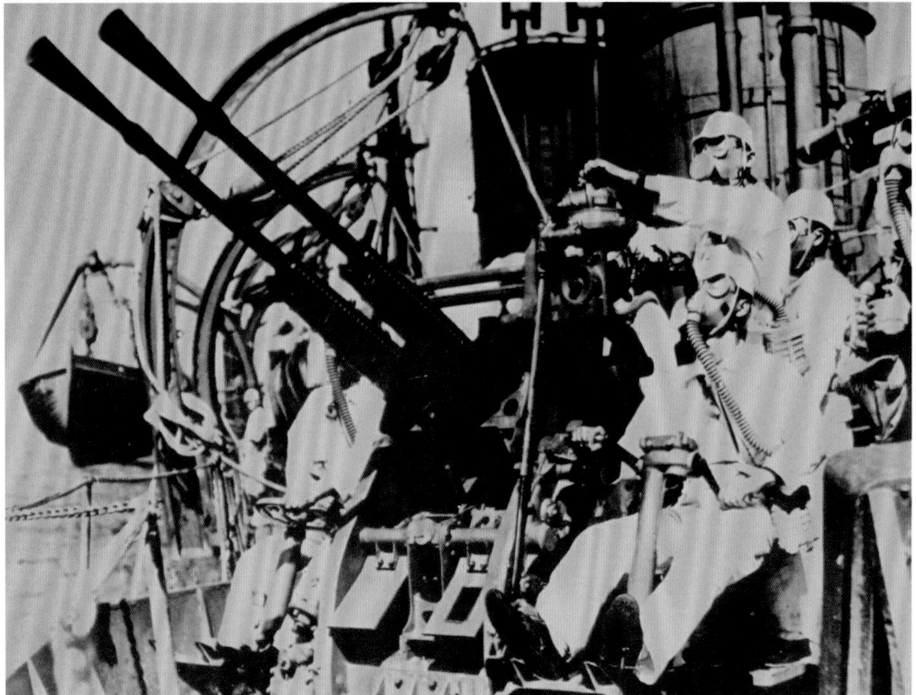

Right: *A Japanese twin 37-mm AA mounting with its crew wearing gas masks in a pre-war drill demonstration.*

THE SECOND WORLD WAR
THE SWANSONG OF THE BATTLESHIP

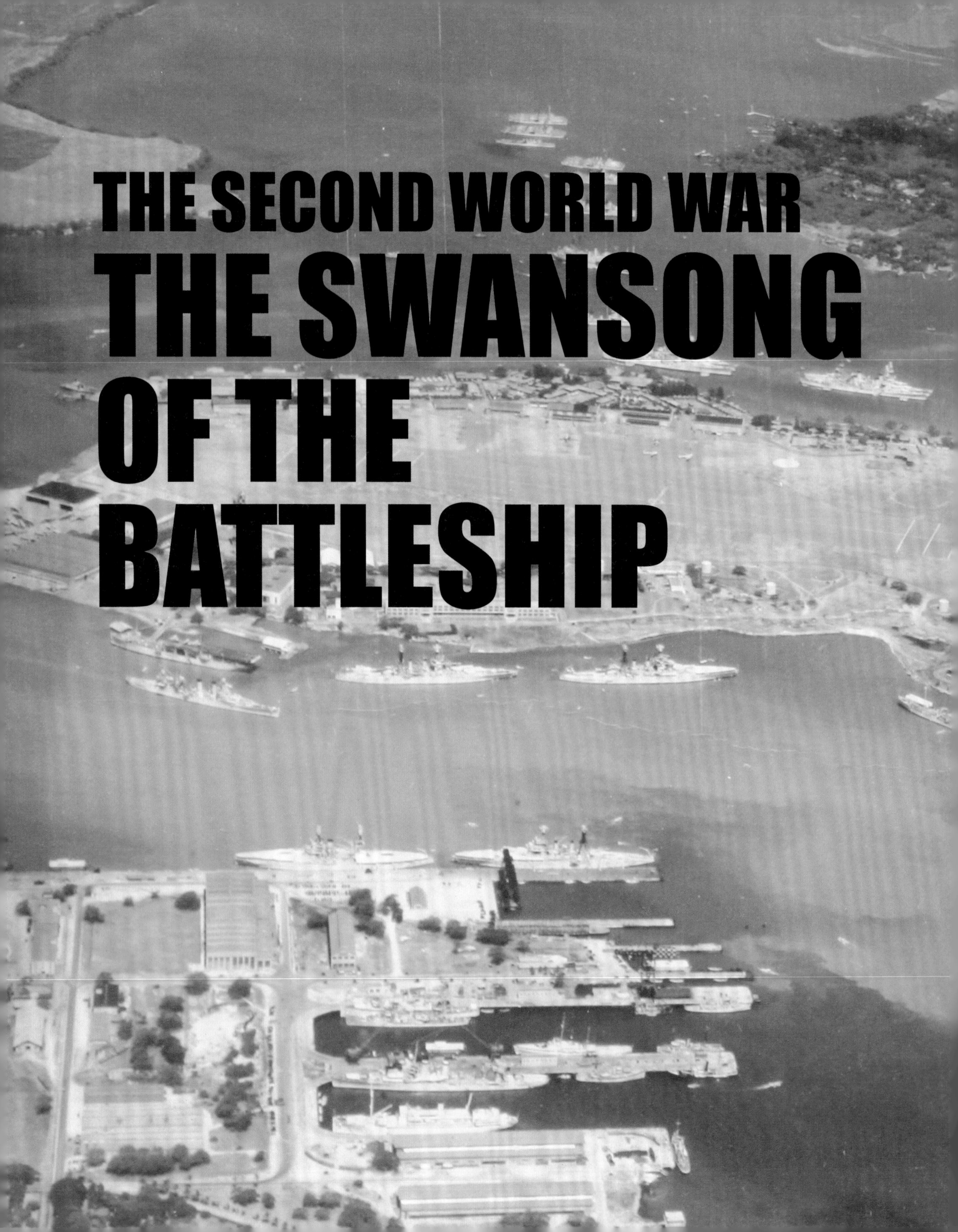

Pearl Harbor, Hawaii, in 1938, almost exactly as Japanese bombers would find it three years later. In the foreground are the lines of battleships moored in the lee of Ford Island, just as they would be on that fateful day in 1941.

The Second World War

When war broke out following the German invasion of Poland on September 1, 1939, the naval situation was very different from that which had existed in 1914. The Royal Navy was not opposed by a large German surface fleet, and a major action such as the Battle of Jutland was not going to occur. The position might have been different if the German's Admiral Raeder had been given time to implement staff plans approved by Adolf Hitler, which envisaged a fleet of ten battleships and battlecruisers, 11 heavy cruisers (including the three *Panzerschiffe* – pocket battleships), five light cruisers, 50 destroyers and more than 200 submarines, all to be ready by 1945.

This would have included six of a new class of super-battleship, nominally termed class H, and in fact, the first two were laid down in the summer of 1939 although all work ceased in the October. In outline, they resembled enlarged Bismarcks, but the main armament was up-rated to 405-mm (16-inch) caliber and displacement was calculated at over 56,000 tons. A major departure was that they would be diesel powered giving a cruising range of over 24,000 km (15,000 miles). In the event, Hitler's ambitions drove him to war long before this grand plan could be implemented and, even had he waited, the pace of British re-armament would have preserved the Royal Navy's numerical superiority in every category (except perhaps in submarines).

The Royal Navy already had the King George V-class battleships under construction and in the summer of 1939 had laid down four new Lion-class ships. These were similar to the earlier ships except that the opportunity was taken to adopt the 16-inch gun of which nine were to be mounted in three triple turrets, two forward and one aft. The 5.25-inch secondary armament was retained, but heavier armor was applied to the turrets. Overall displacement rose to 42,500 tons.

All these vessels were cancelled in 1940 as it was not envisaged that they could be completed before the end of hostilities. One reason for this was the time that would be taken to produce the guns and mountings, but a suggestion was made that one battleship could be built within a reasonable timescale using the 15-inch guns that had previously been removed from the battlecruisers *Courageous* and *Glorious* when they had been converted to aircraft carriers. With encouragement from prime minister Winston Churchill, this project went ahead. The keel of HMS *Vanguard* was laid down in March 1941, although she was not to be completed until after the end of the war. The design was a further enlargement

Above: *The King George V class were the Royal Navy's most modern battleships in World War II. This is HMS* Howe, *the fifth and last to be completed.*

of the Lion class to cater for four twin 15-inch turrets instead of the three triple 16-inch mountings. With a displacement of 44,500 tons as completed, she was to be the last and largest battleship ever built for the once illustrious Royal Navy.

However, at the start of the Second World War, it was German U-boats that drew the first blood, when U-47 commanded by Gunther Prien dramatically

The Bismarck *and* Tirpitz *(shown here) were intended as the start of a much more ambitious German naval construction program.*

Above: *HMS* Royal Oak *was sunk at her Scapa Flow anchorage on the night of 14 October 1939 by torpedoes fired from U47 commanded by Kapitanleutnant Gunther Prien.*

penetrated the weak anti-submarine defenses at Scapa Flow, Orkney, and sank the British R-class battleship HMS *Royal Oak* on October 14, 1939. This caused the Home Fleet's capital ships to be transferred to Loch Ewe on the Scotland's western coast, while Scapa's defenses were being improved. But even here, HMS *Nelson* was seriously damaged by a mine and was out of action for almost a year.

At this stage, Britain's policy was to blockade Germany by sealing off the English Channel, and mounting patrols and laying minefields to prevent access to the Atlantic Ocean by way of the Norwegian Sea or the Denmark Strait. However, the Kriegsmarine had deployed several surface raiders before the outbreak of war including the pocket battleship *Graf Spee*. Away from European waters, the German surface raiders were a significant threat, and in the early stages of the war tied down significant numbers of British and French warships. It was not until mid-December that these efforts bore fruit when the British cruisers *Exeter, Ajax* and *Achilles* intercepted the pocket battleship *Admiral Graf Spee* off the mouth of the River Plate, off the southern coast of Uruguay.

On paper, the *Graf Spee*, armed with 11-inch guns, had a considerable advantage over the 8-inch and 6-inch-gunned cruisers, although the latter were faster. In a spirited action, the British ships under Commodore Henry Harwood harried the larger ship and obtained many hits although little substantial

U47 returns to a heroes' welcome at Wilhelmshaven. Prien was decorated with the Knight's Cross.

Outfought by British cruisers, the pocket battleship Graf Spee *took refuge in neutral Montevideo and was subsequently scuttled.*

Above: Warspite's *Swordfish floatplane is hoisted aboard after a sortie. One of the ship's aircraft succeeded in sinking a U-boat during the Second Battle of Narvik.*

The Scharnhorst *and* Gneisenau, her sister ship (shown here) *provided heavy cover to the German invasion of Norway in April 1940.*

damage was done. On the other hand, the *Exeter* was severely mauled and was forced to pull out of the battle, while both *Ajax* and *Achilles* suffered casualties and damage. Nevertheless the *Graf Spee's* commander, Captain Langsdorff, decided against continuing the fight and sought the sanctuary of a neutral harbor at Montevideo, Uruguay, to effect repairs. After much diplomatic activity, the *Graf Spee* was forced to put to sea again on December 17, but Langsdorff, mistakenly convinced that an overwhelming force was awaiting him outside neutral waters, elected to scuttle his ship. He subsequently committed suicide three days later. This outcome was a major blow for German pride and a great boost to Allied morale.

In the early days of 1940, there was relatively little action until April 9, when German forces occupied Norway, an operation that involved virtually the entire resources of the German navy. Despite the loss of the heavy cruiser *Blucher* to torpedoes fired from a coast defense fort, the German forces quickly achieved their objectives. However, substantial British forces were also at sea. On the afternoon of April 9, the battlecruiser HMS *Renown* accompanied by a flotilla of destroyers intercepted the battlecruisers *Scharnhorst* and *Gneisenau* providing cover for invasion groups heading for Trondheim and Narvik.

The German ships turned away to the north and in the ensuing running fight managed to hit the *Renown* twice without causing any significant damage. In return, *Renown* landed three 15-inch shells on the *Gneisenau*, one of which took out her main armament gunnery director. Although outnumbered, *Renown's* heavier firepower stood a good chance of gaining the upper hand, and so the German ships increased speed and drew away to the north, aided by the poor visibility in the squally weather conditions. This indecisive engagement was one of the few between British and German capital ships, although others were to have more dramatic outcomes.

In the meantime, a flotilla of German destroyers had successfully transported troops to Narvik but was laid up awaiting a fuel tanker. Grasping the opportunity, five British destroyers entered the fiords on April 10, and sank several transports as well as two of the German destroyers, although HMS *Hardy* and *Hunter* were also subsequently sunk and the others damaged. However, the remaining German destroyers remained trapped, and three days later a British force under Vice-Admiral William Whitworth flying his flag in the battleship HMS *Warspite,* re-entered the fiord and proceeded to sink and destroy the remaining eight destroyers. *Warspite* herself survived two U-boat attacks and in return, her catapult-launched Swordfish seaplane bombed and sank U-64.

Virtually the entire home fleet was involved in other Norwegian operations including the battleships *Rodney, Warspite, Valiant* and the battlecruiser *Renown*. The campaign also saw the first major use of aircraft carriers as it became increasingly clear that warships could not operate unsupported in the face of enemy air attack. Unfortunately, the carrier *Glorious* (a converted battlecruiser) was sunk by the *Scharnhorst* and *Gneisenau* on June 8, while proceeding unescorted back to Scapa Flow – a major German success. By this time, British forces were evacuating Norway in the face of events elsewhere. On May 10, 1940, German forces had launched an offensive through Belgium into France, and by the end of the month the British Expeditionary Force and elements of the French army were being evacuated at Dunkirk. Other German forces raced south, captured Paris, and an armistice was signed on June 25. In the meantime, eager to pick easy spoils from his beaten French rivals, Mussolini had led Italy into the war as an Axis power on June 10.

As the Germans advanced westwards, the French admiralty gave orders for the battleships *Richelieu* and *Jean Bart* to sail for French colonial ports. *Richelieu* was almost complete, and was able to leave Brest on June 18, arriving in Dakar, Senegal, five days later. Her sister ship *Jean Bart* under construction at St. Nazaire was not in such a good state, and it was a race against time to get her ready so that she could sail. Eventually, she set off in the early hours of the June 19, but was attacked by German aircraft and took a bomb on the foredeck causing some damage. Nevertheless, she eventually made the open sea and made for Casablanca, where she arrived on June 22. At that time, only the forward main armament turret was installed as well as a few 90-mm (3.5-inch) AA guns hastily fitted at St.Nazaire just before she sailed.

The events in France focused attention on the Mediterranean Sea. Italy already had a powerful fleet including six fast battleships, and if there was the slightest chance that Germany would be able to take over the ships under control of the French Vichy government, then the whole balance of maritime power would be altered. Force H at Gibraltar was commanded by Vice-Admiral James Somerville and included the aircraft carrier *Ark Royal*, battlecruiser *Hood*, and battleships *Resolution* and *Valiant*. His immediate task was, on Churchill's direct orders, to attempt to persuade the French ships in the Algerian ports of Oran and Mers-el-Kebir to join the Allied cause. Various courses of action were offered to the French, but Somerville was ordered to make it clear that he had orders to sink and destroy the French

The French battleship Bretagne *sinking at Mers-el-Kebir, Algeria, after bombardment by British warships in 1940.*

Above: *On paper the Italian Fleet was a formidable force and outnumbered Admiral Cunningham's Mediterranean Fleet.*

ships if they would not accept any of the alternatives. At dawn on July 3, Force H lay off the anchorage at Mers-el-Kebir. Despite protracted negotiations an ultimatum issued by Somerville expired at 5.30 p.m., but he delayed until 5.54 p.m. when, under pressure from Churchill, the order to open fire was given.

The main targets were four French battleships moored by their sterns to the long breakwater mole, and when the British opened fire, they immediately got underway. The *Dunkerque*, was hit by several 15-inch shells, just as she was beginning to gather way and drifted out into mid channel before temporary repairs brought her under control, although she was subsequently beached on the western shore.

Of the older battleships, *Bretagne* was hit almost immediately, and with fierce fires raging she rolled over and sank within ten minutes, taking over 800 of her crew with her. The *Provence* did succeed in getting under way and opened fire before a hit on the stern caused serious damage and effectively put her out of action, although she remained afloat and was eventually beached. The remaining modern battleship, *Strasbourg*, was more fortunate and succeeded in making a prompt get away from the jetty, shells falling into her vacant berth literally seconds after she had left. She set off down the main channel and made open waters accompanied by five destroyers.

The British bombardment lasted only ten minutes and fire was halted when the heavy pall of smoke from the sinking and damaged ships obscured all targets, including the escaping *Strasbourg*. Somerville then ordered his ships to steer to the west, convinced that he had achieved his objective. It was not until a Swordfish aircraft reported that the *Strasbourg* had escaped that he realized the true situation. Two separate attacks were made by aircraft from *Ark Royal*, and although one torpedo hit was claimed the battlecruiser did not slow down and eventually made Toulon, France, in the evening of July 4 to a rapturous reception. Despite a further aerial attack a few days later on the *Dunkerque*, this ship was eventually able to return to Toulon, along with the damaged *Provence*. However, both of these and the *Strasbourg* were scuttled along with the other ships of the French fleet in November 1942 when the Germans occupied Vichy France. This was exactly what the French had promised would happen and served to illustrate that perhaps the action at Mers-el-Kebir had been unnecessary. Churchill had just not been prepared to take that chance, and the action had at least demonstrated to the world at large that Britain was not defeated and was determined to fight to the last. Total French casualties were 1,147 dead and the memories of the event soured Anglo-French relations for years.

The Italian navy still posed a potent threat and initially was intent on flexing its muscles. A substantial force was at sea on July 9 in support of an Italian troop convoy when contact was made with the British Mediterranean Fleet commanded by Admiral Andrew Cunningham. His force included the battleships *Warspite, Malaya* and *Royal Sovereign* supported by five light cruisers and a few destroyers, as well as the carrier HMS *Eagle*. The action was joined off Calabria on the southern tip of Italy. The battle lasted for nearly two

The Italian fleet suffered a severe setback at Taranto. The battleship Littorio *lies on the harbor seabed after taking at least three torpedo hits.*

hours before the Italian fleet withdrew, mainly as a result of a hit on the battleship *Guilio Cesare* by a 15-inch shell fired by *Warspite* at the staggering range of 23,700 meters (26,000 yards) – the longest gunnery hit on a moving target at sea ever recorded.

Nevertheless, the Mediterranean Fleet was still outnumbered, so when Cunningham received reinforcements in the shape of the new armored carrier HMS *Illustrious,* he decided to put into action a pre-war plan for an aerial attack on the Italian port of Taranto. Only 21 Swordfish planes were available for the operation, and they were launched in two waves on the evening of November 11, 1940.

The main targets were the two Littorio-class and three Cavour-class battleship anchored in the Mare Grande, the outer anchorage at Taranto. The first wave succeeded in torpedoing the *Littorio* and *Cavour.* Despite the vicious AA fire and the dangers presented by the barrage balloon wires, only one aircraft was lost, and the survivors headed back to *Illustrious.*

The attack by the second wave followed a similar profile although by now the defenses were thoroughly alerted and put up a tremendous barrage as the Swordfish approached. Five torpedo-armed aircraft went in at low level, hitting both the *Littorio* and *Caio Duilio.* One aircraft was lost in this attack, but the others returned safely. The final attack of the evening was by a straggler from the second flight, which made a leisurely bombing attack on two cruisers. This last aircraft landed on *Illustrious* at 2.55 a.m., and the carrier then turned south to rejoin the fleet.

Subsequent reports determined that the *Littorio* had been hit by three torpedoes and was out of action for five months. The *Caio Duilio* was hit by a single torpedo on the starboard side, which resulted in severe flooding, and the ship was beached in order to prevent her sinking. She was not fully repaired until the following May. The most seriously damaged was the *Conti de Cavour,* which although only hit by a single torpedo nevertheless settled on the bottom with her upper deck submerged. Eventually re-floated in July 1941, she saw no further service. In all, it was an outstanding success by a small number of aircraft, that materially altered the balance of power in the Mediterranean. (The carrier-led action was also noted with interest on the other side of the world in Japan.)

On March 26, 1941, Admiral Angelo Iachino sailed from Naples aboard the modern battleship *Vittorio Veneto* accompanied by four destroyers. His movements were coordinated with a force of three heavy cruisers from Taranto, two light cruisers from Brindisi and three more heavy cruisers from Messina,

Below: *The* Vittorio Veneto *had a lucky escape at Matapan after being hit by an air-launched torpedo.*

Aircraft launched from the aircraft carrier HMS Formidable *played a vital role in the Battle of Cape Matapan.*

each group accompanied by escorting destroyers. On the morning of March 27, the combined Italian fleet set course towards Crete with the intention of attacking British troop convoys to Greece. However, the ships were spotted and reported by an RAF Sunderland. Consequently, the Mediterranean Fleet sailed from Alexandria that same evening to rendezvous with a force of four cruisers and four destroyers off Cape Matapan the following dawn.

The stage was now set for the largest fleet action to be fought by the Royal Navy in the Second World War. Its battle fleet of one carrier, three battleships, four light cruisers and 13 destroyers was heading towards the Italian force of one battleship, six heavy and two light cruisers, and 13 destroyers. Although the British had superiority in battleships, they were all elderly ships, and the fastest (*Valiant*) was only capable of just over 24 knots, while the Italian *Vittorio Veneto* was one of the new breed of heavily armored fast battleships capable of in excess of 30 knots. Also the Italian force included six heavily armored 8-inch cruisers against which the smaller British cruisers with their 6-inch guns were outclassed. Thus, on paper the fleets were very evenly matched – but the British had two priceless advantages of which they made full use: One was an aircraft carrier, although its complement of only 27 aircraft severely limited its offensive capability. The other was radar, which was to prove invaluable, especially in the night actions.

The first contact was made by the opposing cruiser forces, and Vice-Admiral H.D. Pridham-Whipple initially tried to draw the Italian cruisers towards Cunningham's battleships, but the situation was then reversed as the Italians turned north with the British

Above: *The heavy cruiser* Zara *was sunk by gunfire from the battleships* Warspite, Barham *and* Valiant.

light cruisers following. As Cunningham continued towards the scene of the action at a stately 22 knots, he ordered air strikes from Crete and from the carrier *Formidable*. At 10.58 a.m., HMS *Orion*, the leading British cruiser, suddenly sighted the *Vittorio Veneto.* Although Pridham-Whipple immediately ordered his force to turn back to the southeast, they came under heavy and accurate fire from the battleship and heavy cruisers. With Cunningham's battleships still some 125 km (80 miles) away, the British cruisers were in a critical situation, when *Formidable's* strike force arrived on the scene. Although their attack was pressed home with great determination, they did not score any hits, but it did prompt Ianchino to break off the action and alter course to the northwest, his aim now being to return home and escape further air attack.

With the *Vittorio Veneto* drawing away, Cunningham ordered another carrier strike but this comprised only five aircraft and did not catch up with the Italian battleship until 3.19 p.m. However, the carrier planes were assisted by the fact that as they started their attack, a formation of RAF Blenheims were also making a high-level bombing run, which distracted the Italian gunners. One torpedo struck below the stern, damaging the rudders and propellers and bringing the battleship to a temporary halt. There was now every prospect that Cunningham's ships would be able to catch the damaged Italian battleship and finish her off. However, the Italian crew succeeded in getting their ship underway and eventually she was making off at 16 knots.

Further air strikes were ordered, and although the *Vittorio Veneto* escaped damage, one torpedo hit the heavy cruiser *Pola* which came to a dead stop. The 1st Cruiser Division (*Zara* and *Fiume*) together with four destroyers was ordered to remain with the damaged cruiser. During the night, Cunningham's battleships came upon the unsuspecting Italian ships and using radar information until visual contact was achieved opened fire at almost point blank range. Within minutes the *Zara* and *Fiume* were blazing wrecks, and two Italian destroyers were also sunk.

British destroyers subsequently finished off the damaged *Pola* and then made off to the east, joining up with the battle fleet at dawn. It was an outstanding victory for the Mediterranean Fleet under Admiral Cunningham, which had sunk three heavy cruisers and two destroyers for the loss of a single aircraft. They had also demonstrated the extreme vulnerability of battleships to air attack. The *Vittorio Veneto* had been very lucky to escape.

Aircraft were to be the deciding factor in another even more dramatic engagement, which was to be fought out in the vast expanses of the Atlantic Ocean. On May 18, 1941, the new battleship *Bismarck* and heavy cruiser *Prinz Eugen* sailed to the Norwegian port of Bergen with the intention of using it as a base for attacking the Allied Atlantic convoys. Admiral John Tovey, C-in-C of the Home Fleet, immediately planned the deployment of ships to counter any possible breakout by the German force. The cruisers *Norfolk* and *Suffolk* patrolled the Denmark Strait between Iceland and the Arctic ice pack, while Vice-Admiral Lancelot Holland with the battlecruiser *Hood* and the new battleship *Prince of Wales*, was ordered northwards to be ready for a possible engagement.

On May 22, a Fleet Air Arm aircraft finally confirmed that the *Bismarck* and *Prinz Eugen* had left Bergen, and Admiral Tovey immediately left Scapa Flow with the rest of the Home Fleet. It was not until the evening of May 23, that the cruiser *Suffolk* sighted the two German ships in the Denmark Strait. Reports were immediately dispatched, and the two cruisers settled down to shadow the enemy ships, their accurate and effective reporting enabling Holland to bring his two capital ships into contact with the enemy just as dawn was breaking on May 24.

Not wasting any time, Holland ordered the *Hood* and *Prince of Wales* onto a northwest course to close the enemy as quickly as possible. At 5.52 p.m., *Hood* opened fire. *Bismarck* replied two minutes later with very accurate shooting. As the range fell to less than 18,250 meters (20,000 yards). Holland ordered the *Hood* and *Prince of Wales* to turn to port so that all guns could fire. Even as they did so, the *Bismarck*'s fifth salvo crashed home on the *Hood*. Within seconds the great battlecruiser was rent apart by a massive explosion and sank within three minutes, leaving only a pall of smoke and three survivors from a crew of over 1,400 men. It was the Royal Navy's worst ever calamity.

Below: *HMS* Hood *ready for action with her guns trained to starboard, just as she would have appeared seconds before being destroyed by the* Bismarck's *incredibly accurate gunnery.*

Above: *The carrier HMS* Ark Royal *was part of the Gibraltar based Force H. It was her aircraft that delivered the fateful torpedo hits which sealed the* Bismarck's *fate.*

To make matters worse, the German ships quickly concentrated their fire on the *Prince of Wales,* which was hit several times. With her after turret jammed, she was forced to withdraw, and the two German ships made off to the southwest still doggedly shadowed by the cruisers *Norfolk* and *Suffolk*. However, the *Bismarck* had not escaped unscathed having been hit at least twice by heavy caliber shells.

The loss of the *Hood* now made it imperative for the Royal Navy to sink the *Bismarck* if pride was to be restored. Throughout May 24, more ships were ordered to join the hunt including the battleships *Rodney, Ramilles* and *Revenge*.

Force H (*Ark Royal, Renown* and *Sheffield)* was already heading north from Gibraltar. A small strike force of Swordfish torpedo bombers was launched from Home Fleet carrier *Victorious* late in the evening and made a brave night attack through rain showers, claiming at least one hit. By now the German battleship was alone, the *Prinz Eugen* having separated undetected before the air attack, and continued south eluding the shadowing cruisers. Eventually, contact was regained at 10.30 a.m. on the morning of May 26 by a Catalina flying boat. By then the *Bismarck* was far ahead of Tovey in HMS *King George V* and there was little chance of catching her. The only hope lay

Above: *The 16-inch guns of HMS* Rodney *fired 380 rounds during the* Bismarck *engagement.*

in the aircraft aboard the carrier *Ark Royal*, which was ideally placed ahead of the *Bismarck's* track. The first strike of 14 aircraft was flown off at 2.50 p.m. and, sighting a ship through the broken cloud, they dived to the attack. Unfortunately, their target was not the *Bismarck*, but the cruiser *Sheffield*, which had been detached to shadow the German battleship.

Luckily the torpedoes missed although some exploded prematurely. A second strike was hastily arranged, and in the gathering darkness 15 Swordfish began their gallant attacks through heavy anti-aircraft fire, coming in close before dropping their torpedoes. At least two of these hit but initially it was difficult to ascertain what damage had been caused. In fact, one of the torpedoes had struck the starboard quarter damaging the steering gear and jamming the rudders so that the ship began circling uncontrollably before eventually settling on a meandering course to the northwest.

The way was now clear for the *King George V*, with the *Rodney* in company, to engage the *Bismarck*, but Tovey decided to wait for dawn. *Rodney* was the first to open fire with the *King George V* following almost immediately, and for once the British gunnery was as accurate as the Germans. *Rodney* scored a hit with her third salvo, and further hits put the *Bismarck's* fore turrets out of action. The range steadily reduced, as the *Bismarck's* fire slackened under the punishment she was receiving. Finally the two battleships closed to within 2,750 meters (3,000 yards), *Rodney* scoring a hit with one of her 24.5-inch torpedoes – the only recorded instance of a battleship torpedoing another. *Bismarck* was now a blazing wreck and obviously finished so, desperately short of fuel, the British battleships broke off and set course to the northwest, leaving the cruisers to finish her off with torpedoes.

A dramatic action view showing, in the distance, the Bismarck *wreathed in smoke and surrounded by shell splashes from the British 16-inch and 14-inch guns.*

A photo taken from a Japanese aircraft in the opening stages of the attack on Pearl Harbor. Most of the battleships have their awnings spread, ripples from torpedo and bomb explosions can be seen in the water, and in the background smoke rises from burning army aircraft at Hickham Field.

The great German battleship rolled over and sank at 10.40 a.m., but only 110 survivors were eventually rescued before it was necessary to withdraw under threat of possible aircraft and U-boat attacks. The *Hood* had been avenged and one of the greatest and most dramatic sea chases was at an end.

As 1941 drew to a close, the focus of the naval war turned dramatically to the Pacific Ocean where at dawn on December 7, a force of Japanese aircraft from six aircraft carriers made a surprise attack on the battleships of the U.S. Pacific Fleet moored in neat rows at Pearl Harbor, Hawaii. The first bombs fell at 7.55 a.m. as the American sailors prepared for the traditional hoisting of the colors aboard their ships at 8.00 a.m. In the history of warfare, there has been no clearer example of complete and absolute surprise being achieved. Within a couple of minutes, the dramatic signal was broadcast that told the world that the United States was at war, 'Air Raid, Pearl Harbor. This is no drill!' Kate torpedo bombers roared in low over the water, launching their loads at short range where they could hardly miss. At the same time Val dive bombers fell upon the helpless battleships, almost every bomb finding a mark. Within five minutes, the once proud line of battleships was reduced to a flaming mass, individual ships fighting for survival. *Arizona* was wracked by a massive explosion as the forward magazines went up. She quickly settled on the bottom and over 1,100 of her crew of 1,400 were killed. At the front of the line, the *California* was hit by two torpedoes and a bomb, the latter triggering a magazine explosion. The great ship quickly sank, settling upright on the bottom.

Aft of her, *Oklahoma* was the outboard ship and took three torpedoes on her port side. Within 15 minutes, she had capsized and settled hull up in the mud. The inboard ship, *Maryland* was hit by only two bombs and was relatively undamaged. The

Below: *The wreckage of the USS* Oklahoma *(BB37) during salvage operations in 1944 when the upturned hull had been righted.*

Above: *The USS* New Jersey *(BB62), second of the new Iowa-class battleships, joined the Pacific Fleet in the summer of 1943.*

next pair off ships, *Tennessee* and *West Virginia* were similarly attacked. Being the outboard ship, the *West Virginia* took several torpedo hits, but prompt counter flooding by her crew stopped her from capsizing and she settled upright on the bottom, her upper deck awash. *Tennessee* received only two bomb hits but was damaged by fire and debris when the *Arizona* blew up astern of her. The last battleship in the line was the *Nevada* which, despite being the oldest ship present, was also the most wide awake and succeeded in getting its AA armament into action in time to shoot down at least one of her attackers. Despite having taken a torpedo and two bombs, she succeeded in leaving her berth and getting under way.

As the first wave of Japanese aircraft completed their work, a second wave arrived. Lacking the element of surprise, these received a much hotter reception. Nevertheless, they finished off the work of destroying aircraft on the ground and also concentrated on the *Nevada* as she was underway. The gallant ship was beached off Hospital Point to prevent her sinking and blocking the main channel. Out of the 361 Japanese aircraft that had taken part in the raid, some 29 did not return and others were damaged. This was a small price to pay for what they had achieved, sinking or damaging seven battleships, a light cruiser and three destroyers, as well as destroying over 250 aircraft and damaging many others. The US armed forces lost around 2,500 officers and men killed. It was disaster of the first order.

The losses at Pearl Harbor gave added impetus to the US battleship-building program in progress. The four South Dakota class then under construction were all rushed into service in 1942, and four Iowa class had been laid down in 1940–1941.

These were to be the largest and fastest of the American battleships, although armament details were basically the same as the earlier North Carolina and South Dakota classes (nine 16-inch and twenty 5-inch guns, plus numerous light AA). However, four shaft steam turbine machinery with an output of 210,000 horsepower was fitted, and the hull lengthened to 262 meters (861 feet) on the waterline. With a fine bow blending into wide midship and stern hull sections, often referred to as a 'Coke bottle' shape, these battleships could make 33 knots. Displacement increased to 45,000 tons, as permitted from 1938 by the raising of the Washington Treaty limits, of which no less than 18,700 tons (41 per cent) was taken up by armor protection. These fine ships commissioned in 1943–1944, with the USS *New Jersey* being completed within 32 months of her keel laying – another example of the industrial capacity of the United States and a feat that could not have been matched elsewhere.

USS Alaska (CB1), one of a pair of battlecruisers armed with 12-inch guns and completed in 1944.

Two more of this class were ordered and laid down towards the end of the war (*Illinois* and *Kentucky*). The former was canceled at the end of the war in August 1945, and *Kentucky's* fate is described in the next chapter. An enlargement of the Iowa class was planned and these would have carried an additional triple 16-inch mounting on a displacement of just over 60,000 tons. Known as the Montana class, no less than six were ordered in 1940 but due to other commitments, no work had commenced before they were cancelled in 1943.

As the possibility of war with Japan loomed larger in 1940, there were rumors that Japan was building small battlecruisers similar to the German *Scharnhorst*, but armed with 12-inch guns. This resulted in a requirement for fast, well-armed ships to combat these as well as the already existing Japanese 8-inch gun cruisers. The outcome was the Alaska class, the US Navy's first and only battlecruisers (the earlier Lexington class having never been completed) which were very similar to the German design in size and outline. Displacing around 27,500 tons, they were armed with nine 12-inch guns and could make 33 knots although armor protection was more to cruiser standards with a main belt tapering from 22 to 13 cm (9–5 inches) thickness, and 22 cm (9 inches) on the barbettes and conning tower.

Six were ordered and the first two (*Alaska* and *Guam*) were laid down within two months of Pearl Harbor, both commissioning in mid 1944 just in time to take part in the final push against Japan. A third ship, *Hawaii*, was laid down in 1943 but not completed. The remainder were cancelled.

Even while the attack on Pearl Harbor was in progress, other Japanese forces were invading the Philippines and Malaya. In anticipation of such attacks, the Royal Navy had deployed a force commanded by Admiral Tom Phillips to Singapore. This included the battleship HMS *Prince of Wales* and battlecruiser HMS *Repulse*, although the aircraft carrier HMS *Indomitable*, which was to have accompanied this force was not available. Early on December 8 reports were received of Japanese troops landing in the far north of Malaya.

Admiral Phillips decided to sortie in an attempt to attack the Japanese troop transports, and at dawn on December 10 was off Kuantan, although no landing force was found. By now the British ships had been reported by Japanese reconnaissance aircraft and just after 11 a.m., a formation of high-altitude bombers

Below: *The naval base at Singapore had been developed as the base for a major fleet in time of war. However, by December 1941 the only ships available were the* Prince of Wales *(shown here on arrival) and* Repulse.

HMS Repulse **(bottom left)** *experiences several near misses from a high altitude bomb attack while puffs of smoke from the damaged* Prince of Wales **(top right)** *indicates that her starboard 5.25-inch guns are still in action.*

was spotted approaching. Over the next two hours, the two ships were attacked by bombers and skillfully co-ordinated torpedo attacks. Almost immediately, the *Prince of Wales* was hit right aft by one, or possibly two, torpedoes, which blew off one propeller, wrecked the port-side machinery and jammed the rudders. The ship was left barely able to maneuver with half her AA armament out of action due to power failures and listed heavily to port. Subsequently, the *Repulse* suffered several attacks and was eventually hit almost simultaneously by four torpedoes sinking within a few minutes. Three more torpedoes finished off the almost defenseless *Prince of Wales* which rolled over and sank.

The destroyers managed to rescue 1,285 officers and men from the *Prince of Wales* and a further 796 from the *Repulse* out of a combined complement of 2,911. The loss of the two ships, immediately following American losses at Pearl Harbor, gave the Japanese an unrivaled naval superiority that they were quick to exploit. Even more, this attack finally spelt the end of the battleship as the arbiter of sea power and showed clearly that air power was now the decisive factor.

Further disasters befell the Royal Navy at home and in the Mediterranean. Only two weeks before Pearl Harbor, the battleship *Barham* had been torpedoed and sunk off the Egyptian coast by U-331, rolling over so quickly that more than 800 of her crew perished. Even worse was to follow when on December 19, Italian frogmen placed torpedo warheads under the *Queen Elizabeth* and *Valiant* while the battleships were at anchor in Alexandria, Egypt. The charges exploded causing major damage to both ships, putting them out of action for 12 months and effectively eliminating Cunningham's Mediterranean Fleet.

More embarrassment was to occur closer to home in early 1942. The *Bismarck* sortie had been intended to build on the success of an earlier operation by the battlecruisers *Scharnhorst* and *Gneisenau*, which had safely arrived in the French port of Brest on March 22, 1941, having sunk or captured 21 allied merchant ships. On June 1, they were joined by the cruiser *Prinz Eugen*, which had been accompanying the *Bismarck*. All three German ships, were subjected to continuous heavy air attacks over the next few months and each received substantial damage. If they remained at Brest it was almost inevitable that they would eventually be sunk by bombing and, at Hitler's instigation, an audacious and detailed plan was drawn up to get them back to Germany.

The chosen route was not through the vast expanses of the Atlantic Ocean, but through the narrow waters of the English Channel, right under the noses of the Royal Navy and the RAF. Luck was with the Germans from the very start, and through a series of mishaps it was not until late morning that the ships were spotted already past Le Havre.

Below: *Cunningham's flagship HMS* Queen Elizabeth *was put out of action for almost 18 months following a daring attack by Italian frogmen.*

As they swept through the Straits of Dover at high speeds, the German ships were attacked by British MTBs (Motor Torpedo Boat) and a suicidally brave attack by six Swordfish planes, which were all shot down. Shore batteries at Dover had briefly opened fire at 12.15 p.m. but by then the German ships were rapidly moving out of range and no damage was done. The German force continued to head north east for another two hours without further attacks, their progress uncontested until at 2.30 p.m., the *Scharnhorst* slowed to stop off the Belgian coast. She had hit a mine but was not badly damaged and was soon under way again. For the next two-and-half hours, the German ships were harassed by uncoordinated air attacks but again no hits were scored and they continued steadily northwards. A brave attack by a Harwich-based squadron of destroyers was also beaten off.

Nothing further could be done to stop the German ships, although the *Gneisenau* also hit a mine while north of Vlieland. However, damage was again slight, and she was soon underway again at 25 knots. Almost two hours later, the *Scharnhorst* struck a second mine which caused more-serious damage than the first. All engines were stopped, and she shipped 1,000 tons of water before the flooding was brought under control. Eventually, she got underway again and limped into Wilhelmshaven the next morning. Nevertheless, the outcome was an undoubted tactical victory for the German navy – although in strategic terms little was actually gained. The *Gneisenau* was seriously damaged in a bombing raid only two weeks later and she was never again fit for service. The *Scharnhorst* went on to join German naval forces in Norway, but at least the Royal Navy could now concentrate its own forces to

Below: *For almost three years, the mere presence of the* Tirpitz *in Norwegian fiords posed a threat to allied convoys which tied down the heavy units of the Home Fleet.*

meet this threat without also having to guard against a breakout by other ships based on the French ports.

This was just as well as the German invasion of Russia in May 1941 had brought Russia into the Allied camp, which in turn resulted in supply convoys being run through the Arctic seas to Murmansk. In this situation, German naval and air forces based in Norway posed a dangerous threat. Greatest of these was the *Bismarck's* sister ship *Tirpitz*.

Although she was never actually in action with Allied naval forces, her very presence required that the battleships of the Home Fleet were held available to guard against the possibility that she would attack a convoy. The most graphic illustration of her potential occurred when the large convoy PQ17 set out on June 27, 1942.

This consisted of 37 merchant ships with a heavy escort including distant cover by the battleships HMS *Duke of York* and the USS *Washington*. On July 3, the British Admiralty, under the impression that the *Tirpitz* had left port and was about to attack, ordered the convoy to scatter. By this time the convoy had passed beyond the protection of the Allied heavy units, and it fell easy prey to aircraft and U-boats. The *Tirpitz*, by her mere presence and potential, had been the instrument of a major success for the German forces without herself firing a single shot. The statistics made grim reading. Out of 33 ships which comprised the convoy (four others having turned back due to various problems) no less than 24 were sunk. This was a major victory for the German forces, and it resulted in the immediate suspension of Russian convoys for the rest of the summer. In addition, the Royal Navy had

The audacious escape of the battlecruisers Scharnhorst *and* Gneisenau *from Brest to Germany through the English Channel was achieved by meticulous planning, helped by a series of lucky co-incidences that left the ships undetected until it was too late to mount effective counter actions.*

The Tirpitz *lies in Alten Fiord surrounded by anti-torpedo nets. It was these obstacles that the midget submarines X6 and X7 had to penetrate in their partially successful attack on September 22, 1943.*

suffered a rare and resounding defeat that was to tarnish its reputation for many years to come.

In fact, the *Tirpitz* continued to tie down considerable Allied resources for another two years, even though she rarely went to sea. In September 1943, a daring attack by British midget submarines was partially successful, and on April 3, 1944, an attack by dive bombers from carriers escorted by the battleships *Duke of York* and *Anson* inflicted considerable damage. This was Operation Tungsten that was followed by Operations Mascot and Goodwood in July and August although the later attacks were less successful. In September, RAF Lancasters flying from bases in Russia made a very near miss with a five-ton bomb, which caused considerable damage, rendering the battleship unseaworthy. She was moved to Tromso Fiord, where she was to act as floating battery but was finally destroyed by a further Lancaster attack in November 12, 1944, capsizing with the loss of 1,204 members of her crew.

By this time the Kreigsmarine's surface fleet no longer represented a threat to Allied convoys, as the *Scharnhorst* had been sunk in the last big gun battle in European waters on December 26, 1943. On this occasion, she had left Altenfiord, Norway, to attack convoy JW55B, but had been intercepted during the night by elements of the Home Fleet commanded by Admiral Sir Bruce Fraser flying his flag in the battleship HMS *Duke of York*.

Holding the *Scharnhorst* in radar contact until the range dropped 10,900 meters (12,000 yards), he surprised the German battlecruiser, which then increased speed to escape. However, several hits from 14-inch shells slowed her down, and she was finished off with considerable assistance from the gunfire and torpedoes of accompanying cruisers and destroyers.

Allied fortunes in the Mediterranean began to revive towards the end of 1942, and the invasion of North Africa, Operation Torch, was launched in November. A US task force was responsible for landings around Casablanca and was supported by the battleships *Massachusetts* and *Texas*. Among the opposition encountered was fire from the single turret of the partially completed but immobile French battleship *Jean Bart*. Subsequently, the *Jean Bart* was severely damaged by gunfire from the *Massachusetts* and

Below: *After a distinguished war career, the* Scharnhorst *was finally brought to bay and sunk by the battleship HMS* Duke of York *in a night action on Boxing Day 1943.*

air attacks from carrier-based aircraft. Consequently, when the fighting ended, she played no further part in the war, although was eventually repaired and fully commissioned after 1945. Her sister ship, *Richelieu,* was still at Dakar and was not involved in any fighting. When French forces rejoined the Allied cause, she was sent to New York for repairs and a refit and subsequently served with the British Far East Fleet.

In the Pacific, 1942 had been a year of mixed fortunes, as the Japanese initially swept all before them. However, they were checked at the Battle of the Coral Sea in May and decisively defeated at Midway in June. These battles were a new type of naval engagement in which the surface ships never came within sight of enemy forces, the actions being entirely fought by carrier-based aircraft. After Midway, US forces were able to begin the long haul back across the Pacific in an attempt to reach the Japanese homeland and end the war. It was to be a long and bloody path in which battleships would play their part but now as a subsidiary element of the new carrier-based task forces. In this, they would find new roles suited to their size and firepower and, in particular the new fast battleships capable of operating in close company with the aircraft carriers soon showed their worth as anti-aircraft escorts. By virtue of their size, they were able to mount substantial batteries of 20-mm (0.75-inch) and 40-mm (1.5-inch) AA guns to supplement the controlled fire of the 5-inch guns. For example, by 1945, the USS *North Carolina* carried no less than ninety-six 40-mm (1.5-inch) AA guns in twenty-four quadruple mountings, and these were supplemented by several single 20-mm (0.75-inch) guns.

The new battleships first proved their worth in the Battle of Santa Cruz in October 1942. This was one of a series of battles fought in the waters around the Solomon Islands following the landing of US Marines on the island of Guadalcanal in August of that year.

In the Santa Cruz battle, the USS *South Dakota* operated in close company with the carrier *Enterprise,* shooting down several of her attackers and taking hits that might otherwise have been directed at the more vulnerable carrier. Despite the emphasis now placed on aircraft carrier operations, attempts by the Japanese to eliminate the US presence on Guadalcanal resulted in some fierce night actions known as the Naval Battles of Guadalcanal in the period November 12 to 15, 1942, in which battleships played a major part. Action started on the night of the November 12, when strong Japanese forces, which included the 11th Battle Squadron comprising the *Hiei* and *Kirishima,* moved into Iron Bottom Sound off the island with the intention of bombarding US positions ashore. They were intercepted by a force of US destroyers and cruisers, and a wild mêlée resulted in which the Americans came of worst, losing several destroyers and two cruisers. Japanese losses amounted only two destroyers, although the battleship *Hiei* had taken

Below: *The incomplete* Jean Bart *lying at Casablanca, Morocco, in November 1942 after the Allied invasion of North Africa. She shows obvious damage incurred while assisting Vichy forces to resist the landings.*

Above: *Japanese torpedo bombers approach the USS* South Dakota *(***top left***) on October 26, 1942, during the Battle of Santa Cruz. The battleship's AA firepower was instrumental in protecting the aircraft carrier USS* Enterprise.

numerous hits from 8-inch shells fired by the USS *Portland* and USS *San Francisco*, as well as a couple of torpedo hits. Consequently, her speed was reduced, and the next day she fell easy prey to aircraft operating from Henderson Field on Guadalcanal and from the carrier *Enterprise* approaching from the south.

The night of the November 14 saw an even more dramatic engagement. To add to the pressure on Guadalcanal, a substantial force drawn from Admiral Kondo's 2nd Fleet was detailed to carry out a further bombardment. Led by the battleship *Kirishima*, the force included two heavy cruisers and two divisions of destroyers, each led by a light cruiser. However, the Americans were reinforced by Task Force 64 consisting of the battleships *South Dakota* and *Washington* under the command of Rear-Admiral Willis 'Ching' Lee. This officer had firm ideas about the tactical handling of battleships and, unlike many of his contemporary flag officers, was thoroughly acquainted with use of the latest radar equipment. Setting up a patrol at the entrance to Iron Bottom Sound, a radar contact was picked up on the starboard beam at a range of around 9. 5 km (6 miles). The battleships opened fire on this target, which turned out to be the light cruiser *Sendai*, and she promptly reversed course and made off. Shortly afterwards, the four U.S. destroyers scouting

Below: *The USS* Washington *sank the Japanese battleship* Kirishima *with radar-directed gunfire on the night of November 14, 1942, in one of the few Second World War battleship vs. battleship engagements during the Naval Battle of Guadalcanal.*

Above: *The battle plot aboard a US battleship. Here details of the enemy ship's range, course and speed, obtained from radar and visual rangefinders are fed into the gunnery computer, so that the guns can be set at the correct bearing and elevation to hit the target.*

ahead of the battleships, ran into a pack of Japanese destroyers and were badly mauled, three being sunk and one badly damaged. While the destroyer action was going disastrously wrong, Lee suffered another setback when the *South Dakota* suffered an electrical power failure that put her radar and fire control out of action. She was therefore in no fit state to take on the combined fire of the battleship *Kirishima* and heavy cruisers *Atago* and *Takao*, which between them scored more than 40 hits on the superstructure.

While *South Dakota* was forming the center of a lot of unwelcome attention, Lee continued steadily ahead in the *Washington* and right on midnight, he surprised the Japanese battleship *Kirishima* with several radar-directed salvoes at a range of 7,680 meters (8,400 yards). In only seven minutes, nine 16-inch and forty 5-inch shells crashed into the *Kirishima*, starting countless uncontrollable fires and turning her into a helpless wreck. After checking fire, Lee ordered the *Washington* to continue to the northwest in what proved to be a successful attempt to draw off the ships engaging the embattled *South Dakota*.

By 12.25 a.m., Admiral Kondo had decided to abandon the bombardment mission and ordered his ships to withdraw. Once again, Henderson Field had been saved from a major bombardment and a second battleship had been sunk. In three days of continuous action, the Japanese had lost two battleships, a heavy cruiser and at least three destroyers. American losses stood at two light cruisers and seven destroyers, while both sides had several ships seriously damaged and out of action for some time. Neither side could claim a decisive victory, but from this point on the initiative began to pass to the US Navy.

The fighting continued on and around Guadalcanal for several more weeks, but by February

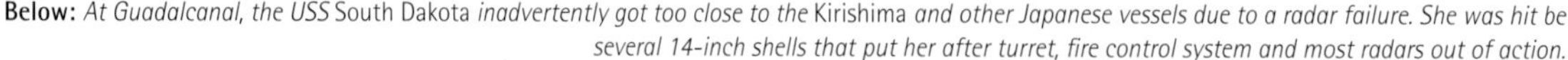

Below: *At Guadalcanal, the USS* South Dakota *inadvertently got too close to the* Kirishima *and other Japanese vessels due to a radar failure. She was hit be several 14-inch shells that put her after turret, fire control system and most radars out of action.*

1943, the Japanese had evacuated the island, and US forces began advancing up the chain of the Solomon Islands towards the major Japanese Navy base at Rabaul. In the meantime, the build up of carrier task forces had allowed an advance to begin across the central Pacific. Amphibious operations began in the Gilbert Islands in November 1943, followed by the Marianas (February 1944), and Saipan (June 1944).

The latter was an important operation, as it secured a base for B-29 bombers to operate against Japan. In all of these operations, US Navy battleships played an important part, the new fast battleships operating with the carrier task forces and the older classes (including an increasing number of repaired Pearl Harbor survivors) performed the vital task of fire support for the US Army and Marine invading forces.

In October 1944, a major operation was mounted to regain the Philippines, and a strong invasion force was landed on Leyte, a southern island. The supporting fleet comprised over 700 warships including six fast battleships under Admiral Lee operating with the carriers and a fire-support group of six older battleships under Rear-Admiral Jesse Oldendorff. Faced with this challenge, the Imperial Japanese Navy embarked on a complicated plan to disrupt the invasion and committed virtually its entire fleet including the hybrid battleships *Hyuga* and *Ise*.

Above: *Despite the fierce battles in the Pacific, sailors were quick to take the opportunity to relax between periods of action.*

After the carrier losses at Midway, these two ships had their after turrets removed and a hangar and short flight deck erected on the stern. They were intended to carry up to 20 dive-bomber seaplanes that would be launched by catapult and recovered by crane after landing on the water. In practice, they were never used in this role as the necessary aircraft were not produced. Also, at the earlier Battle of the Philippine Sea, the Japanese carrier air groups had been decimated, and so a force of four carriers and two hybrid battleships was now deployed well to the north to merely act as

Below: *The Japanese Ise-class battleships were modified to act as hybrid battleship-aircraft carriers in 1943, but the concept was impractical. By the end of the war, the aircraft had been landed and multiple AA weapons erected on the flight decks.*

a decoy. In this it was completely successful, drawing Admiral William Halsey's Task Force 38 and Lee's battleships of Task Force 34 well away from the main action around Leyte.

The main Japanese attack was two pronged, and the first to attract US attention on October 24 was Vice-Admiral Takeo Kurita's First Striking Force, which was headed by the two large battleships, *Yamato* and *Musashi*, and also included the *Nagato*, *Kongo*, and *Haruna*. As these passed through the Sibuyan Sea north of Leyte, they were soon the attention of repeated attacks by US carrier-based aircraft, which concentrated on the *Musashi*, and she was eventually sunk, but only after absorbing 20 torpedoes and over a dozen heavy bombs.

The *Nagato* was also hit by two torpedoes, and in the evening Kurita ordered his ships to reverse course and withdraw. The second prong was led by Admiral Shoji Nishimura and consisted of the battleships *Fuso* and *Yamashiro* as well as several cruisers and destroyers. At nightfall on October 24, they approached Leyte from the south, passing through the Surigao Strait, where they were subjected to constant torpedo attacks by US Navy destroyers and PT boats. The battleship *Fuso* took a torpedo and sheared out of line on fire, while *Yamashiro* was also hit. Ten minutes later, another group of American destroyers pitched in, scoring another hit on *Yamashiro*, while *Fuso* was also attacked again and the cumulative damage was such that she later sank. Nevertheless, Admiral Nishimura pressed steadily onwards in his flagship *Yamashiro*, now only accompanied by the cruiser *Mogami* and destroyer *Shigure*.

He appeared to be unaware of the massive concentration of firepower that awaited him in the form of Oldendorf's six battleships, not to mention nine heavy and light cruisers. Steaming steadily on an east-west patrol line and tracking the Japanese ships on radar, Oldendorf's battlewagons were perfectly placed and opened fire at 3.53 a.m. The *Yamashiro* quickly became a battered wreck, and was eventually finished off by torpedoes from American destroyers. This was the last occasion in which battleships fought each other, and the honor of firing the last salvo in

Below: Musashi *comes under attack by aircraft from the USS* Enterprise *while underway in the Sibuyan Sea on October 24, 1944. The ship subsequently sank after numerous bomb and torpedo hits.*

Above: *While approaching Leyte from the southwest, the battleship* Yamashiro *is attacked by US carrier-based aircraft in the morning of October 24, 1944. No damage was caused in this attack, but the ship was sunk early the next morning by the gunfire of US battleships in the Surigao Straits.*

such an engagement is generally accorded to the USS *Mississippi* that fired a full 12-gun broadside at 4.08 a.m. on October 25.

Unfortunately for the Americans, the Japanese had not quite finished. During the night, Kurita had again reversed course and at daylight on October 25, he brought the battleship *Yamato* and the rest of his force including three other battleships through the San Bernardino Strait north of Leyte and fell upon the escort carriers and destroyers of Task Force 77, which was supporting the troops ashore and was not equipped to fight a fleet action.

Kurita succeeded in sinking the carrier USS *Gambier Bay* and three destroyers, but he was increasingly harassed by aircraft from the other escort carriers and after losing three cruisers to air attack, finally turned away, fearful of being trapped by Halsey's carriers to the north. In fact, Kurita's force should have been intercepted by the fast battleships of Task Force 34, but these had been drawn away by the earlier Japanese decoy tactics, and the chance of a major and well-matched battleship action was lost.

After the Leyte battles, the remaining Japanese ships returned home and for the most part lay immobilized due to lack of fuel. The elderly battleship *Kongo* was torpedoed and sunk off Taiwan in November 1944 by the US submarine *Sealion.* A more spectacular coup was achieved by the USS *Archerfish* on November 29, when she sank the 65,000-ton carrier *Shinano* on her maiden voyage from Tokyo Bay. The *Shinano* had originally been laid down in 1940 as the third Yamato-class battleships, but after the disastrous losses at Midway, the decision was made to make her an aircraft carrier. The skipper of the *Archerfish* could not believe his luck when she steamed into his sights, and he put four torpedoes into the great ship.

Above: *On a desperate one-way sortie to Okinawa, the mighty* Yamato *comes under concentrated air attack on April 7, 1945.*

The end. The last battleship sunk in action at sea, Yamato's *magazines explode as she sinks taking 2,488 of her crew with her.*

Only the original *Yamato* now remained, and she sailed on her final mission on April 6, 1945, accompanied by a light cruiser and several destroyers to attack the US forces then invading the Japanese island of Okinawa. This was a suicide mission in more ways than one.

Apart from the fact that *Yamato* would almost certainly be overcome by the massed US naval and air forces, she only carried enough fuel for the one-way voyage to Okinawa. Inevitably, she was spotted by American submarines and aircraft, and at noon on April 7, the giant battleship was subjected to continuous air attack. In less than two hours, she was reduced to a sinking hulk by at least 10 torpedo and 23 bomb hits. Thus, the last of the world's most powerful battleships was gone, although it is interesting to note that at one time the Japanese navy had considered construction of even larger 70,000-ton ships armed with six 20-inch guns. Work on these was never started, and the project was abandoned after the defeat at Midway in 1942.

The other Japanese battleships anchored in home waters were pounded into wrecks by a sustained campaign of carrier-launched strikes in July 1945, part of the preparations for landings on the Japanese mainland that were expected to be difficult and costly. Consequently, there was great relief when the war was ended by the dropping of atomic bombs on Hiroshima and Nagasaki.

It was perhaps fitting that the final surrender document was signed aboard a battleship, the USS *Missouri*, in Tokyo Bay on September 2, 1945. One of the signatories was the C-in-C of the British Pacific Fleet, Admiral Sir Bruce Fraser, who flew his flag aboard the battleship HMS *Duke of York*, with HMS *King George V* in company. Apart from the American fast battleships accompanying the carrier task forces, the older battleships *New Mexico, Mississippi, Idaho, Colorado* and *West Virginia* were present. The last named, of course, being a survivor of Pearl Harbor.

The gathering in Tokyo Bay was a fitting climax to the career of the battleship, and the last time that so many would be seen together. With the war ended the fleets dispersed, and for all practical purposes the development and career of the great ships whose story started with the armored steamships of the 19th century had almost come to an end.

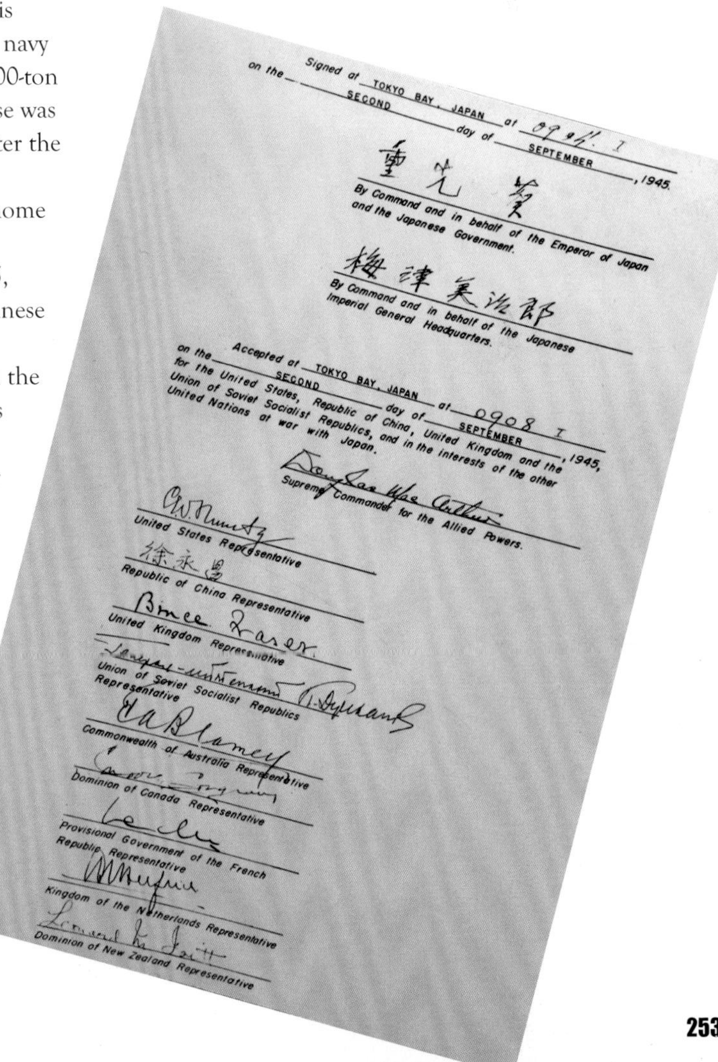

Signed at TOKYO BAY, JAPAN at 0904 I
on the SECOND day of SEPTEMBER, 1945.

重光葵

By Command and in behalf of the Emperor of Japan and the Japanese Government.

梅津美治郎

By Command and in behalf of the Japanese Imperial General Headquarters.

Accepted at TOKYO BAY, JAPAN at 0908 I
on the SECOND day of SEPTEMBER, 1945,
for the United States, Republic of China, United Kingdom and the Union of Soviet Socialist Republics, and in the interests of the other United Nations at war with Japan.

Supreme Commander for the Allied Powers.

United States Representative

Republic of China Representative

United Kingdom Representative

Union of Soviet Socialist Republics Representative

Commonwealth of Australia Representative

Dominion of Canada Representative

Provisional Government of the French Republic Representative

Kingdom of the Netherlands Representative

Dominion of New Zealand Representative

Right: *The signatories on the surrender document signed aboard the USS* Missouri *included Fleet Admiral Chester Nimitz USN for the United States and Admiral Bruce Fraser RN for Great Britain.*

Radar

The invention of radar in the 1930s was to have a far-reaching effect on the conduct of air and sea operations in the Second World War. The first sets were fitted to warships just before the outbreak of hostilities in 1939, but by 1945 battleships would be equipped with a wide range of specialized radar systems. The basic principle of radar is that a transmitted pulse of electromagnetic energy is reflected by a solid object and then picked up by a receiver. Although there was a general awareness of this principle, in Britain the scientist Sir Robert Watson Watt perfected the first practical radar sets which were initially developed by the RAF to give warning of enemy aircraft approaching British shores. The Royal Navy was quick to recognize the potential of such systems, and by 1938 the first Type 79Y radar was fitted to the cruiser HMS *Sheffield*. Trials demonstrated that an aircraft flying at 3,000 meters (10,000 feet) could be detected at 85 km (53 miles), reducing to 56 km (30 miles) when the target was at 1,500 meters (5,000 feet). This type of radar was known as an Air Warning (AW) system, because although it would give reasonably accurate readings of range, it would only give a general indication of the direction of the target. A Type 79Y set was installed in the battleship *Nelson* by January 1939, and it was this set which was first used in action when it gave warning of German aircraft approaching *Nelson* and other units of the Home Fleet in the North Sea in September 1939.

Operating on the relatively low frequency of 75 MHz (megahertz) the Type 79 could only act as a warning radar, but by 1937, the German navy had a set operating on 375 MHz which, although it had a range of only 16 km (10 miles), was accurate enough to be used as a gunnery set. Known as Seetakt, it was fitted to two ships including the *Graf Spee* in 1939. Inspection of the wreckage of this vessel off Montevideo gave the first indication that the enemy possessed such equipment.

However, the German navy seems to have made little effort to develop other radars in contrast to the Royal Navy which, due to the close links between

Below: *This view of USS* Pennsylvania *in 1944 shows the large antenna associated with the SC search radar on the mainmast.*

A Mark 37 HA director aboard USS New Jersey *(BB62). The larger antenna is for the Mark 12 centimetric gunnery radar and the smaller one is a Mark 22 height finder operating on the 3-cm wavelength for very accurate resolution of low targets.*

British scientists and the armed forces, rapidly developed a variety of specialist radars. A good example was the Type 281, which served as a long-range AW set, detecting aircraft up to 160 km (100 miles) away, and also as a surface-warning (SW) set with a range of 7.5 km (12 miles). In gunnery ranging mode it was accurate within 25 meters (27 yards) at a distance of 20,000 km (22,000 yards). HMS *Prince of Wales* was one of the first battleships to receive this equipment. A more specialized gunnery radar was the Type 284 fitted to *King George V*. This had a 6.4-meter (21-foot) wide aerial array that was capable of determining bearings to within half a degree. In contrast to the warning and surveillance radars, which rotated to give continuous coverage, gunnery radars were fixed and aligned by the gunnery director. In order to ensure that the director was pointing in the right direction so that the Type 284 could pick up the target, the bearing information was taken from one of the other surveillance radars operating as a target indicator (TI). A modified Type 284M could measure bearing accuracy to within 5 minutes of arc (one twelfth of a degree.) and the *Duke of York* made good use of this equipment when she sank the *Scharnhorst* in December 1943.

Further radar improvements later in the war came about as the result of the British invention of the cavity magnetron. Where previously radars had worked on wavelengths measured in meters, new radars, such as the Type 271 SW operated on the 10-cm band, while the Type 274 gunnery radar went down to 3 cm, giving excellent resolution in range and azimuth. Another British device was IFF (Identification Friend or Foe) in which aircraft and vessels were fitted with a transponder that responded to ship or ground-based radar pulses, allowing the operator to identify friendly forces. Consequently, by 1945 a battleship such as HMS *King George V* was equipped with a bewildering array of radar equipment including Type 279B AW, Type 277P AW/SW with height finding capability, Type 293 TI , Type 275 gunnery for the main armament, Type 285 gunnery for the four high-angle directors, and Type 282 on each of the multiple 2-pounder mountings. In addition, she carried a Type 242 IFF interrogator and a Type 251 responder.

US radar research started in 1934, and the first operational AW set designated XAF was fitted to the battleship *New York* in December 1938. Using the 200 MHz frequency it had a similar performance to the British Type 79 but provided offered considerably better azimuth resolution. By the time of Pearl Harbor, several battleships including *Texas, California* and *West Virginia* were fitted with improved CXAM or SC radars. Ironically, indications of the approaching Japanese aircraft on a land-based Air Corps radar were assumed to be friendly B-17s and so were disregarded. Subsequent, US Navy radar development followed the British pattern. When the USS *Washington* sank the Japanese battleship *Kirishama* off Guadalcanal in November 1942, she utilized the metric Mark 3 gunnery and surface-warning radar for range information and to maintain the action when visual contact was lost. In 1941, the British-invented magnetron became available, and centimetric Mark 8 and Mark 13 sets were developed. These were fitted to the battleships *California, Tennessee* and *West Virginia* which used them to good effect when they sank the *Yamashiro* in the Battle of Surigao Strait in October 1944. The SK and SP series of long-range search radar were distinguished by their large rotating parabolic aerials mounted atop the foremast of the Iowa-class battleships among others.

Given their modern day dominance of the electronics market, it is surprising that the Japanese navy failed to develop a significant range of radar equipment. From 1942, most of their battleships were eventually fitted with the Type 1 AW radar on they mainmast and Type 2 SW on the foremast. The performance of these was similar to the British Type 79 or American CXAM and operated on metric wavelengths, as the Japanese were not aware of the magnetron development, which remained a closely guarded Allied secret.

Admirals of the Second World War

Above: *Universally known as ABC from his initials, Cunningham was cast in the Nelson mold - vigorous in action but always considerate of his men.*

Admiral of the Fleet Andrew Cunningham RN (1883–1963)

Andrew Cunningham was Britain's outstanding naval leader of the Second World War. Joining the Navy 1897, he saw distinguished service as a destroyer captain during the First World War, winning the DSO three times.

Cunningham progressed to the rank of admiral in the interwar years, and was made commander-in-chief (C-in-C) of Britain's Mediterranean Fleet in June 1939. His record in this command was outstanding throughout several critical engagements, notably Taranto (1940), Cape Matapan (1941), Crete (1941) and the defense of Malta (1940–2). He also commanded the naval forces supporting the landings in North Africa, Sicily and Italy.

In October 1943, Cunningham became First Sea Lord, and oversaw the strategic direction of Britain's naval forces for the rest of the war and until his retirement in May 1946.

Admiral of the Fleet John Tovey RN (1885–1971))

Like Cunningham, John Tovey was a destroyer captain in the First World War, and rose to the rank of admiral in the interwar years.

He was Cunningham's Rear-Admiral Destroyers and second-in-command in the Mediterranean until November 1940, when he was given command of the Home Fleet. In this capacity, he was in charge during the pursuit and sinking of the *Bismarck*, and had onerous responsibilities involving the protection of Atlantic and Arctic convoys.

In 1943, Tovey became Commander-in-Chief Nore, responsible for the East-coast convoys and mine-sweeping operations, and was heavily involved in the naval preparations for D-Day. He retired in 1946.

Above: *Admiral Sir John Tovey (left) aboard his flagship King George V with Rear Admiral Brind, his Chief of Staff during the Bismarck hunt.*

Below: *Admiral Bruce Fraser RN (right) at a meeting with Admiral Nimitz USN after the British Pacific Fleet joined the US Navy for the final push against Japan.*

Admiral of the Fleet Bruce Fraser RN (1888–1981)
Bruce Fraser was a specialist gunnery officer in the First World War. By the outbreak of the Second World War, he was Third Sea Lord and Controller of the Navy, but in May 1943 he succeeded Tovey as commander of the Home Fleet. Here, he was in command during one of the few surface battleship engagements of the war, the Battle of the North Cape (December 1943), which resulted in the destruction of the *Scharnhorst*.

In the summer of 1944, Fraser became C-in-C of the Eastern Fleet, and subsequently named the British Pacific Fleet. In this capacity, he was the British officer who signed the Japanese Instrument of Surrender aboard the USS *Missouri* in Tokyo Bay in September 1945. He went on to become First Sea Lord and Chief of the Naval Staff in 1948, retiring in 1951.

Fleet Admiral Chester Nimitz USN (1885–1966)
Chester Nimitz was selected as C-in-C of the US Navy's Pacific Fleet immediately after the attack on Pearl Harbor. In March 1942, he was additionally appointed C-in-C Pacific Ocean Areas, with operational control over all Allied air, land and sea

Left: *Admiral Chester Nimitz, C-in-C Pacific Fleet, presents a unit citation to the aircraft carrier USS* Enterprise *in June 1943.*

Below: *Nimitz wears the five stars denoting Fleet Admiral rank on his uniform lapels.*

Above: *As the effective head of the US Navy, Admiral King was singleminded in his pursuit of the defeat of Japan of which he was the principal architect*

forces in the central Pacific. He retained this post to the end of the war.

Nimitz's strategic skill was evident during the rebuilding and development of the US Navy, and in the many successful campaigns and battles leading to the final Japanese defeat. When the grade of Fleet Admiral was created in December 1944, he was the first officer appointed to that rank.

Nimitz signed for the United States at the Japanese surrender in 1945. After the war, he became Chief of Naval Operations until retiring in 1949.

Fleet Admiral Ernest 'Ernie' King USN (1878–1956)
Along with General Marshall (army) and General Arnold (air force), Ernest King was one of the three service chiefs who formed the Joint Chiefs of Staff, responsible for directing the U.S. military in the Second World War. From December 1941, he was C-in-C U.S. Fleet, and from March 1942 Chief of Naval Operations as well, the only officer ever to combine the two posts. King was therefore the most important figure in developing and executing U.S. naval strategy in all theaters of conflict. Often described as argumentative and abrasive, he was also a highly capable and effective strategist. From the British perspective he is remembered as an opponent of the deployment of the British Pacific Fleet, an opposition seen as justified by many recent commentators.

Vice-Admiral Willis Augustus Lee USN (1888–1945)
Willis Lee is famous for commanding Task Force 64 at the Second Naval Battle of Guadalcanal (November 14 and 15, 1942), the culmination of US attempts to prevent the Japanese reinforcing the island. It was one of only two battleship versus battleship actions in the Pacific war.

Below: *Rear-Admiral Willis A Lee, victor of the Battle of Guadalcanal when gunfire from his flagship USS* Washington *sank the Japanese battleship* Kirishima.

Lee's task force contained the battleships USS *Washington* (his flagship) and *South Dakota*. The larger Japanese force was led by the battleship *Kirishima*, but in the ensuing night action she was sunk by gunfire from the *Washington*. Lee's expert use of his ship's radar was a feature of this successful action.

He was appointed Commander Battleships Pacific Fleet in 1944 but subsequently died suddenly from a heart attack in August 1945.

Naval Marshal General (Fleet Admiral) Isoroku Yamamoto (1884–1943)

Isoroku Yamamoto was C-in-C of Japan's Combined Fleet from 1939 to 1943 and was the main architect of his nation's naval strategy, despite being opposed to the idea of war with the Allies.

He originated the plan for the Pearl Harbor attack, and was particularly known for his expertise and innovations in the field of naval aviation. Yamamoto was a gifted naval commander, who retained his popularity with the armed forces and the Japanese people even when Japan's fortunes declined after the Battle of Midway in 1942.

Yamamoto decided on an inspection tour of the South Pacific in April 1943, but his itinerary was decoded by US Naval Intelligence. Long-range fighters intercepted his aircraft, and Yamamoto was killed.

Vice-Admiral Takeo Kurita (1889–1977)

One of Japan's most actively engaged flag officers, Takeo Kurita commanded Cruiser Division 7 at the outbreak of war, and led the division during the Battle of Midway (1942). In May 1942, he was promoted to vice-admiral and given command of Battleship Division 3, which participated in the Guadalcanal campaign of that year.

In 1943, Kurita received command of the 2nd Fleet, which included the largest battleships in the world, *Yamato* and *Musashi*. His fleet was heavily engaged during the Battle of Leyte Gulf (1944). Kurita eventually withdrew without accomplishing his mission, refusing to sacrifice his forces in a futile fight to the death. Consequently, Kurita lost his command in disgrace and finished the war in charge of Japan's Naval Academy.

Above: *Flying his flag on the battleship* Yamato, *Vice-Admiral Takeo Kurita commanded the Japanese Center Force at Leyte Gulf but failed to capitalize on his success in surprising the US forces off Samar.*

Grand Admiral Erich Raeder (1876–1960)

Erich Raeder was Admiral Franz von Hipper's Chief of Staff in the First World War, taking part in the Battle of Jutland. Steadily promoted in the interwar years, by 1939 he was the first officer since Tirpitz to become a Grand Admiral.

Raeder supervised the growth of the Kriegsmarine (German navy) under Adolf Hitler, and was responsible for the construction programs which produced the German battleships and battlecruisers. His greatest success was the invasion of Norway (1940). He supported a strategic focus in the Mediterranean, while having doubts about Operation Sea Lion, the German plan to invade the British Isles.

Subsequent naval failures, particularly the Battle of the Barents Sea (1942), combined with the success of Donitz's U-boat fleet, led to Raeder's replacement by Donitz in 1943, following which Raeder resigned.

Found guilty at the post-war tribunals in Nuremberg of conspiring to wage aggressive war, Erish Raeder was imprisoned by the Allies powers from 1945 to 1955.

THE END OF THE LINE

Nagato was the only Japanese battleship left afloat at the end of the war. Here, she is being prepared as a target ship for the atomic bomb trials at Bikini Atoll in 1946.

The End of the Line

When the Second World War finally ended in August 1945, the battleships of the Axis nations had virtually ceased to exist as effective operational units. During the war, the German navy had lost the *Bismarck, Tirpitz, Scharnhorst* and *Graf Spee* to enemy action, while *Gneisenau* had been seriously damaged in an air raid only a few days after the spectacular Channel dash in February 1942. Work on her reconstruction was halted in January 1943. She was subsequently scuttled and was broken up after the war. The *Admiral Scheer* almost survived, but was sunk at Kiel by British bombers on April 9, 1945, while the *Lutzow* (previously *Deutschland)* fought right to the end supporting German troops attempting to hold off the advancing Russian Red Army, and was blown up by her crew on May 4, 1945, having previously been beached due to bomb damage.

By July 1945, the surviving Japanese battleships were anchored in home waters, where the *Ise, Hyuga* and *Haruna* were sunk in concentrated attacks by carrier-based aircraft. After the war, the wrecks were raised and broken up. The only battleship afloat at the time of the Japanese surrender was the heavily damaged *Nagato* (her sister ship *Mutsu* had been destroyed by an internal explosion on June 8, 1943) which lay at Yokosuka. She was taken over by the occupying U.S. forces and subsequently sunk in the atomic bomb tests at Bikini Atoll in July 1946.

Only the Italian navy retained a significant battle fleet, although the *Roma* had been sunk on September 9, 1943, as she made her way in company with the *Vittorio Veneto* and *Italia* (previously *Littorio)* to Malta as part of the armistice agreement made the previous day. While on the way, the ships were attacked by German aircraft, which launched radio-controlled FX 1200 guided bombs and, surprisingly, a single hit by one of these was enough to sink the modern battleship. Ultimately, five Italian battleships reached Malta, and only the *Conte di Cavour* was left in Italy. She had been scuttled at Trieste on September 10, while still not repaired from damaged inflicted in the 1940 Taranto raid. Although raised by the Germans, she was sunk again by Allied air attack and broken up after the war. The *Caio Duillio* and *Andrea Doria* were returned to Italy in 1944 and served as training ships until 1956, when they were laid up and scrapped. The *Giulio Cesare* was transferred to Russia in February 1947 as part of the war reparations scheme. It was incorporated into the Black Sea Fleet as the *Novorossijsk*. Based at Sevastopol, she sank after hitting

Below: Caio Duillio, *shown at Malta shortly after the end of the war, was one of two battleships returned to the Italian navy in 1944.*

Above: *As finally completed the* Jean Bart *carried an exceptionally heavy secondary battery of twenty-four 100-mm guns and twenty-eight 57-mm AA guns. She could also be distinguished from the* Richelieu *by the greatly enlarged bridge deck.*

a mine in October 1955. The modern battleships *Vittorio Veneto* and *Italia* were laid up and interned in the Suez Canal. Although subsequently allocated to the United States and Britain as war reparations, they were handed back to Italy on the condition that they would be scrapped, and this process commenced at La Spezia in 1948.

By 1945, the French navy possessed only the battleships *Richelieu, Jean Bart, Lorraine* and *Paris,* the others having been either sunk at Oran in 1940 or scuttled at Toulon in November 1942. The *Richelieu* had joined the Free French Navy in late 1942 following the Allied invasion of North Africa, and had been sent to New York Navy Yard for repairs and modernization. These repairs were completed in August 1943, and later that year she joined the British Home Fleet at Scapa Flow and then the Far East Fleet in March 1944. Here, she remained for the rest of the war and saw considerable action. She was present at the capitulation of Japanese forces in Singapore in September, and subsequently assisted with the re-occupation of French Indochina before returning home to Toulon in February 1946. This was the first time she had been in a French home port since her hurried departure from Brest in June 1940. After a refit, she served as flagship of the French Mediterranean Fleet until 1950. After a further refit, she saw further service until being laid up at Brest as a training vessel in 1956. She was sold in 1967 and towed to Genoa for breaking up in 1968.

The incomplete *Jean Bart* lay at Casablanca, where she had been seriously damaged during the fighting before the Vichy forces came over to the Allied side. Due to lack of resources, little work was done on her until she was sailed for France in August 1945. Despite plans to convert her to an aircraft carrier, she was finally completed at the Brest naval yard as a battleship to the original design but with a modern anti-aircraft armament and the latest radars. She finally joined the French fleet in April 1950, the last battleship in the world to be completed although her battery of 57-mm (2.25-inch) AA guns was not fitted until 1952. Throughout her subsequent career she remained with the Mediterranean fleet, taking part in support of the

Suez operations in October 1956, before being laid up as a training ship. She was not finally scrapped until 1970. The two older ships (*Lorraine, Paris*) had been laid up in 1945 and were scrapped in the 1950s.

Interestingly, the *Jean Bart* was not the last surviving ship of its kind in European waters. That record went to one of the oldest ships, the ex-German battlecruiser *Goeben*, which had been handed over to the Turkish navy after its escape from the Royal Navy in August 1914. She had remained in commission until 1950, when she was laid up and subsequently stricken from the navy list in 1954. Although put up for sale, an offer from West Germany to purchase the ship was declined in 1963 and she was not finally sold until 1971. Even then it was not until 1973 that she was towed away for scrapping.

Of the British and US navies in 1945, the former had suffered the most grievous losses including the *Royal Oak, Barham, Repulse,* as well as the modern *Prince of Wales.* The surviving ships had all been worked hard, none more than the redoubtable *Warspite*, which had experienced the most active war of any battleship. Starting at Narvik in 1940, she had taken part in numerous actions in the Mediterranean and had finally almost succumbed to hits by two glider bombs off Salerno in September 1943. Although repairs were effected, by the time she supported the Normandy landings in June 1944, one boiler room and X turret were permanently out of action. Subsequently she suffered damage from a ground mine, which caused considerable damage to the machinery and propeller shafts. Temporary repairs were effected, which allowed her to carry out further gunfire support missions, the last at Walcheren off the Scheldt Estuary, by which time she was running on only three shafts and could make only 15 knots. She was finally placed in reserve in February 1945, and due to her condition was the first of the Royal Navy's capital ship to be sold for scrap. However, the grand old lady had the last word, running ashore at Prussia Cove in Cornwall while under tow in April 1947 and was finally broken up where she lay. The rest of the older capital ships (*Nelson, Rodney, Renown* and the remaining Queen Elizabeth and R-class battleships) were all sent to the ship breakers in 1948, leaving only the four King George V class and the new *Vanguard*, which was commissioned in April 1946. While the four older battleships spent various periods with the Home Fleet or acted as training ships, they were all laid up in reserve by 1950 and then sold for scrap in 1957. At one time, serious consideration was given to converting them to guided-missile ships, but for both financial and technical reasons this was not done.

As well as being the last, HMS *Vanguard* was probably Britain's best and fastest battleship. Had she been available, she would have been a valuable

Below: *HMS* Warspite *aground at Prussia Cove where she was finally broken up.*

Above: Vanguard *incorporated all the lessons learnt from war experience. and carried a heavy radar-directed AA armament. With the sweeping sheer of the bow and capped funnels she was a handsome ship.*

addition to the British Pacific Fleet in 1945, but by 1946 the day of the battleship was over, and she fell into a routine of refits and training exercises although for obvious reasons of prestige she was used to convey the royal family to South Africa for a state visit in 1947. In 1954, she entered Devonport dockyard for a refit and thereafter was placed in reserve. Sold for scrap in 1959, she ran aground while leaving Portsmouth under tow in August 1960 but was refloated and was finally broken up at Faslane in Scotland. By this time, the Royal Navy was operating jet aircraft from modern aircraft carriers, building guided-missile destroyers, and was in the process of commissioning its first nuclear-powered submarine. Although much mourned, the battleship had become obsolete as far as the Royal Navy was concerned.

And yet, some battleships still lingered on and found roles to play. At the end of the Second World War, the US Navy possessed ten modern battleships all less than eight years old, as well as two new battlecruisers. During the war, it had lost only two of the older battleships, both at Pearl Harbor, where *Arizona* had blown up and *Oklahoma* had capsized (although the latter was refloated and later foundered while under tow to San Francisco in 1947). The remaining ships were all repaired and modernized and returned to service. However, with a surfeit of modern ships, the older battleships were all available for disposal, and four (*Arkansas, New York, Nevada, Pennsylvania*) were allocated to the atomic bomb trials at Bikini Atoll in July 1946. Only *Arkansas* was actually sunk during the tests, the others being subsequently expended as targets for conventional ordnance. *Wyoming*, which had been used as a gunnery training ship during the war was scrapped in 1948, and *Texas* was handed to her name state and preserved as a memorial. *Idaho* and *New Mexico* were laid up in 1946 and both were scrapped within a couple of years. The five ships of the Tennessee and Maryland classes were all laid up by the start of 1947, but lingered on until 1959 when they were all disposed for scrap. The only active survivor of this group of older battleships was *Mississippi*, which was converted to a training and trials ship, remaining in service until 1955. At one point a Terrier guided-missile system was installed in the positions of the former X and Y gun turrets.

There was little use for even the newer ships as the US Navy concentrated resources on its carriers. The two North Carolinas and four South Dakotas were laid up in 1947, and all were disposed of in the early 1960s.

North Carolina, *Massachusetts*, and *Alabama* survive as museum ships and can be visited today. This left the four large Iowa class of which three were paid off into reserve in 1948 and 1949, leaving the USS *Missouri* as the only US battleship in commission. Consequently when the Korean War broke out she was immediately rushed into action to provide fire support for the hard-pressed ground troops ashore. Her three sister ships were each reactivated, and between them provided a continuous battleship presence throughout the conflict until 1953. Thereafter, the battleships were gradually withdrawn, the last (*Iowa*) being laid up in reserve in 1958, so that for the first time since the USS *Indiana* (BB1) was commissioned in 1895, the US Navy had no battleships in service. This might have been the end of the line except for the fact that the United States found itself in another bitter Asian war, and the USS *New Jersey* was re-commissioned in 1968 to provide fire support for troops in Vietnam. Recent information suggests that instead of conventional 16-inch shells, the *New Jersey* was also equipped with sub-caliber rocket-propelled 14-inch shells with a range of 144 km (90 miles), enabling her to engage targets far inland with the assistance of spotting aircraft. *New Jersey* returned stateside in April 1969, but after a refit was again placed in reserve.

Above: *USS* Mississippi *(BB41) replaced* Wyoming *as a training and trials ship and from 1952 was involved in guided missile firing trials, in this case Terrier surface-to-air missiles.*

However, in a surprise twist, all four ships were reactivated from 1982 onwards under President Reagan's plan for a 600-ship navy. As part of this plan, they were extensively modified to carry 32 Tomahawk cruise missiles and 16 Harpoon anti-ship missiles. The secondary armament was reduced to twelve 5-inch DP guns in three twin mountings on either beam but this was augmented by four Phalanx automatic CIWS (close-in weapon system) for close-range defense. A full outfit of modern radars was also installed. Work was quickly found for these ships. USS *New Jersey*

The last moments of the USS Pennsylvania *(BB38). She survived the 1946 atomic bomb tests at Bikini Atoll but was sunk as a target by conventional weapons in 1948.*

USS Iowa (BB61) in action carrying out a shore bombardment off Korea in 1952. Another Iowa class battleship, USS New Jersey (BB62) performed similar duties in 1968 during the Vietnam war.

Above: *A close -up of the* Iowa *in 1985. Although some of the venerable 5-inch, 38-caliber DP guns are retained, they are backed up by Harpoon anti-ship missiles and the Phalanx CIWS with their distinctive white radar domes.*

was involved in bombarding Syrian artillery positions during the Lebanese civil war in 1982. However, the ships were expensive to maintain and also engaged the resources of several thousand crew who could be better employed elsewhere. Consequently, by the time the Gulf War broke out in 1991, the *Iowa* and *New Jersey* had already been laid up. However, the other two contributed materially to the successful outcome of the fighting, launching their full complement of cruise missiles against targets up to 1,250 km (800 miles) away – a distance that Admiral Fisher and the early proponents of the battleship could hardly have dreamed of. During the actions, the *Missouri* was targeted by an Iraqi Chinese-made Silkworm anti-ship missile fired from a shore position. This was picked up by an alert radar operator on the British destroyer HMS *Gloucester*, which successfully engaged it with her Sea Dart missiles. Again, a type of warfare undreamt of only 50 years earlier.

However, this really was the end for the battleship. *Wisconsin* was paid off in September 1991, although *Missouri* was retained for a few months longer so that she could participate in ceremonies at the end of the year marking the 50th anniversary of the Japanese attack on Pearl Harbor. Officially stricken from the navy list in 1995, all four remain in existence and except for *Iowa* are available for public viewing as museum ships.

Finally, mention should be made of the Russian navy which, by a bizarre twist, has now reinvented the battlecruiser as a modern missile ship. Seven dreadnoughts were commissioned before the 1917 revolution of which three were still in existence in 1939. The Marat class displaced around 25,000 tons and carried a main armament of twelve 12-inch guns in four triple turrets unusually arranged with one each fore and aft, and two amidships on the centerline fore and aft of the second funnel. All were badly damaged by German air attacks during the war and played little part in naval operations. Two (*Gangut* and *Sevastopol*) saw brief service after 1945 but were scrapped in the mid 1950s. Under Stalin, Russia had ambitious plans to build modern battleships and battlecruisers. Two incomplete Krondstat-class battlecruiser hulls (35,000 tons, nine 12-inch guns) were available in 1945, but little work was done before they were broken up. Another hull for the battlecruiser *Stalingrad* was laid down in 1949, but work progressed slowly and ceased completely after Stalin's death in 1953.

However, the Russian navy still had a predilection for large warships and, unable to match the US Navy's carrier fleet, came up with the concept of a large nuclear-powered missile-armed capital ship. For want of any other name to apply to these unique ships they are known as battlecruisers, a not inappropriate title given their size, speed and powerful armament. Displacing just over 20,000 tons, they can make 30 knots and have a range of at least 22,500 km (14,000 miles) at that speed. In addition to the nuclear power plant, there are two conventional steam turbines. The range of missile systems carried is staggering, and includes SS-N-19 Shipwreck anti-ship missiles with a range of 400 km (250 miles) carrying nuclear or conventional warheads, three different types of surface-to-air missiles systems (SA-N-20 Grumble, SA-N-4 Gecko, SA-N-9 Gauntlet), and SS-N-15 anti-submarine missiles. In addition, there are six CIWS with 30-mm Gatling guns, and one twin 130-mm DP gun mounting. There are also torpedoes and other anti-submarine weapon systems as well as provision for up to three Ka-27 helicopters.

In all, four of these formidable Kirov-class battlecruisers were commissioned between 1982 and 1988 and were partly responsible for the re-commissioning of the US Iowa-class battleships at that time. With the end of the Cold War in the early 1990s, their running cost became astronomically high, and most were withdrawn from service and at least one has been scrapped. Nevertheless, the Russian battlecruisers remain possibly the most powerful surface warships ever built and have carried the battleship tradition into the 21st century.

Below: *The Soviet navy gave a new and potent meaning to the term* battlecruiser *with the four nuclear-powered Kirov class*.

Museum Ships: Preserved Battleships around the World

Amazingly the ironclad HMS Warrior *is still in existence, 150 years after she was launched in 1860.*

Ten true battleships are currently preserved as museum ships – and eight of those are US Navy vessels at various locations in the United States. They were saved from being scrapped following public campaigns to preserve them as memorials and museums. Of the other great naval nations, only Japan still has a battleship to show to the public, although in Britain, the ironclad HMS *Warrior* has also been restored.

HMS Warrior (9,200 tons)

Launched in December 1860, *Warrior* was the Royal Navy's first ironclad battleship, and the most powerful warship afloat when completed. She represents a unique historical resource, and her survival to the present day is remarkable. HMS *Victory* and HMS *Gannet* (a steam-powered sloop) are the only other surviving British warships from the 19th century – neither of which are ironclad. *Warrior* never saw action during her career. Withdrawn as a fighting ship in 1883, she spent over 40 years as a storage hulk and depot ship before becoming a floating oil jetty for a further 50 years. Saved by the Maritime Trust in 1979, an extraordinary eight-year restoration ended with her berthed as a museum at Portsmouth Historic Dockyard in the UK, alongside *Victory*, Nelson's flagship, and the wooden wreck of the *Mary Rose*, the pride of Henry VIII's navy, which sunk suddenly at Portsmouth in 1545.

USS Texas (BB-35, 27,000 tons)

Texas is the only surviving true dreadnought. The New York-class ship was launched in 1912 and served in both world wars, being modified numerous times. She only fired her guns in anger during the Second World

Below: *USS* Texas *in San Jacinto State Park.*

Above: *USS* Alabama, *a South Dakota Class battleship now preserved at Mobile, Alabama.*

War, providing fire support to landings in North Africa, Normandy, Iwo Jima and Okinawa.

In 1948, the ship became the first US battleship memorial museum. She is berthed at San Jacinto State Park, near Houston, Texas. Deterioration of her hull has prompted plans to place her in permanent dry dock, possibly by 2011.

USS North Carolina (BB55, 37,500 tons)
Launched in 1940 as the lead ship of her class, *North Carolina* took part in every major naval offensive in the Pacific theater. Although decommissioned in 1947, she did not become a museum ship until 1961. She is berthed at the port of Wilmington, North Carolina.

USS Massachusetts (BB-59, 35,000 tons)
Massachusetts was launched in 1941 as a battleship of the South Dakota class. She first joined the Atlantic fleet, seeing action during Operation Torch, then was transferred to the Pacific in 1943, where she saw further extensive action.

Decommissioned in 1947 she stayed in reserve until 1962, being subsequently saved from scrapping and becoming a museum in 1965. She can be seen at Battleship Cove, Fall River, Massachusetts.

USS Alabama (BB-60, 35,000 tons)
Alabama was the fourth South Dakota-class vessel, launched in 1942. In 1943 she and *South Dakota* were operational as part of the British Home Fleet for about four months before returning to the US and being assigned to the Pacific theater. Here she fired her main armament many times in support of various amphibious landings.

Like *Massachusetts*, she was decommissioned in 1947, then stayed in reserve until 1962. She became a museum ship in 1964 and is berthed at Battleship Memorial Park, Mobile, Alabama.

USS Iowa (BB-61, 45,000 tons)
Iowa was the lead ship of her class of battleships, and was launched in 1942. She transported President Roosevelt to the Tehran Conference in late 1943, then transferred to the Pacific fleet in 1944 to perform the usual battleship duties – screening aircraft carriers and shelling shore installations. Decommissioned in 1949, she was reactivated for the Korean War, before being again placed in reserve in 1958.

Under the Reagan plan for a 600-ship navy, Iowa was reactivated in 1984 and extensively modernized, with Harpoon and Tomahawk missiles being fitted. Although deployed to the Middle East in 1987–8, *Iowa* did not fire her guns in anger during this last phase of her career. In 1989, 47 sailors from the Iowa were killed in an accidental turret explosion, and the damage kept her out of the Desert Storm action in the Persian Gulf in 1991.

Decommissioned again in 1990, *Iowa* remains on the naval register, berthed at Suisun Bay, California, as part of the Reserve Fleet. In spring 2010, she was still awaiting release for use as a museum ship, the only member of her class not currently open to the public.

USS New Jersey (BB-62, 45,000 tons)
The second Iowa-class ship to be built, *New Jersey* was launched in 1942. Earning more battle stars for combat actions than any of the other three Iowa-class vessels, *New Jersey* saw action in the Pacific in the Second World War, the Korean War and the Vietnam War. Reactivated in 1982 and modernized like her three sister ships, she fired her guns during the Lebanese civil war (1983–4).

New Jersey was decommissioned in 1991, at the same time as *Missouri* and *Wisconsin* were taking part in Desert Storm. She was finally released for museum use in 1999 and can now be visited at Camden Waterfront, New Jersey.

USS Missouri (BB-63, 45,000 tons)
An Iowa-class vessel launched in 1944, *Missouri* was the last battleship built by the United States. She saw action in the Pacific theater and also in Korea. Decommissioned in 1955, she was reactivated and modernized in 1984 and provided fire support to land forces during Operation Desert Storm in 1991.

Decommissioned again in 1992, she was eventually donated as a museum ship in 1998, and is docked at Pearl Harbor, Hawaii.

63

USS Missouri*, now preserved at Pearl Harbour, Hawaii*

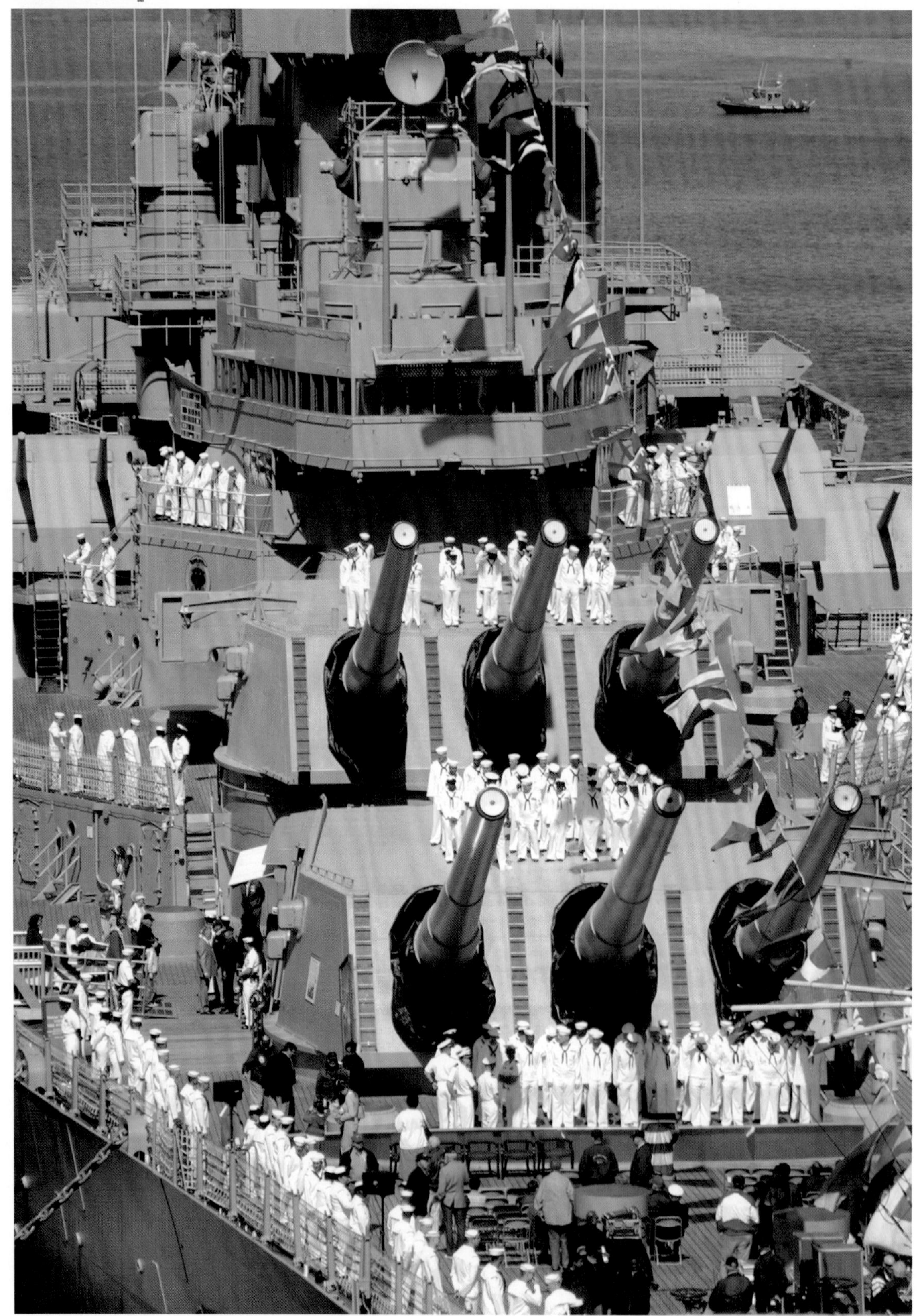

Above: *Iowa class battleship USS* Wisconsin *dressed overall on the occasion of her handover to the City of Norfolk, Virginia.*

USS Wisconsin (BB-64, 45,000 tons)

Launched in 1943, *Wisconsin* saw action in the Pacific during the Second World War, and later in Korea. Used extensively as a training ship, she remained in commission until 1958. She was reactivated and modernized in 1986. In 1991, she fired her guns and Tomahawk missiles in anger during Desert Storm, operating in company with *Missouri* for much of the time. *Wisconsin* became the last battleship to fire her guns in war.

Decommissioned in 1991, Wisconsin remained on the naval register until 2009, although during this time she was open to the public at her berth at the Hampton Roads Naval Museum, Norfolk, Virginia. *Wisconsin* was finally transferred to the City of Norfolk as a museum ship in late 2009.

Mikasa (15,000 tons)

A remarkable survivor, *Mikasa* is a pre-dreadnought battleship built by Vickers and launched in Britain in 1900. Serving as Admiral Togo's flagship at the Battle of the Yellow Sea (1904) and the Battle of Tsushima (1905), she remained in commission until 1921. She became a museum ship at Yokosuka in 1925, having a significance in Japan similar to the position of HMS *Victory* in British minds.

After the Second World War, the ship was in a very poor state, having been bombed and then having had her guns removed by the occupying forces. Between 1958 and 1961 the ship was restored. A number of missing parts and fittings (including the current 12-inch guns) came from the Chilean battleship *Almirante Latorre*, which was being scrapped in Japan at the time.

Below: *The pre-dreadnought* Mikasa *was Admiral Togo's flagship at the Battle of Tsushima in 1905. Built in Britain, she is now preserved at Yokosuka in Japan.*

List of Battleships and Battlecruisers

The following list gives details of all battleships and battlecruisers laid down in the post-dreadnought era (from 1905 onwards). Details of ships that were planned or projected but that were not laid down are not included.

Ships displacement is given in the column headed Tons. The figures given are the standard displacement. The year given relates to the year in which the ship was launched, unless otherwise stated.

Ship	Class	Tons	Year	Notes
Argentina				
Moreno	Rivadavia	28000	1911	Built in USA
Rivadavia	Rivadavia	28000	1911	Built in USA
Austro-Hungary				
Viribus Unitis	Tegetthoff	21750	1911	
Prinz Eugen	Tegetthoff	21740	1912	
Tegetthoff	Tegetthoff	21750	1912	
Szent Istvan	Tegetthoff	21750	1914	
Brazil				
Minas Gerais	Sao Paulo	19280	1908	Built in UK
Sao Paulo	Sao Paulo	19280	1909	Built in UK
Britain				
Dreadnought	Dreadnought	18110	1905	
Invincible	Invincible	17420	1907	Battlecruiser
Inflexible	Invincible	17290	1907	Battlecruiser
Indomitable	Invincible	17410	1907	Battlecruiser
Superb	Bellopheron	18800	1907	
Temeraire	Bellopheron	18800	1907	
Bellopheron	Bellopheron	18800	1907	
St Vincent	Collingwood	19560	1908	
Collingwood	Collingwood	19560	1908	
Vanguard	Collingwood	19560	1909	
Neptune	Colossus	19680	1909	
Hercules	Colossus	20225	1910	
Colossus	Colossus	20225	1910	
Indefatigable	Indefatigable	18500	1909	Battlecruiser
New Zealand	Indefatigable	18500	1911	Battlecruiser
Australia	Indefatigable	18500	1911	Battlecruiser
Orion	Orion	22200	1910	
Monarch	Orion	22200	1911	
Conquerer	Orion	22200	1911	
Thunderer	Orion	22200	1911	
Lion	Lion	26270	1910	Battlecruiser
Princess Royal	Lion	26270	1911	Battlecruiser
Queen Mary	Lion	27300	1912	Battlecruiser
King George V	King George V	23300	1911	
Centurion	King George V	23300	1911	
Ajax	King George V	23300	1912	
Audacious	King George V	23300	1912	
Iron Duke	Iron Duke	25820	1912	
Marlborough	Iron Duke	25820	1912	
Emperor of India	Iron Duke	25820	1913	
Benbow	Iron Duke	25820	1913	
Tiger	Tiger	28430	1913	Battlecruiser
Queen Elizabeth	Queen Elizabeth	29150	1913	
Warspite	Queen Elizabeth	29150	1913	
Barham	Queen Elizabeth	29150	1914	
Valiant	Queen Elizabeth	29150	1914	
Malaya	Queen Elizabeth	29150	1915	
Royal Oak	Royal Sovereign	28000	1914	
Royal Sovereign	Royal Sovereign	28000	1915	
Resolution	Royal Sovereign	28000	1915	
Revenge	Royal Sovereign	28000	1915	
Ramilles	Royal Sovereign	28000	1916	
Erin	Erin	22780	1913	ex-Turkish *Reshadije*
Agincourt	Agincourt	27500	1913	Acquired fromTurkey
Canada	Canada	28600	1913	*Almirante Latorre*
Repulse	Renown	27333	1916	Battlecruiser
Renown	Renown	27947	1916	Battlecruiser
Courageous	Courageous	19320	1916	Battlecruiser

Appendix i

Ship	Class	Tons	Year	Notes
Furious	Courageous	19513	1916	Battlecruiser
Glorious	Courageous	19320	1916	Battlecruiser
Hood	Hood	36300	1918	Battlecruiser
Nelson	Nelson	35500	1925	
Rodney	Nelson	35500	1925	
King George V	King George V	38000	1939	
Prince of Wales	King George V	38000	1939	
Howe	King George V	38000	1940	
Duke of York	King George V	38000	1940	
Anson	King George V	38000	1940	
Lion	Lion	40000		Laid down 1939. Not completed
Temeraire	Lion	40000		Laid down 1939. Not completed
Vanguard	Vanguard	44500	1944	

France

Ship	Class	Tons	Year	Notes
Danton	Danton	18400	1909	Mixed main armament
Mirabeau	Danton	18400	1909	Mixed main armament
Condorcet	Danton	18400	1909	Mixed main armament
Diderot	Danton	18400	1909	Mixed main armament
Voltaire	Danton	18400	1909	Mixed main armament
Vergniaud	Danton	18400	1910	Mixed main armament
Jean Bart	Courbet	23000	1911	
Courbet	Courbet	23000	1911	
France	Courbet	23000	1912	
Paris	Courbet	23000	1912	
Lorraine	Bretagne	23230	1913	
Provence	Bretagne	23230	1913	
Bretagne	Bretagne	23230	1913	
Normandie	Normandie	24832	1914	Not completed
Flandre	Normandie	24832	1914	Not completed
Gascogne	Normandie	24832	1914	Not completed
Languedoc	Normandie	24832	1915	Not completed
Bearn	Normandie	24832	1920	Completed as aircraft carrier 1927
Dunkerque	Dunkerque	30750	1935	Battlecruiser
Strasbourg	Dunkerque	31400	1936	Battlecruiser
Richelieu	Richelieu	40900	1939	
Jean Bart	Richelieu	40900	1940	
Clemenceau	Richelieu	40900	1940	Not completed

Germany

Ship	Class	Tons	Year	Notes
Nassau	Nassau	18569	1908	Mixed main armament
Westfallen	Nassau	18569	1908	Mixed main armament
Rheinland	Nassau	18569	1908	Mixed main armament
Posen	Nassau	18569	1908	Mixed main armament
Blucher	Blucher	15550	1908	Battlecruiser
Helgoland	Helgoland	22437	1909	
Thurigen	Helgoland	22437	1909	
Ostfriesland	Helgoland	22437	1909	
Oldenburg	Helgoland	22437	1910	
Van der Tann	Van der Tann	19064	1909	Battlecruiser
Moltke	Moltke	22616	1910	Battlecruiser
Goeben	Moltke	22616	1911	Battlecruiser
Seydlitz	Seydlitz	23707	1912	Battlecruiser
Kaiser	Kaiser	24333	1911	
Friedrich der Grosse	Kaiser	24333	1911	
Kaiserin	Kaiser	24333	1911	
Konig Albert	Kaiser	24333	1912	
Prinzregent Luitpold	Kaiser	24333	1912	
Konig	Konig	25391	1912	
Grosser Kurfurst	Konig	25391	1912	
Markgraf	Konig	25391	1913	
Kronprinz	Konig	25391	1914	
Derfflinger	Derfflinger	28180	1913	Battlecruiser
Lutzow	Derfflinger	26318	1913	Battlecruiser
Hindenburg	Derfflinger	26513	1915	Battlecruiser
Baden	Baden	28061	1915	
Bayern	Baden	28061	1915	
Sachsen	Baden	28345	1916	Not completed
Wurttemberg	Baden	28061	1916	Not completed
Mackensen	Mackensen	30510	1917	Battlecruiser. Not completed
Graf Spee	Mackensen	30510	1917	Battlecruiser. Not completed
Prince Eitel Friedrich	Mackensen	30510	1920	Battlecruiser. Not completed
Furst Bismarck	Mackensen	30510		Laid down 1915. Not completed
Ersatz Yorck	Ersatz Yorck	32971		Laid down 1916. Not completed
Ersatz Gneisenau	Ersatz Yorck	32971		CB.Laid down 1916. Not completed
Ersatz Scharnhorst	Ersatz Yorck	32971		CB.Laid down 1916. Not completed

Battleships

Ship	Class	Tons	Year	Notes
Gneisenau	Scharnhorst	34841	1936	Battlecruiser
Scharnhorst	Scharnhorst	34841	1936	Battlecruiser
Deutschland	Deutschland	13000	1931	Panzerschiff (*Lutzow*)
Admiral Scheer	Deutschland	13000	1933	Panzerschiff
Admiral Graf Spee	Deutschland	13880	1934	Panzerschiff
Bismarck	Bismarck	45712	1939	
Tirpitz	Bismarck	46400	1939	
Battleship H	H Class	55453		Laid down 1939. Not completed
Battleship J	H Class	55453		Laid down 1939. Not completed

Italy

Ship	Class	Tons	Year	Notes
Dante Alighieri	Dante Alighieri	19500	1910	
Conte di Cavour	Cavour	23088	1911	
Giulio Cesare	Cavour	23088	1911	
Leonardo da Vinci	Cavour	23088	1911	
Caio Dulio	Dulio	22694	1913	
Andrea Doria	Dulio	22694	1913	
Cristoforo Colombo	Caracciolo	32800		Laid down 1915. Not completed
Francesco Morosini	Caracciolo	32800		Laid down 1915. Not completed
Marcantonio Colonna	Caracciolo	32800		Laid down 1915. Not completed
Francesco Caracciolo	Caracciolo	32800	1920	Not completed
Italia (Littorio)	Littorio	43835	1937	
Vittorio Veneto	Littorio	43624	1937	
Impero	Littorio	44050	1939	Not completed
Roma	Littorio	44050	1940	

Japan

Ship	Class	Tons	Year	Notes
Satsuma	Satsuma	19372	1906	Designed armament not fitted
Aki	Aki	19800	1907	Designed armament not fitted
Kawachi	Kawachi	20823	1910	
Settsu	Kawachi	21443	1911	
Kongo	Kongo	27500	1912	Battlecruiser. Built in UK
Hiei	Kongo	27500	1912	Battlecruiser
Haruna	Kongo	27613	1913	Battlecruiser
Kirishima	Kongo	27613	1913	Battlecruiser
Fuso	Fuso	30600	1914	
Yamashiro	Fuso	30600	1915	
Ise	Ise	31260	1916	
Hyuga	Ise	31260	1917	
Nagato	Nagato	33800	1919	
Mutsu	Nagato	33800	1920	
Kaga	Tosa	39330	1921	Completed as aircraft carrier
Tosa	Tosa	39330	1921	Not completed
Amagi	Amagi	41217		Laid down 1920. Not completed
Atago	Amagi	41217		Laid down 1921. Not completed
Takao	Amagi	41217		Laid down 1921. Not completed
Akagi	Amagi	41217	1925	Completed as aircraft carrier
Yamato	Yamato	69100	1940	
Musashi	Yamato	69100	1941	
Shinano	Yamato	69100	1944	Completed as aircraft carrier
No.111	No.111	69100		Laid down 1940. Not completed

Russia

Ship	Class	Tons	Year	Notes
Gangut	Gangut	23000	1911	
Poltava	Gangut	23000	1911	
Sevastopol	Gangut	23000	1911	
Petropavlovsk	Gangut	23000	1911	
Imperatritsa Maria	Imperatritsa Maria	22800	1913	
Ekaterina II	Imperatritsa Maria	22800	1914	
Imperator Aleksander III	Imperatritsa Maria	22800	1915	
Imperator Nikolai I	Imperatritsa Maria	22800	1916	Not completed
Borodino	Borodino	32500	1915	Not completed
Izmail	Borodino	32500	1915	Not completed
Kinburn	Borodino	32500	1915	Not completed
Navarin	Borodino	32500	1916	Not completed
Sovietski Soyuz	Sovietski Soyuz	59000		Laid down 1938. Not completed
Sovietskaya Ukraina	Sovietski Soyuz	59000		Laid down 1938. Not completed
Sevastapol	Kronstadt	35000		Laid down 1939. Not completed
Kronstadt	Kronstadt	35000		Laid down 1939. Not completed
Stalingrad	Stalingrad	42000		Laid down 1949. Not completed

Spain

Ship	Class	Tons	Year	Notes
Espana	Espana	15500	1912	Built in UK
Alfonso XIII	Espana	15500	1913	Built in UK
Jaime I	Espana	15500	1914	Built in UK

Turkey

Ship	Class	Tons	Year	Notes
Fatikh	Fatikh	24700		Laid down 1914. Not Completed

Appendix i

Ship	Class	Tons	Year	Notes
United States				
South Carolina	South Carolina	16000	1908	BB26
Michigan	South Carolina	16000	1908	BB27
Delaware	Delaware	20380	1909	BB28
North Dakota	Delaware	20000	1908	BB29
Florida	Florida	21825	1910	BB30
Utah	Florida	21825	1909	BB31
Wyoming	Wyoming	26000	1911	BB32
Arkansas	Wyoming	26000	1911	BB33
New York	New York	27000	1912	BB34
Texas	New York	27000	1912	BB35
Nevada	Nevada	27500	1914	BB36
Oklahoma	Nevada	27500	1914	BB37
Pennsylvania	Pennsylvania	31400	1915	BB38
Arizona	Pennsylvania	31400	1915	BB39
New Mexico	New Mexico	32000	1917	BB40
Mississippi	New Mexico	32000	1917	BB41
Idaho	New Mexico	32000	1917	BB42
Tennessee	Tennessee	32300	1919	BB43
California	Tennessee	32300	1919	BB44
Colorado	Colorado	32600	1921	BB45
Maryland	Colorado	32600	1920	BB46
West Virginia	Colorado	32600	1921	BB48
Washington	Colorado	32600	1921	BB47 Not completed
South Dakota	South Dakota	43200		BB49. Laid down 1919. Not completed
Indiana	South Dakota	43200		BB50. Laid down 1919. Not completed
Montana	South Dakota	43200		BB51. Laid down 1919. Not completed
North Carolina	South Dakota	43200		BB52. Laid down 1919. Not completed
Iowa	South Dakota	43200		BB53. Laid down 1919. Not completed
Massachusetts	South Dakota	43200		BB54. Laid down 1920. Not completed
Lexington	Lexington	43500	1925	CC1. Completed as aircraft carrier
Saratoga	Lexington	43500	1925	CC3. Completed as aircraft carrier
Constitution	Lexington	43500		CC5. Laid down 1920. Not completed
Constellation	Lexington	43500		CC2. Laid down 1920. Not completed
Ranger	Lexington	43500		CC4. Laid down 1920. Not completed
United States	Lexington	43500		CC6. Laid down 1920. Not completed
North Carolina	North Carolina	38000	1940	BB55
Washington	North Carolina	38000	1940	BB56
South Dakota	South Dakota	38000	1941	BB57
Indiana	South Dakota	38000	1941	BB58
Massachusetts	South Dakota	38000	1941	BB59
Alabama	South Dakota	38000	1942	BB60
Iowa	Iowa	48500	1942	BB61
New Jersey	Iowa	48500	1942	BB62
Missouri	Iowa	48500	1944	BB63
Wisconsin	Iowa	48500	1943	BB64
Illinois	Iowa	48500		BB65. Laid down 1945. Not completed
Kentucky	Iowa	48500	1950	BB66 Not completed
Alaska	Alaska	29000	1943	CB1
Guam	Alaska	29000	1943	CB2
Hawaii	Alaska	29000	1945	CB3 Not completed

Battleship Specifications 1905–1945

The following notes give the main details of the major battleship and battlecruisers built since HMS *Dreadnought* in 1905. For comparison purposes, the Standard Displacement is given which is defined as the mass of the ship including hull, machinery, armor, armament as well as crew, normal ammunition stocks and fresh water for domestic purposes. It does not include oil fuel, boiler feed water and additional equipment, which in total could add several thousand tons and the more realistic full-load displacement is therefore quoted in most cases.

Armor thickness relates to the maximum figure in each case.

See **Appendix i** for a list of ships in each class.

Great Britain

HMS Resolution, *R Class, launched 1915*

Dreadnought. Data as completed 1906

Displacement: 17,900 tons
Length: 161 meters; 527 feet
Beam: 25 meters; 82 feet
Draught: 8 meters; 27 feet
Machinery: 18 boilers. Parsons steam turbines. 4 shafts. 23000 shp.
Speed: 21 knots
Protection: Main belt 28 cm (11 inches), end bulkheads 20 cm (8 inches), decks 10 cm (4 inches), turrets 28 cm (11 inches), barbettes 28 cm (11 inches) max.
Armament: Guns: Ten 12-inch (5 x 2), twenty-seven 12-pounders (27 x 1) Torpedoes: Five 18-inch TT (fixed)
Complement: 697

Invincible/Indefatigable-class battlecruisers.
Data HMS *Invincible* 1908

Displacement: 17,250 tons
Length: 173 meters; 567 feet
Beam: 24 meters; 78.5 feet
Draught: 8 meters; 27 feet
Machinery: 31 Yarrow boilers, Parsons turbines, 4 shafts. 41,000 shp.
Speed: 25 knots
Protection: Main belt 15 cm (6 inches), end bulkheads 18 cm (7 inches), decks 5 cm (2 inches), turrets 18 cm (7 inches), barbettes 18 cm (7 inches).
Armament: Guns: Eight 12-inch (4 x 2), sixteen 4-inch (16 x 1). Torpedoes: Five 18-inch TT (fixed)
Complement: 784
Notes: *Indefatigable* class similar but lengthened hull (180 meters; 590 feet) and displacement 18,800 tons

Bellerophon/St.Vincent/Neptune Classes.
Data HMS *Neptune* 1911

Displacement: 19,900 tons
Length: 166 meters; 546 feet
Beam: 26 meters; 85 feet
Draught: 8.5 meters; 29 feet (full load)
Machinery: 18 boilers, Parsons turbines, 4 shafts. 25,000 shp
Protection: Main belt 25 cm (10 inches), end bulkheads 20 cm (8 inches), decks 10 cm (4 inches), turrets 28 cm (11 inches), barbettes 23 cm (9 inches).
Armament: Guns: Ten 12-inch (5 x 2), sixteen 4-inch (16 x 1), four 3-pounders (4 x 1). Torpedoes: Three 18-inch TT (fixed)

Complement: 755
Notes: These three classes were progressive improvements of the Dreadnought design with only minor variations although displacement increased slightly in each class.

Orion/King George V class. Data HMS *Orion* 1912
Displacement: 22,500 tons
Length: 177 meters; 581 feet
Beam: 27 meters; 88.5 feet
Draught: 8.5 meters; 28 feet
Machinery: 18 boilers, Parsons turbines, 4 shafts. 27,000 shp.
Speed: 21 knots.
Protection: Main belt 30 cm (12 inches), end bulkheads 25 cm (10 inches), decks 10 cm (4 inches) max, turrets 28 cm (11 inches), barbettes 25 cm (10 inches).
Armament: Guns: Ten 13.5-inch (5 x 2), sixteen 4-inch (16 x 1), four 3-pounders (4 x 1). Torpedoes: Three 21-inch TT (fixed)
Complement: 752
Notes: *King George V* class similar. Displacement 23,000 tons, length 597 feet.

Lion-class battlecruisers. Data HMS *Lion* 1912
Displacement: 26,350 tons (25,870 tons full load)
Length: 213 meters; 700 feet
Beam: 27 meters; 88.5 feet
Draught: 8.8 meters; 29 feet
Machinery: 42 Yarrow boilers, Parsons turbines, 4 shafts. 70,000 shp.
Speed: 27 knots
Protection: Main belt 23 cm (9 inches), end bulkheads 10 cm (4 inches), decks 2.5 cm (1 inch), turrets 23 cm (9 inches), barbettes 23 cm (9 inches).
Armament: Guns: Eight 13.5-inch (4 x 2), sixteen 4-inch (16 x 1), four 3-pounders (4 x 1). Torpedoes: Two 21-inch TT (fixed)
Complement: 997

Iron Duke class. Data HMS *Iron Duke* 1914
Displacement: 26,100 tons (30,380 tons full load)
Length: 190 meters; 622.75 feet
Beam: 27.5 meters; 90 feet
Draught: 9 meters; 30 feet
Machinery: 18 boilers, Parsons turbines, 4 shafts. 29,000 shp.
Speed: 21 knots
Protection: Main belt 30 cm (12 inches), end bulkheads 20 cm (8 inches), decks 6 cm (2.5 inches), turrets 28 cm (11 inches), barbettes 25 cm (10 inches).
Armament: Guns: Ten 13.5-inch (5 x 2), twelve 6-inch (12 x 1), four 3-pounders (4 x 1). Torpedoes: Four 21-inch TT (fixed)
Complement: 952

Tiger-class battlecruiser. Data HMS *Tiger* 1914
Displacement: 28,500 tons
Length: 214.5 meters; 704 feet
Beam: 27.5 meters; 90.5 feet
Draught: 9.75 meters; 32 feet
Machinery: 39 boilers, Brown-Curtis turbines, 4 shafts. 108,000 shp.
Speed: 29 knots
Protection: Main belt 23 cm (9 inches), decks 7.5 cm (3 inches), turrets 23 cm (9 inches), barbettes 23 cm (9 inches).
Armament: Guns: Eight 13.5-inch (4 x 2), twelve 6-inch (12 x 1), four 3-pounders. Torpedoes: Four 21-inch TT (fixed)
Complement: 1,121

Agincourt class. Data HMS *Agincourt* 1914
Displacement: 27,500 tons
Length: 204 meters; 671.5 feet
Beam: 27 meters; 89 feet
Draught: 9.5 meters; 31 feet
Machinery: 22 boilers, Parsons turbines, 4 shafts. 34,000 shp.
Speed: 22 knots
Protection: Main belt 23 cm (9 inches), bulkheads 15 cm (6 inches), decks 6 cm (2.5 inches), turrets 30 cm (12 inches), barbettes 23 cm (9 inches).
Armament: Guns: Fourteen 12-inch (7 x 2), twenty 6-inch (20 x 1), ten 3-inch (10 x 1). Torpedoes: Three 21-inch TT (fixed)
Complement: 1,115

Queen Elizabeth class. Data HMS *Queen Elizabeth* as modernized
Displacement: 31,585 tons (36,500 tons full load)
Length: 196 meters; 643 feet
Beam: 27.5 meters; 90.5 feet (104 feet across bulges)
Draught: 10.5 meters; 35 feet at full load
Machinery: 8 boilers, 4 shafts, Parsons SR geared turbines. 80,000 shp.

Speed:	24 knots
Protection:	Main belt 33 cm (13 inches), upper belt 15 cm (6 inches), end bulkheads 15 cm (6 inches), funnel casing and uptakes 10 cm (4 inches), decks 9 cm (3.5 inches), over magazines 12.5 cm (5 inches). Turrets 33 cm (13 inches) on faces, 28 cm (11 inches) sides, 12.5 cm (5 inches) crowns, barbettes 25 cm (10 inches) max. Hull bulges.
Armament:	Eight 15-inch (4 x 2), twenty 4.5-inch DP (10 x 2), thirty-two 2-pounders AA (4 x 8), sixteen 0.5-inch AA (4 x 4).
Complement:	1,124+
Aircraft:	3. One catapult

Royal Sovereign class. Data HMS *Resolution* 1916

Displacement:	27,500 tons (31,290 tons full load)
Length:	190 meters; 624.25 feet
Beam:	27 meters; 88.5 feet
Draught:	8.8 meters; 29 feet
Machinery:	18 Yarrow boilers, Parsons direct and geared turbines, 4 shafts. 40,000 shp.
Speed:	23 knots
Armament:	Guns: Eight 15-inch (4 x 2), fourteen 6-inch (14 x 1), two 3-inch AA (2 x 1). Torpedoes: Four 21-inch TT (fixed)
Complement:	936

Renown-class battlecruisers. Data HMS *Renown* as modernized 1940

Displacement:	32,000 tons (37,410 tons full load)
Length:	229 meters; 750 feet (pp), 794 feet
Beam:	26.5 meters; 87 feet (31 meters; 103 feet over bulges)
Draught:	9.6 meters; 31.5 feet (full load)
Machinery:	42 boilers, 4 shafts, Brown-Curtis turbines. 112.000 shp.
Speed:	29 knots
Protection:	Main belt 23 cm (9 inches), bulkheads 10 cm (4 inches), main deck 12.5 cm (5 inches) max. Turrets 28 cm (11 inches), faces and barbettes 18 cm (7 inches) max. Externally bulged
Armament:	Guns: Six 15-inch (3 x 2), twenty 4.5-inch DP (10 x 2), twenty-four 2-pounders AA (3 x 8), sixteen 0.5-inch AA (4 x 4). Torpedoes: eight, 18-inch fixed tubes (4 x 2)
Complement:	1,309
Aircraft:	4. One athwartships catapult

Hood (battlecruiser). Data as at May 1941

Displacement:	42,100 tons (46,200 full load)
Length:	262 meters; 861 feet
Beam:	29 meters; 95 feet
Draught:	9.6 meters; 31.5 feet (full load)
Machinery:	24 Yarrow boilers, 4 shafts, Brown-Curtis turbines. 144,000 shp.
Speed:	31 knots
Protection:	Main belt 30 cm (12 inches) max., bulkheads 23 cm (9 inches), decks 7.5 cm (3 inches). Turrets 38 cm (15 inches) face, 30 cm (12 inches) sides max., 12.5 cm (5 inches) crowns. Barbettes 30 cm (12 inches) max. External bulges
Armament:	Guns: Eight 15-inch (4 x 2), fourteen 4-inch AA (6 x 2), twenty-four 2-pounders AA (3 x 8), six 20-mm AA (6 x 1). Rockets: Five 20-barreled UP rocket projectors. Torpedoes: Four fixed 21-inch torpedo tubes.
Complement:	1,420

Nelson class. Data HMS *Nelson* 1939

Displacement:	33,950 tons (38,000 tons full load)
Length:	216 meters; 710 feet
Beam:	32 meters; 106 feet
Draught:	9.6 meters; 31.5 feet (full load)
Machinery:	8 boilers, 2 shafts, Brown-Curtis SR geared turbines. 45,000 shp.
Speed:	23 knots
Protection:	Main belt 36 cm (14 inches), bulkheads 23 cm (9 inches), middle deck 15 cm (6 inches) maximum. Turrets 41 cm (16 inches) faces, 30 cm (12 inches) sides, 23 cm (9 inches) crowns, barbettes 36 cm (14 inches). Internal bulges.
Armament:	Guns: Nine 16-inch (3 x 3), twelve 6-inch (6 x 2), six 4.7-inch AA (3 x 2), thirty-two 2-pounders AA (3 x 8 and 8 x 1), sixteen 0.5-inch AA (4 x 4). Torpedoes: Two 24.5-inch (2 x 1) fixed torpedo tubes.
Complement:	1,314
Aircraft:	1 (2 in *Rodney*)

King George V class. Data as designed
Displacement: 35,000 tons (40,000 full load)
Length: 227 meters; 745 feet
Beam: 31 meters; 103 feet
Draught: 9.6 meters; 31.5 feet (full load)
Machinery: 8 boilers, 4 shafts, Parsons SR geared turbines. 110,000 shp.
Speed: 29 knots
Protection: Main belt 38 cm (15 inches) (maximum, bulkheads 30 cm (12 inches), Main deck 15 cm (6 inches). Turrets, 33 cm (13 inches) faces, 23 cm (9 inches) sides, 18 cm (7 inches) rear, 15 cm (6 inches) crowns. Barbettes 33 cm (13 inches). Internal bulges
Armament: Ten 14-inch (2 x 4, 1 x 2), sixteen 5.25-inch DP (8 x 2), thirty-two 2-pounders AA (4 x 8), sixteen 0.5-inch AA (4 x 4).
Complement: 1,612
Aircraft: 3. Fixed athwartships catapult

United States

USS *New York (BB34)* in 1935.

South Carolina class. Data USS *South Carolina (BB26)* 1910
Displacement: 16,000 tons
Length: 138 meters; 452.75 feet
Beam: 24.5 meters; 80.25 feet
Draught: 7.5 meters; 24.5 feet
Machinery: 12 boilers, VTE reciprocating machinery, 2 shafts. 16,500 ihp.
Speed: 18.5 knots
Protection: Main belt 28 cm (11 inches), end bulkheads 25 cm (10 inches), decks 7.5 cm (3 inches), turrets 30 cm (12 inches), barbettes 25 cm (10 inches).
Armament: Eight 12-inch (4 x 2), twenty-two 3-inch (22 x 1). Torpedoes: Two 21-inch TT (fixed)
Complement: 869

Delaware/Florida class. Data USS *Delaware (BB28)* 1910
Displacement: 20,380 tons
Length: 158 meters; 518.75 feet
Beam: 26 meters; 85.25 feet
Draught: 8.8 meters; 29 feet
Machinery: 14 boilers, VTE reciprocating machinery, 2 shafts. 25,000 ihp.
Speed: 21 knots
Protection: Main belt 28 cm (11 inches), turrets 30 cm (12 inches), barbettes 25 cm (10 inches).
Armament: Guns: Ten 12-inch (5 x 2), fourteen 5-inch (14 x 1), two 3-pounders (2 x 1). Torpedoes: Two 21-inch TT (fixed)
Complement: 945
Notes: *Florida* class similar but turbine powered, 4 shafts, 28,000 shp, 20,75 knots.

Wyoming class. Data USS *Wyoming (BB32)* 1912
Displacement: 26,000 tons
Length: 171 meters; 562 feet
Beam: 28.5 meters; 93.25 feet
Draught: 8.8 meters; 29 feet
Machinery: 12 boilers, Parsons turbines, 4 shafts. 26,000 shp.
Speed: 20.5 knots
Protection: Main belt 28 cm (11 inches), end bulkheads 28 cm (11 inches), turrets 30 cm (12 inches), barbettes 28 cm (11 inches).
Armament: Guns: Twelve 12-inch (6 x 2), twenty-one 5-inch (21 x 1). Torpedoes: Two 21-inch TT (fixed)
Complement: 1,063

Texas class. Data USS *Texas* 1944
Displacement: 27,000 tons (32,000 tons full load)
Length: 174.5 meters; 573 feet
Beam: 30 meters; 95 feet
Draught: 9.6 meters; 31.5 feet full loaf
Machinery: 6 boilers, VTE reciprocating machinery, 2 shafts. 28,100 ihp.

Speed: 21 knots
Protection: Main belt 30 cm (12 inches) max, bulkheads 25 cm (10 inches), main deck 6 cm (2.5 inches) (max, lower deck 3.5in (max). Turrets 36 cm (14 inches) max, barbettes 30 cm (12 inches). External bulges
Armament: Ten 14-inch (5 x 2), six 5-inch (6 x 1), ten 3-inch AA (10 x 1), forty 40-mm AA(10 x 4), forty 20-mm AA (40 x 1)
Complement: 1,530
Aircraft: 3. Catapult mounted on Q turret amidships

Nevada class. Data USS *Oklahoma (BB37)* 1940
Displacement: 29,000 tons (34,000 tons full load)
Length: 177.5 meters; 583 feet
Beam: 29 meters; 95.25 feet (33 meters; 108 feet over bulges)
Draught: 9.75 meters; 32 feet full load
Machinery: Oklahoma: 6 boilers, VTE reciprocating machinery, two shafts. 24,800 ihp (Nevada: geared turbines, 26,500 shp).
Speed: 20.5 knots
Protection: Main belt 33 cm (13 inches), bulkheads 33 cm (13 inches), decks 7.5 cm (3 inches) max. Turrets 45 cm (18 inches) faces, 25 cm (10 inches) sides, 23 cm (9 inches) rears, 12.5 cm (5 inches) crowns. Barbettes 13.5in (above decks). External bulges.
Armament: Ten 14-inch (2 x 3, 2 x 2), twelve 5-inch, 51 caliber (12 x 1), eight 5-inch, 25 caliber AA (8 x 1).
Complement: c.2,000
Aircraft: 3. Two catapults–stern and atop X turret

Pennsylvania class. Data USS *Pennsylvania (BB38)* 1943
Displacement: 33,100 tons (36,500 tons full load)
Length: 185 meters; 608 feet
Beam: 29.5 meters; 97 feet (32 meters; 106.25 feet over bulges)
Draught: 10 meters; 33 feet full load
Machinery: 6 boilers, geared turbines, 4 shafts. 31,500 shp.
Speed: 21 knots
Protection: Main belt 36 cm (14 inches), bulkheads 36 cm (14 inches), decks 10 cm (4 inches), funnel and boiler uptakes 18 cm (15 inches). Turrets 46 cm (18 inches) faces, 25 cm (10 inches) sides, 23 cm (9 inches) rear, 12.5 cm (5 inches) crowns. Barbettes 36 cm (14 inches). External bulges.
Armament: Twelve 14-inch (4 x 3), sixteen 5-inch DP (8 x 2), forty 40-mm AA (10 x 4), fifty 20-mm AA (50 x 1).
Complement: 2,290
Aircraft: 3. One stern catapult

New Mexico/Tennessee classes. Data USS *New Mexico (BB40)* 1940
Displacement: 33,400 tons (36,000 tons full load)
Length: 190 meters; 624 feet
Beam: 29.5 meters; 97.5 feet (32 meters; 106.25 feet over bulges)
Draught: 10.25 meters; 34 feet full load
Machinery: 4 (6 in *Mississippi* and *Idaho*) boilers, geared turbines, four shafts. 40,000 shp
Speed: 21.5 knots
Range: 9000 sm at 12 knots
Protection: Main belt 36 cm (14 inches), bulkheads 36 cm (14 inches), uptakes and funnel 41 cm (16 inches), decks 15 cm (6 inches) max. Turrets 46 cm (18 inches), barbettes 36 cm (14 inches). External bulges.
Armament: Twelve 14-inch (4 x 3), twelve 5-inch, 51 caliber (12 x 1), eight 5-inch, 25 caliber AA (8 x 1), twelve 1.1-inch AA (3 x 4)
Complement: 1,930
Aircraft: 3. Two catapults

Colorado class. Data USS *Maryland (BB46)* as reconstructed 1944-45
Displacement: 31,500 tons (39,100 tons full load)
Length: 190 meters; 624 feet
Beam: 29.5 meters; 97.5 feet (33 meters; 108 feet over bulges)
Draught: 10.5 meters; 35 feet full load
Machinery: 8 boilers, Curtis geared turbines (28,900shp), electric motors (27,200shp), four shafts.
Speed: 21 knots
Protection: Main belt 41 cm (16 inches), bulkheads 36 cm (14 inches),

	uptakes 41 cm (16 inches), decks 6 cm (2.5 inches), turrets 46 cm (18 inches), barbettes 41 cm (16 inches) (max). Externally bulges.
Armament:	Eight 16-inch (4 x 2), sixteen 5-inch DP (8 x 2), forty 40-mm (10 x 4), thirty-six 20-mm AA (36 x 1).
Complement:	c.2,000
Aircraft:	3. Stern catapult

North Carolina class. Data USS *Washington (BB56)* as completed 1941

Displacement:	35,000 tons (45,370 tons full load)
Length:	222 meters; 729 feet
Beam:	33 meters; 108 feet
Draught:	10.5 meters; 35 feet
Machinery:	8 boilers, General Electric geared turbines, 4 shafts. 121,000 shp.
Speed:	28 knots
Protection:	Main belt 41 cm (16 inches) max, bulkheads 41 cm (16 inches), main deck 15 cm (6 inches), lower deck 10 cm (4 inches), turrets 46 cm (18 inches) (max), barbettes 41 cm (16 inches).
Armament:	Nine 16-inch (3 x 3), twenty 5-inch DP (10 x 2), sixteen 1.1-inch AA (4 x 4), twelve 0.5-inch AA (12 x 1)
Complement:	2,339
Aircraft:	3. Two stern catapults

South Dakota class. Data USS *Indiana (BB50)* as completed 1942

Displacement:	35,000 tons (44, 370 tons full load)
Length:	207.25 meters; 680 feet
Beam:	33 meters; 108.25 feet
Draught:	11 meters; 36 feet full load
Machinery:	8 boilers, geared turbines, 4 shafts. 130,000 shp.
Speed:	28 knots
Protection:	Main belt 41 cm (16 inches) max, bulkheads 41 cm (16 inches), main deck 15 cm (6 inches), lower deck 10 cm (4 inches), turrets 46 cm (18 inches) (max), barbettes 41 cm (16 inches).
Armament:	Nine 16-inch (3 x 3), twenty 5-inch DP (10 x 2), fifty six 40-mm AA (14 x 4), forty 20-mm AA (40 x 1).
Complement:	c.2,300
Aircraft:	3. Two stern catapults

Iowa class. Data USS *New Jersey (BB62)* as completed 1943

Displacement:	45,000 tons (57,450 tons full load)
Length:	270 meters; 887 feet
Beam:	33 meters; 108 feet
Draught:	11 meters; 36 feet full load
Machinery:	8 boilers, geared turbines, 4 shafts. 212,000 shp.
Speed:	33 knots
Protection:	Main belt 41 cm (16 inches) max, bulkheads 41 cm (16 inches), main deck 15 cm (6 inches), lower deck 10 cm (4 inches), turrets 46 cm (18 inches) max, barbettes 41 cm (16 inches).
Armament:	Nine 16-inch (3 x 3), twenty 5-inch DP (10 x 2), sixty-four 40-mm AA (16 x 4), sixty 20-mm AA (60 x 1).
Complement:	2,750–3,000
Aircraft:	3. Two stern catapults

Alaska-class battlecruisers. Data USS *Alaska (CB1)* as completed

Displacement:	27,500 tons (34,250 tons full load)
Length:	246 meters; 808.5 feet
Beam:	27.75 meters; 91 feet
Draught:	9.75 meters; 32 feet full load
Machinery:	8 boilers, geared turbines, 4 shafts. 150,000 shp.
Speed:	33 knots
Protection:	Main belt 23 cm (9 inches) max, bulkheads 23 cm (9 inches), decks 11 cm (4.5 inches). Turrets 32 cm (12.5 inches) faces, 12.5 cm (5 inches), sides, rear, crown, barbettes 23 cm (9 inches).
Armament:	Nine 12-inch (3 x 3), twelve 5-inch DP (6 x 2), fifty six 40-mm AA (14 x 4), thirty-four 20-mm (34 x 1).
Complement:	2,250
Aircraft:	4 . Two catapults

France

Courbet class. Data *Courbet* 1913

Displacement:	23,190 tons
Length:	168 meters; 551 feet
Beam:	27.75 meters; 91.5 feet
Draught:	9 meters; 30 feet
Machinery:	24 Belville boilers, Parsons turbines, 4 shafts. 28,000 shp.

Speed:	21 knots
Protection:	Main belt 30 cm (12 inches), decks 7.5 cm (3 inches), turrets 32 cm (12.5 inches), barbettes 28 cm (11 inches).
Armament:	Guns: Twelve 12-inch (6 x 2), twenty-two 5.5-inch (22 x 1). Torpedoes: Four 17.7-inch TT (fixed)
Complement:	1,108

Bretagne class. Data *Lorraine* 1916

Displacement:	23,320 tons (28,500 tons full load)
Length:	166 meters; 544.75 feet
Beam:	27 meters; 88.5 feet
Draught:	9.75 meters; 32 feet
Machinery:	24 boilers, Parsons turbines, 4 shafts. 29,000 shp.
Speed:	20 knots
Protection:	Main belt 28 cm (11 inches), decks 5 cm (2 inches), turrets 43 cm (17 inches), barbettes 28 cm (11 inches).
Armament:	Guns: Ten 13.4-inch (5 x 2), twenty-two 5.5-inch (22 x 1), four 47-mm AA. Torpedoes: Four 17.7-inch TT (fixed)
Complement:	1,113

Dunkerque class. Data *Dunkerque* as completed

Displacement:	26,500 tons (33,000 tons full load)
Length:	214.5 meters; 704 feet
Beam:	31 meters; 102 feet
Draught:	9.6 meters; 31.5 feet full load
Machinery:	6 boilers, 4 shafts, Parsons SR geared turbines. 112,500 shp.
Speed:	29.5 knots
Protection:	Main belt 25 cm (9.75 inches) max, bulkheads 23 cm (9 inches) max, main deck 12.5 cm (5 inches). Turrets 33 cm (13 inches) faces, 25 cm (10 inches) sides, 15 cm (6 inches) crowns. Internal anti-torpedo bulkheads.
Armament:	Eight 13-inch (2 x 4), sixteen 5.1-inch DP (3 x 4, 2 x 2), eight 37-mm AA (4 x 2), thirty-two 13.2-mm AA (8 x 4).
Complement:	1,431
Aircraft:	4. Stern mounted catapult

Richelieu class. Data *Richelieu* final design

Displacement:	35,000 tons (47,500 full load)
Length:	248 meters; 813 feet
Beam:	33 meters; 108 feet
Draught:	9.5 meters; 31.75 feet full load
Machinery:	6 boilers, 4 shafts, Parsons SR geared turbines. 150,000 shp.
Speed:	30 knots
Protection:	Main belt 34 cm (13.5 inches), bulkheads 38 cm (15 inches) max, main deck 17 cm (6.75 inches). Turrets 45 cm (17.5 inches) faces, 27 cm (10.5 inches) sides, 19 cm (7.75 inches) crowns.
Armament:	Eight 15-inch (2 x 4), nine 6-inch DP (3 x 3), twelve 3.9-inch AA (6 x 2), twelve 37-mm AA (6 x 2), twenty-four 13.2-mm AA (6 x 4)
Complement:	1,550
Aircraft:	3. Two stern catapults.

Germany

SMS Westfalen. Nassau class. Launched 1908

Nassau class. Data *Nassau* 1909

Displacement:	18,875 tons
Length:	146 meters; 479.5 feet
Beam:	27 meters; 88.5 feet
Draught:	8.8 meters; 29 feet
Machinery:	12 boilers, VTE reciprocating machinery, 3 shafts. 22,000 ihp.
Speed:	19.5 knots
Protection:	Main belt 29 cm (11.4 inches), decks 8 cm (3.2 inches), turrets 28 cm (11 inches), barbettes 28 cm (11 inches).
Armament:	Guns: Twelve 11-inch (6 x 2), twelve 5.9-inch (12 x 1), sixteen 3.5-inch. Torpedoes: Six 17.7-inch TT (fixed)
Complement:	1,008

Von der Tann-class battlecruiser. Data *Von der Tann* 1910

Displacement:	19,370 tons

Length: 171.5 meters; 563.25 feet
Beam: 26.5 meters; 87.25 feet
Draught: 9 meters; 30 feet
Machinery: 18 boilers, Parsons turbines, 4 shafts. 42,000 shp.
Speed: 24.75 knots
Protection: Main belt 25 cm (10 inches), decks 7.5 cm (3 inches), turrets 23 cm (9 inches), barbettes 23 cm (9 inches).
Armament: Guns: Eight 11-inch (4 x 2), ten 5.9-inch (10 x 1), sixteen 3.5-inch (16 x 1). Torpedoes: Four 17.7-inch TT (fixed)
Complement: 910

Helgoland class. Data *Helgoland* 1911
Displacement: 22,800 tons
Length: 167 meters; 548.5 feet
Beam: 28.5 meters; 93.5 feet
Draught: 9 meters; 29.25 feet
Machinery: 15 boilers, VTE reciprocating machinery, 3 shafts. 28,000 ihp.
Speed: 20.3 knots
Protection: Main belt 29.5 cm (11.75 inches), decks 6 cm (2.25 inches), turrets 29.5 cm (11.75 inches), barbettes 27 cm (10.5 inches).
Armament: Guns: Twelve 12-inch (6 x 2), fourteen 5.9-inch (14 x 1), fourteen 3.5-inch (14 x 1). Torpedoes: Six 19.7-inch TT (fixed)
Complement: 1,100

Moltke/Seydlitz-class battlecruisers. Data *Moltke* 1911
Displacement: 22,980 tons
Length: 186.5 meters; 612 feet
Beam: 29.5 meters; 96.75 feet
Draught: 9 meters; 30 feet
Machinery: 24 boilers, Parsons turbines, 4 shafts. 52,000 shp.
Speed: 25.5 knots
Protection: Main belt 28 cm (11 inches), decks 6 cm (2.5 inches), turrets 25 cm (10 inches), barbettes 25 cm (10 inches).
Armament: Guns: Ten 11-inch (5 x 2), twelve 5.9-inch (12 x 1), twelve 3.5-inch (12 x 1). Torpedoes: Four 19.7-inch TT (fixed)
Complement: 1,107
Notes: *Seydlitz* similar but larger, 24,990 tons, 67,000 shp, 26.5 knots.

Kaiser/Konig class. Data *Friedrich der Grosse* 1912
Displacement: 24,725 tons
Length: 172.5 meters; 566 feet
Beam: 30 meters; 95 feet
Draught: 9 meters; 30 feet
Machinery: 16 boilers, Parsons turbines, 3 shafts. 31,000 shp.
Speed: 21 knots
Protection: Main belt 34 cm (13.5 inches), decks 7.5 cm (3 inches), turrets 29.5 cm (11.75 inches), barbettes 29.5 cm (11.75 inches).
Armament: Ten 12-inch (5 x 2), fourteen 5.9-inch (14 x 1), eight 3.5-inch (8 x 1). Torpedoes: Five 19.7-inch TT (fixed)
Complement: 1,088
Notes: *Konig* class similar but with all main armament turrets on the centerline.

Derfflinger-class battlecruisers. Data *Defflinger* 1914
Displacement: 26,600 tons
Length: 210 meters; 690.25 feet
Beam: 29 meters; 95 feet
Draught: 9.5 meters; 31 feet
Machinery: 14 twin coal-fired and 2 oil-fired double-ended boilers, Parsons geared turbines, 4 shafts. 63,000 shp.
Speed: 26.5 knots
Protection: Main belt 30 cm (12 inches), decks 6 cm (2.5 inches), turrets 28 cm (11 inches), barbettes 27 cm (10.5 inches).
Armament: Guns: Eight 12-inch (4 x 2), twelve 5.9-inch (12 x 1), twelve 3.5-inch (12 x 1). Torpedoes: Four 19.7-inch TT (fixed)
Complement: 1,215

Baden class. Data *Baden* 1916
Displacement: 28,600 tons (32,200 tons full load)
Length: 180 meters; 590.5 feet
Beam: 30 meters; 98.5 feet
Draught: 9.5 meters; 31 feet
Machinery: 11 boilers, Parsons geared turbines, 3 shafts. 35,000 shp.
Speed: 22 knots
Protection: Main belt 13.75in, decks 10 cm (4 inches), turrets 34 cm (13.75 inches), barbettes 34 cm (13.75 inches).
Armament: Guns: Eight 15-inch (4 x 2), sixteen

5.9-inch (16 X1), eight 3.5-inch (8 x 1). Torpedoes: Five 23.6-inch TT (fixed)

Complement: 1,171

Deutschland-class armored ships. Data *Deutschland* 1933

Displacement: 11,700 tons (15,900 tons full load)
Length: 187.75 meters; 616 feet
Beam: 20.75 meters; 68 feet
Draught: 7 meters; 23 feet full load
Machinery: 2 shafts. 8 diesel motors (four per shaft). 56,800 bhp.
Speed: 26 knots
Protection: Main belt 8 cm (3.25 inches) max, main deck 4 cm (1.5 inches), 7.5 cm (3 inches) over magazines. Turrets 14 cm (5.5 inches) faces, 10 cm (4 inches) sides. Barbettes 10 cm (4 inches). External bulges.
Armament: Guns: Six 11-inch (2 x 3), eight 5.9-inch (8 x 1), six 4.1-inch AA (3 x 2), eight 37-mm AA, ten 20-mm AA. Torpedoes: Eight 21-inch tubes (2 x 4)
Complement: 1,150
Aircraft: 2. One catapult

Scharnhorst-class battlecruisers. Data as completed

Displacement: 31,800 tons (38,900 tons full load)
Length: 235 meters; 771 feet
Beam: 30.5 meters; 100 feet
Draught: 9.75 meters; 32 feet full load
Machinery: 12 high pressure boilers, Brown Boveri geared turbines, 3 shafts. 160,000 shp.
Speed: 32 knots
Protection: Main belt 34 cm (13 inches) amidships. Main deck 12 cm (4.5 inches) max. Turrets 36 cm (14.25 inches) in faces, 25 cm (9.75 inches) sides, 10 cm (4 inches) rear. Barbettes 36 cm (14 inches). Secondary turret 15 cm (6 inches).
Armament: Guns: Nine 11-inch (3 x 3), twelve 5.9-inch (4 x 2 and 4 x 1), fourteen 4.1-inch AA (7 x 2), sixteen 37-mm AA (8 x 2). Torpedoes: Six 21-inch tubes (2 x 3)
Complement: 1,800
Aircraft: 4. Two catapults

Bismarck class. Data *Bismarck* 1940

Displacement: 41,700 tons (50,900 tons full load)
Length: 251 meters; 823 feet
Beam: 36 meters; 118 feet
Draught: 10 meters; 33 feet full load
Machinery: 12 boilers, Brown-Boveri geared turbines, 3 shafts. 138,000 shp.
Speed: 29 knots
Protection: Main belt 32 inches (12.75 inches) max, decks 12 cm (4.5 inches). Turrets 36 cm (14 inches) face, 22 cm (8.5 inches) sides, 12.5 cm (5 inches) crown. Barbettes 34 cm (13.5 inches).
Armament: Guns: Eight 15-inch (4 x 2), twelve 5.9-inch (6 x 2), sixteen 4.1-inch AA (8 x 2), sixteen 37-mm AA (8 x 2), thirty-six 20-mm AA (4 x 4, 6 x 2, 8 x 1) Torpedoes: Eight 21-inch tubes (2 x 4) in *Tirpitz* only.
Complement: 2,200
Aircraft: 6. Fixed athwartships catapult

Italy

Doria/Cavour classes. Data *Andrea Doria* 1940 as modernized

Displacement: 25,924 tons (29,000 tons full load)
Length: 187 meters; 613 feet
Beam: 28 meters; 92 feet
Draught: 8.8 meters; 29 feet full load
Machinery: 8 boilers, Belluzo geared turbines, 2 shafts. 85,000 shp.
Speed: 27 knots
Protection: Main belt 24.5 cm (9.75 inches) max, decks 9 cm (3.5 inches), turrets 28 cm (11 inches) faces, barbettes 28 cm (11 inches).
Armament: Ten 12.6-inch (2 x 3, 2 x 2), twelve 5.3-inch (4 x 3), ten 3.5-inch AA (10 x 1), nineteen 37-mm AA, twelve 20-mm AA.
Complement: 1,490

Littorio class. Data *Littorio* as completed 1940

Displacement: 41,377tons (46,000 tons full load)
Length: 237 meters; 780 feet
Beam: 32.5 meters; 107 feet
Draught: 9.75 meters; 32 feet full load
Machinery: 8 boilers, Belluzo geared turbines, 4 shafts. 139,000 shp.

Speed: 30 knots
Complement: c.1,900
Protection: Main belt 30 cm (12 inches), decks 15 cm (6 inches) max, turrets 34 cm (13.5 inches) max, barbettes 34 cm (13.5 inches). Pugilise system of internal anti-torpedo spaces.
Armament: Nine 15-inch (3 x 3), twelve 6-inch (4 x 3), twelve 3.5-inch AA (12 x 1), twenty 37-mm AA (10 x 2), twenty 20-mm AA (10 x 2)
Complement: c.1,900
Aircraft: 3. One stern catapult

Japan

IJN Ise. Japan. Launched 1916

Kongo class Data *Kongo* 1940
Displacement: 31,720 tons (36,300 tons full load)
Length: 222 meters; 728.5 feet
Beam: 29 meters; 95 feet
Draught: 9.75 meters; 32 feet full load
Machinery: 8 boilers, Kanpon geared turbines, 4 shafts. 136,000 shp.
Speed: 30.5 knots
Protection: Main belt 20 cm (8 inches), deck 7 cm (2.75 inches), turrets 23 cm (9 inches)
Armament: Guns: Eight 14-inch (4 x 2), fourteen 6-inch (14 x 1), eight 5-inch AA (4 x 2), twenty 25-mm AA (10 x 2)
Complement: 1,437
Aircraft: 3. One catapult abaft X turret

Fuso/Ise classes. Data *Ise* 1937
Displacement: 35,800 tons (40,100 tons full load)
Length: 215.75 meters; 708 feet
Beam: 32 meters; 104 feet
Draught: 9 meters; 30 feet full load
Machinery: 8 boilers, Kanpon geared turbines, 4 shafts. 80,825 shp.
Speed: 25.25 knots
Protection: Main belt 30 (12 inches) max, decks 6 cm (2.5 inches). Turrets 30 cm (12 inches) faces, 20 cm (8 inches) sides.
Armament: Twelve 14-inch (6 x 2), sixteen 5.5-inch (16 x 1), eight 5-inch AA (4 x 2), twenty 25-mm AA (10 x 2)
Complement: 1,376
Aircraft: 3. One stern catapult

Nagato class. Data *Nagato* 1944
Displacement: 39,130 tons (46,350 tons full load)
Length: 223.75 meters; 734 feet
Beam: 34.5 meters; 113.5 feet
Draught: 9.5 meters; 31 feet full load
Machinery: 10 boilers, Kanpon geared turbines, 4 shafts. 82,300shp.
Speed: 25 knots
Protection: Main belt 33 cm (13 inches) max, decks 12 cm (4.5 inches) max. Turrets 36 cm (14 inches) faces. External bulges
Armament: Eight 16-inch (4 x 2), sixteen 5.5-inch (16 x 1), eight 5-inch AA (4 x 2), ninety eight 25-mm AA
Complement: 1,368
Aircraft: 3. One catapult abaft mainmast, offset to port

Yamato class. Data *Yamato* as completed 1941
Displacement: 64,170 tons (71,660 tons full load)
Length: 263 meters; 863 feet
Beam: 40 meters; 127.75 feet
Draught: 11 meters; 35.5 feet
Machinery: 12 boilers, Kanpon geared turbines, 4 shafts. 150,000 shp.
Speed: 27.5 knots
Protection: Main belt 41 cm (16 inches), decks 20 cm (7.75 inches), turrets 63 cm (25 inches)
Armament: Nine 18-inch (3 x 3), twelve 6.1-inch DP (6 x 2), twelve 5-inch AA (6 x 2), twenty-four 25-mm (8 x 3), four 13-mm MG (2 x 2)
Complement: c.2500
Aircraft: 6. Two stern catapults

The Big Guns

The whole purpose of a battleship was to carry into action a battery of long-range heavy guns. Consequently, the relative power of a particular battleship depended mainly on the numbers and characteristics of the guns that made up its main armament. The table below gives brief details of a selection of heavy ordnance mounted on battleships and battlecruisers since 1905.

Caliber	Shell weight (lb/kg)	Range (yds/m)	Notes
Great Britain			
12in/50 cal	850/386	20,960/19,200	St.Vincent, Neptune, Colossus classes
13.5in/45 cal	1400/635	23,740/21,710	Orion to Iron Duke classes and some battlecruisers.
14in/45 cal	1590/721	38,560/35,260	King George V class
15in/42 cal	1938/879	33,550/30,680	Data refers to modified mountings with 30 degree elevation
16in/45 cal	2048/929	39,780/36,375	*Nelson, Rodney*
United States			
12in/50 cal	870/395	23,500/21,490	Wyoming class
14in/50 cal	1500/680	36,300/33,190	New Mexico, California classes
16in/45 cal	2700/1225	36,900/33,740	North Carolina, South Dakota classes
16in/50 cal	2700/1225	42,345/38,720	Iowa class

Caliber	Shell weight (lb/kg)	Range (yds/m)	Notes
Germany			
11in/51 cal	728/330	44,760/40,930	*Scharnhorst, Gneisenau*
12in/47 cal	626/284	42,400/38,600	*Moltke, Seydlitz* (WWI)
15in/42 cal	1653/750	22,200/20,300	Baden class (WWI)
15in/48 cal	1764/800	38,880/35,550	*Bismarck, Tirpitz*
Japan			
12in/50 cal	850/386	27,600/25,250	Kawachi class
14in/45 cal	1485/673	38,770/35,450	Kongo, Fuso, Ise classes
16.1in/45 cal	2249/1020	42,000/38,400	*Nagato, Mutsu*
18in/45 cal	3219/1460	45,960/42,030	*Yamato/Musashi*
Italy			
12in/46 cal	981/445	25,200 / 24,000	Dante Alighieri, Duilio and Cavour classes as built.
12.6in/44 cal	1157/525	31,280/28,600	Modernized Duilio and Cavour classes
15in/50	1951/885	46,216/42,260	Littorio class
France			
12in/45 cal	679/308	28,800/26,300	Courbet class
13in/50 cal	1235/560	45,600/41,700	*Dunkerque, Strasbourg*
13.4in/46 cal	1268/575	29,090/26,600	Bretagne class
15in/45 cal	1949/884	45,600/41,700	*Richelieu, Jean Bart*

Aircraft carried by battleships

This table lists details of a selection of seaplanes operated from battleships. In most cases these were launched by catapult and then landed on the water to be recovered by crane. The table should be read in conjunction with the following notes.

Aircraft Type: Manufacturer and designation. Data may relate to a specific version as noted.
Engine: All engines drive tractor propellers unless otherwise noted. Radial engines are all air cooled.
Type: Abbreviations are used. First letter indicates monoplane (M) or Biplane (B). Remaining letters indicate float or hull configuration, single float with stabilizing wingtip floats (1F), twin floats (2F), hulled flying boat (FB).
Crew; Numbers include pilot.
Span and Length: Dimensions in meters / feet and inches
Speed: Maximum in km per hour / miles per hour. In practice this was rarely attained and a typical cruising speed would be between half and two thirds of this figure.
MAUW: Maximum Weight given kg / pounds.
Date: Year in which first aircraft of the series made its maiden flight.

Aircraft	Type	Crew	Span m/ft and in	Length m/ft and in	Speed km/m	MAUW kg/lbs	Date
Britain (Royal and Commonwealth Navies)							
Fairey IIID	B2F	3	14.05 / 46'1"	11/ 36'1"	188 / 117	2290 / 5050	1920
Fairey Flycatcher	B2F	1	8.83 / 29'	8.83 / 29'	203 / 126	1602 / 3531	1922
Fairey IIIF	B2F	3	13.97 / 45'10"	11 / 36'4"	193 / 120	2858 / 6301	1926
Hawker Osprey	B2F	2	11.27 / 37'	8.93 / 29'4"	272 / 169	2527 / 5570	1930
Fairey Swordfish	B2F	2/3	13.88 / 45'6"	12.34 / 40'6"	206 / 128	3679 / 8110	1933
Supermarine Walrus	BFA	3/4	13.97 / 45'10"	11.43 / 37'7"	217 / 135	3266 / 7200	1933
Blackburn Shark	B2F	3	14.02 / 46'	11.63 / 38'5"	230 / 143	3722 / 8250	1934
France							
Gourdou-Leseurre GL810	M2F	3	16 / 52'6"	10.49 / 34'5"	180 / 112	2460 / 5423	1926
Loire 130	MFB	3	16 / 52'6"	11.3 / 37'1"	220 / 137	3260 / 7187	1934

A Supermarine Walrus being recovered by HMS Rodney.

Notes	Engine
First standard RN catapult a/c.	450hp Napier Lion V 12-cylinder in-line liquid cooled
Flown off platforms and catapults	400hp Armstrong Siddeley Jaguar III radial
Data for Mk.IIIB	570hp Napier Lion XIA in-line liquid cooled
Data for Osprey IV	640hp Rolls-Royce Kestrel V in-line liquid cool
	870hp Bristol Pegasus 30 9-cylinder radial
Standard in WWII	775hp Bristol Pegasus VI 9-cylinder radial (pusher mounted)
	746hp Armstrong Siddeley Tiger VIc 14-cylinder radial
GL811 and GL812 similar	420hp Gnôme-Rhône 9Ady Jupiter 9-cylinder radial
Over 100 built	720hp Hispano-Suiza 12Xirl 12-cylinder in-line (pusher mounted)

Battleships

Aircraft	Type	Crew	Span m/ft and in	Length m/ft and in	Speed km/m	MAUW kg/lbs	Date
Germany							
Heinkel He.60	B2F	2	13.5 / 44'4"	11.5 / 37'9"	240 / 149	3400 / 7495	1933
Heinkel He.114	B2F	2	13.58 / 44'7"	11.06 / 36'4"	335 / 208	3480 / 7672	1936
Arado Ar.196	M2F	2	12.44 / 40'10"	11 / 36'1"	311 / 193	3719 / 8200	1938
Italy							
I.M.A.M. Ro.43	B1F	2	11.55 / 37'11"	9.69 / 31'10"	300 / 186	2400 / 5291	1936
Reggiane Re.2000 Falco II°	MW	1	11 / 36'1"	8 / 26'3"	525 / 326	2596 / 5722	1938
Japan (allocated Allied code names in parenthesis)							
Aichi HD25	B2F	2	13.97 / 48'10"	9.68 / 31'9"	204 / 127	2350 / 5180	1926
Navy Type 15 (E2N1/2)	B2F	2	13.5 / 44'4"	9.54 / 31'4"	172 / 107	1950 / 4299	1926
Nakajima E4N2/3	B1F	2	10.97 / 36'	8.86 / 29'1"	232 / 144	1800 / 3968	1930
Nakajima E8N1/2 (Dave)	B1F	2	10.05 / 33'	8.78 / 28'10"	296 / 184	2050 / 4519	1934
Mitsubishi F1M1/2 (Pete)	B1F	2	11 / 36'1"	9.49 / 31'2"	370 / 230	2550 / 5622	1936
Aichi E13A1 (Jake)	M2F	3	14.17 / 46'6"	11.32 / 36'11"	377 / 234	4000 / 8818	1938
Aichi E16A1 Zui-un (Paul)	M2F	2	12.8 / 42'	10.82 / 35'6"	439 / 273	4500 / 9920	1942
United States							
Vought VE-7SF	B1F	1	10.39 / 34'1"	7.44 / 24'5"	188 / 117	953 / 2100	1918
Vought UO	BIF	2	10.45 / 34'3"	7.44 / 24'5"	200 / 124	1046 / 2305	1921
Vought FU-1	BIF	1	10.48 / 34'4"	8.63 / 28'4"	196 / 122	1258 / 2774	1926
Vought O2U-1 Corsair	B1F	2	10.51 / 34'6"	7.46 / 24'6"	241 / 150	1649 / 3635	1926
Vought O3U Corsair	B1F	2	10.97 / 36'	8.3 / 27'3"	264 / 164	2019 / 4451	1930
Curtiss SOC-1 Seagull	B1F	2	10.97 / 36'	9.61 / 31'5"	266 / 165	2466 / 5437	1934
Vought OS2U-1 Kingfisher	M1F	2	10.95 / 35'11"	10.13 / 33'10"	264 / 164	2722 / 6000	1938
Curtiss SC-1 Seahawk	M1F	1	12.49 / 41'	11.06 / 36'4"	504 / 313	3600 / 7936	1944

Notes	Engine
	600hp BMW VI 6.0 ZU 12-cylinder liquid cooled Vee
Limited catapult use	970hp BMW 132K 9-cylinder radial
Standard in WWII	970hp BMW 132K 9-cylinder radial
Standard in WWII	700hp Piaggio P.XR 9-cylinder radial
Single seat fighter flown from Littorio class	1025hp Piaggio P.XIbis R.C.40 radial
Navy Type 2	500hp Napier Lion 12 cylinder liquid cooled W type
Data relates to E2N1	300hp Mitsubishi Type Hi 8-cylinderin-line liquid cooled
Modified version of Vought O2U Corsair	460-580hp Nakajima Kotobuki 2-kai 1 9-cylinder radial
Data for E8N2	580hp Nakajima Kotobuki 2 Kai I 9-cylinder radial
(Data for F1M2)	875hp Mitsubishi MK2 Zuizei 13 14-cylinder
Widely used by IJN	1080hp Mitsubishi MK8 Kinsei 43 14-cylinder radial
	1300hp Mitsubishi Kinsei 54 14-cylinder radial
2 seat VE-7H and VE-9H similar	180hp Wright-Hispano E-2 8-cylinder liquid cooled in-line
Based on earlier VE-9	200hp Wright/Lawrence J-1 or J-3 9-cylinder radia
Single seat fighter version of Vought UO	220hp Wright J-5 9-cylinder radial
Standard USN type	450hp Pratt & Whitney R-1340-88 Wasp 9-cylinder radial
Improved O2U	550hp Pratt & Whitney R-1340-12 Wasp 9-cylinder radial
Widely used in WWII	600hp Pratt & Whitney R-1340-18 Wasp 9-cylinder radial
Widely used in WWII	450hp Pratt & Whitney R-985-AN-2 Wasp Junior 9-cylinder radial
Last USN floatplane	1350hp Wright R-1820-62 Cyclone 9-cylinder radial

Selected Bibliography

Battleship, H.P. Willmott. Cassell. 2002

Battleships and Battlecruisers, 1905–1970, Siegfried Breyer, MacDonald and Jane's, 1973

Battleships of the US Navy in World War II, Stefan Terzibaschitsch, Brasseys Publishers, 1977

Chronology of the War at Sea, 1939–1945, J. Rohwer and G. Hummelchen, Greenhill Books, 1992

Directory of the World's Capital Ships, Paul Silverstone, Ian Allan, 1984

French Warships of World War I, Jean Labayle Couhat, Ian Allan, 1974

German Warships of World War I, John C. Taylor, Ian Allan, 1969

Janes Fighting Ships 1906–7, Fred T. Jane, David and Charles, 1970

Narrative of the Battle of Jutland, HMSO, 1924

Naval Battles of the First World War, Geoffrey Bennett, B.T. Batsford Ltd, 1968

Naval Weapons of World War Two, John Campbell, Conway Maritime Press, 1985

Navies of the Second World War, Macdonald, 1966–1973

The Battleship Era, Peter Padfield, Rupert Hart-Davies Ltd, 1972

The Big Gun, Battleship Main Armament 1860–1945, Peter Hodges, Conway Maritime Press, 1981

The Grand Fleet, Warship Design and Development 1906–1922, D.K. Brown, Chatham Publishing, 1999

The Metal Fighting Ship in the Royal Navy 1860–1970. E.H.H. Archibald, Blandford Press, 1971

The Two Ocean War, A short history of the US Navy in the Second World War, Samuel Elliott Morison, Galahad Books, 1997

US Warships of World War I, Paul Silverstone, Ian Allan, 1970

Warship Profile 1: HMS Dreadnought, John Wingate DSC, Profile Publications, 1970

Glossary

AA	Anti-aircraft
AMC	Armed Merchant Cruiser
BB	Battleship, US Navy designation
BCS	Battlecruiser Squadron
BL	Breech-loading
BS	Battle squadron
Caliber	Measure of the internal diameter of a gun barrel. Also the length of a gun barrel is expressed in multiples of the caliber (e.g a 12-inch, 45-caliber gun would have a barrel 45 feet long.
CB	Battlecruiser, US Navy designation
C-in-C	Commander in Chief
CIWS	Close-in Weapon System
CSS	Confederate States Ship
DCT	Director Control Tower
DP	Dual-purpose gun
HA	High-angle (guns or associated equipment intended for use against aerial targets)
HMAS	His/Her Majesty's Australian Ship
HMS	His/Her Majesty's Ship
ihp	Indicated horsepower (in respect of steam reciprocating machinery)
LA	Low-angle guns or associated equipment intended for use against surface targets only
MG	Machine gun
ML	Muzzle-loading
MLR	Muzzle-loading rifle
rpm	Rounds per minute
RAF	Royal Air Force
RMLI	Royal Marine Light Infantry
RN	Royal Navy
SG	Scouting Group
shp	Shaft horsepower
TF	Task Force
TT	Torpedo Tube
USS	United States Ship
VC	Victoria Cross, Britain's highest gallantry award.
VTE	Vertical, triple expansion (reciprocating steam

Picture Credits

Images supplied by Cody Images

All cover images and pages 1, 2, 4, 6/7, 8, 9, 10, 11 top, 14/15, 16, 20 inset, 20/21, 22, 24/25, 26, 27 top, 33, 34, 35, 36, 37, 39 bottom, 40 inset, 41 inset, 42, 44 inset, 46/47, 48/49, 50/51, 58/59, 62/63, 64/65, 66, 67 top right, 68 top, 70/71, 72, 73, 76/77, 83, 84, 85, 86 inset, 86/87, 89, 90 94/95, 98 inset, 98/99, 100/101, 101 inset, 102/103, 105, 108/109, 120, 121, 126, 127 bottom, 128 inset, 130/131, 133 top, 134/135, 136/137, 140/141, 142/143, 142 inset, 144, 146/147, 152, 153, 154/155, 156/157, 158, 159, 160, 161, 172, 184/185, 186, 187, 188/189, 190, 191, 192, 196/197, 199 inset, 200/201, 204/205, 218/219, 218 inset, 224/225, 227, 228, 231, 232, 233, 239, 240, 242/243, 244, 249 bottom 252, 252 inset, 257, 258, 259, 260, 261, 22/262, 264, 267, 271, 274, 276/277, 278, 294/295.

Images supplied by Air Sea Media Services

Pages 11 bottom, 12/13, 17, 18/19, 23, 27 bottom, 28, 29, 30/31, 32, 38, 39 top, 40/41, 43, 44/45, 52, 53, 54/55, 56/57, 60/61, 74, 75, 78, 79, 81, 82, 89 inset, 91, 92/93, 96/97, 104, 106/107, 107 inset, 110, 112, 113, 114, 115,116, 117/118, 122, 123, 124, 125, 127 top, 128/129, 132, 133 bottom, 138/139, 145, 148/149, 150 inset, 150/151, 162, 163, 164, 165, 166/167, 168/169, 170, 171, 173, 174, 175, 176/177, 178/179, 180, 181, 182 inset, 182/183, 193, 194, 195, 198/199, 202/203, 202 inset, 206, 208, 208/209, 210, 211, 212, 214,/215, 216/217, 217 inset, 220/221, 222/223, 222 inset, 226, 229, 230, 234/235, 236, 237, 238, 241/242, 242 inset, 245/246, 247, 248, 249 top, 50, 251, 253, 254, 255, 265, 268, 270, 272, 279, 284, 287, 288, 290, 293, 297.

Images in the public domain

Pages 67, 273.

World Ship Society, D.K.Brown collection

Pages 67, 28 bottom, 269.

Packaged by BlueRed Press Ltd

Index

Names of ships may refer to more than one vessel.